# Drink Like A Lady

# Cry Like A Man

# Drink Like A Lady Cry Like A Man

The Love Story of a Man and His Recovering Alcoholic Wife

By Jack Nero

Published by

publications

2415 Annapolis Lane, Suite 140
Minneapolis, Minnesota 55441
A division of Comprehensive Care Corporation

(Ask for our catalog. 800/328-3330, toll free outside Minnesota
or 612/559-4800, Minnesota residents)

*Dedicated with love to my recovering alcoholic wife.*

# Contents

# Acknowledgments

I give my heartfelt thanks to Jay T. and Kitty S. and to all the men and women of Al-Anon and Alcoholics Anonymous, who, by sharing their experience, strength and hope, helped me to find the pathway to personal growth and freedom.

# Introduction

## Alcoholism — Through the Looking Glass

Anyone who has been exposed recently to newspapers, magazines or television is aware that alcoholism is a disease. Since most diseases can be treated, this is a comforting thought, particularly if you don't have the disease yourself and if no one in your immediate family has it.

It's not so comfortable, gentlemen, if the disease victim is your wife, your mother or your daughter. If she's sick, she should be seeing a doctor, spending a few days in a hospital, taking her medicine, recovering, and then returning to her old routine, right?

On the contrary, the alcoholic probably has already seen a doctor, been to a hospital, added tranquilizers and mood-elevators to her diet, sought out a psychiatrist and prayed with her priest or minister or rabbi. But nothing seems to work. By this time, she knows that something is terribly wrong, but she denies that her drinking just might be a symptom of alcoholism.

You—and others close to her—notice that she has become childish, swinging from hysterical gaiety to suicidal depression; she cries often and easily, moving in a fantasy world that is bounded by her hidden bottles of booze. She's unable to make a rational decision. More often than not, she needs someone to take care of her, someone to clean her up and nurse her through the aftereffects of a binge.

The *Big Book* of Alcoholics Anonymous describes the illness as "cunning, baffling and powerful." The spouse or family member of an alcoholic readily accepts the "baffling" portion of the description, reserves the "cunning" to describe the alcoholic's behavior, and, all too often, assumes that "powerful" refers to his own personal, heroic role of solving her problem for her. Unwittingly, he joins his alcoholic "child" in her games. His part in the game may be that of the persecutor (she'd better damn well shape up—or else!), the martyr (poor long-suffering me, putting up with an alcoholic wife) or the enabler (she can always count on me, the supermate, to come to her rescue). But most often, he moves into the role of stern parent, judge, jury. Finally, he becomes the Almighty—all-powerful, wise beyond words, but also merciful and just; he's God.

He's sick.

Professionals in the field of chemical dependency tell us that the families of alcoholics contract an illness that, in some respects, is equally as devastating as alcoholism. In fact, a family member exhibits many of the same characteristics as the alcoholic. The spouse of an alcoholic wife, for instance, becomes anxious and neurotic, deeply depressed and quick to anger, filled with resentment and frustration, along with fear and guilt. True, he's not addicted to alcohol, but that's understandable; after all, God doesn't need a drink, does He?

These professionals say that it's often easier to spot the spouse of an alcoholic than it is to identify the alcoholic. They use the terms "co-alcoholic," "non-alcoholic family member" or, more aptly, in my estimation, "mirror alcoholic."

This book was written especially for men whose wives, mothers, daughters, sisters or girl friends are having problems with chemical dependency. This may involve alcohol or pills or other mood-altering chemicals, either singly or in combination. For the record, men, if your spouse is a souse, you've joined a not-so-exclusive club with twelve million or so unwilling members in the United States alone, a club comprised of the families of the approximately three million women who have the disease of alcoholism or other drug addiction. Maybe seven to ten percent of these women have learned how to arrest the illness—the statistics are shadowy and uncertain.

Nine out of ten husbands of alcoholic wives—as estimates have it—choose to leave their mate and her problems behind, out of despair, disgust, or just because they can no longer communicate. The percentage of co-alcoholic wives who leave their practicing alcoholic husbands is considerably smaller.

The sickness has been with us for many years, but only recently has it been brought out in the open. Our fathers and mothers—or grandparents and great-grandparents—bemoaned the sot, the tippler, the inebriate, the drunkard. But if there was an unfortunate member of the family with a drinking problem it was a tightly guarded secret.

Our ancestors, masters of tact and delicacy, often wrote about touchy or complex subjects, political or personal, in the form of allegories. Over a hundred years ago, Lewis Carroll, an English mathematician whose real name was Charles Lutwidge Dodgson, wrote *Alice's Adventures in Wonderland* (1865) and *Through the Looking Glass* (1871). I first read the books, which have long been recognized as children's classics, when I was ten or eleven. I still re-read them regularly. Lately, I've been mulling over my growing suspicion that there may be more to these stories than simply free-wheeling fantasies about a White Rabbit, a Mad Hatter, a Mock Turtle or a pair of fighting twins, Tweedledee and Tweedledum. I cannot vouch for the author's allegorical intent, but somehow he must have had a first-hand knowledge of chemical dependency. In spite of his lifelong bacherlorhood, which rules out a drunken wife or daughter, Carroll does a remarkably accurate job in these two books of describing the antics, emotions and progress of the related diseases of alcoholism and mirror alcoholism.

If you have never thought of "Alice" this way, let me give you a little synopsis:

In *Alice's Adventures in Wonderland*, a shy, dreamy girl follows a talking rabbit down a hole, falls into a well and discovers a tiny door which leads to a diminutive garden. But she is too big to enter. She spots a bottle labeled "Drink Me," tries it, likes the taste, and downs the entire contents.

"What a curious feeling," said Alice, "I must be shutting up like a telescope!"

Reduced to only ten inches tall, she is the right scale for the garden, but too small to reach the key. She comes upon a pill-size cake labeled "Eat Me," which she does. Now she feels that she's nine feet tall, but nobody loves her and she's in tears, believing that she's lost her identity.

Alice imagines herself saying, to whoever might call to her down the rabbit hole, "Who am I then? Tell me first, and then, if I like being that person, I'll come up; if not, I'll stay down here till I'm somebody else" ... But she admits, tearfully, "I'm so very tired of being all alone here!"

Further along in the story, Alice gets hooked on mushrooms. A large blue caterpillar smoking a water pipe is the pusher, who explains that she can get high if she eats from one side of the mushroom; the other side is a downer. Since the mushroom bits can make her feel just the right size for any situation, Alice takes along a good "stash" of them and joins the Mad Hatter, the March Hare and a Dormouse for a drinking party. The Dormouse is sleeping off the effects of his earlier libations. Alice, disgusted, leaves the party, nibbling at her mushrooms.

"Now I'll manage better this time," she says to herself.

The mushroom does its work, and Alice finds herself at last in the garden at the Red Queen's croquet party—with no knowledge of how she got there.

She ends up in court, defies the judge, interferes with the jury and protests the verdict—death by decapitation (the legal system overreacted somewhat, even then).

If you don't agree that Alice had a problem with chemical dependency, I suggest that you attend any open meeting of Alcoholics Anonymous to hear similar stories.

If you've ever tried to trim your hair with the aid of a mirror, you can appreciate Alice's puzzlement and frustration in *Through the Looking Glass*. If someone in your family is an alcoholic, you can more than appreciate Alice's dilemma; you will identify directly with her.

In this later book, Alice, a confident and well-adjusted youngster, steps through a mirror hanging over a fireplace mantel into a world that turns backwards. Cast in the role of a pawn in a gigantic chess game, she finds that she must walk backward in order to go forward. Here, the White Queen tells her, one must run furiously just to stay in the same place.

Bewildered, Alice boards a train in the company of some outlandish insects and animals, each filled with advice, instructions and admonitions concerning her trip. Tweedledee and Tweedledum ping away at her self-esteem by insisting that she's nothing more than "a sort of thing," in the Red King's dream. "If that there king was to wake ... you'd go out —bang!—just like a candle!"

The White Queen, whose memory works both forward and backward, teaches Alice to anticipate—even suffer over— events that are to happen week after next.

"For instance, now ... there's the King's Messenger," the Queen said, "He's in prison now, being punished; and the trial doesn't even begin till next Wednesday: and, of course, the crime comes last of all."

Humpty Dumpty has glib answers for all of Alice's questions, takes serious offense when she calls him an "egg" and sums up his opinion of her like this:

"'Some people,' said Humpty Dumpty, looking away from her as usual, 'have no more sense than a baby!'"

Continuing the chess game, Alice reaches the eighth square and gains confidence when she discovers that she is, in fact, a queen. However, the Red Queen and the White Queen quickly deflate her. The accepted rules of normality do not apply here.

"Alice was puzzled. 'In our country,' she remarked, 'there's only one day at a time.'

"The Red Queen said, 'That's a poor thin way of doing things. Now, *here* we mostly have days and nights two or three at a time, and sometimes in winter we take as many as five nights together—for warmth, you know.'"

"Alice sighed and gave it up. 'It's exactly like a riddle with no answer!' she thought."

The climax occurs when the Red and White Queens escort Alice to a party given in her honor, and the guests drink too much.

"'Just like pigs in a trough!' thought Alice."

Alice had had it.

"'I can't stand this any longer!' she cried, as she jumped up and seized the tablecloth with both hands; one good pull, and plates, dishes, guests, and candles came crashing down together in a heap on the floor."

When Alice recovers, she is uncertain about whose dream she has just experienced.

"You see, Kitty, it *must* have been either me or the Red King. He was part of my dream, of course—but then I was part of his dream, too!"

So that's the way it was with Alice. That's the way it was with me, too. As I said, I identify with her.

Possibly Lewis Carroll wrote a third book, but the manuscript has never been unearthed. If it were found and published today, I am confident that it would deal with Alice's return to reality and would be titled *Alice Anonymous*.

Alcoholism is full of paradoxes: No one ever started drinking with the idea of becoming an alcoholic; virtually no alcoholic who is still drinking will admit that he or she has a problem with booze; alcoholics who first approach Alcoholics Anonymous (AA) for help usually don't want to quit drinking; those who are recovering in AA will tell you that they maintain their sobriety by giving it away—carrying the message to other alcoholics.

Mirror alcoholism also has its paradoxes: the spouse of a souse tries in every way she or he knows—or has heard about —to dry up the drunk, and ends up doing all the wrong things for the right reasons; to help the alcoholic, you must let her go; to help the alcoholic, you must help yourself first.

To add to the craziness, those who have this disease won't

admit it, their families insist on treating it with home remedies, and many professionals, who ought to know better, often compound and prolong the sickness.

That's what this book is all about. I'm Jack, and my wife is Maggie. She's a recovering alcoholic. This book recounts the wild, insane games that Maggie and I played. It also includes experiences of other men and women we met along the way as we began to learn how to give up our deadly game-playing.

I choose to be anonymous, to use a pen name rather than my own. Neither my wife nor I is at all ashamed to tell our story, but the tenets of our newly won philosophies suggest that we take no personal credit for the events leading to our recoveries, and that we protect the anonymity of others who have found or are still searching for answers to their similar problems.

As for these others, I've changed names, scrambled characters and their experiences and switched locales, so that no one described is even an approximation of the original person. That's been fun, and leftover from my days when I played God.

Since Maggie and I were pretty well scrambled to begin with, only our names are changed. The story is very real, just as it happened.

I have used the actual names of several staff members at Hazelden, a chemical dependency treatment and rehabilitation center located in Minnesota—the place where Maggie finally learned to be honest and to face reality.

Finally, I want to thank my wife for being an alcoholic. Although this may seem hard to believe, I sincerely mean it. Through her illness and the eventual steps she took to find a happy sobriety, I was forced to find a pathway of my own, to take a long and searching look at myself, to learn who and what was underneath those masks that I wore and to evolve a new set of goals and a worthwhile personal philosophy. I'm still recovering. I have a long way to go. But I know this: I'm on the right road.

# Drink Like A Lady
# Cry Like A Man

# 1

## Very Ill

"Once upon a time there were three little sisters," the Dormouse began in a great hurry; "and their names were Elsie, Lacie and Tillie; and they lived at the bottom of a well."

"What did they live on?" said Alice, who always took a great interest in questions of eating and drinking.

"They lived on treacle," said the Dormouse, after a minute or two.

"They couldn't have done that, you know," Alice gently remarked; "they'd have been very ill."

"So they were," said the Dormouse; "very ill."

Early on in my introduction to the Twelve Steps of Al-Anon Family Groups, it was evident to me that a certain amount of editing and judicious revision of the Steps would be helpful. It wasn't that the authors hadn't done an excellent job—the philosophy expressed in the Steps was simple and explicit— it was just that Step One was a little misstated.

It read: We admitted that we were powerless over alcohol and our lives were unmanageable.

My revision: We admitted *our* prowess over alcohol but our *wives* were unmanageable.

I handled *my* liquor properly; but my wife, Maggie, was a drunken, irrational, completely unpredictable witch, who was willfully destroying herself and her life despite everything I did for her! The people of Al-Anon were wrong—dead wrong!

Within a few weeks, I admitted my error.

Alcoholism, I learned, was an illness of the body, the mind and the spirit. Insanity, Webster's Dictionary says, implies unfitness to manage one's own affairs or safely enjoy liberty. My Maggie, in addition to her physical and spiritual problems, was also mentally incompetent—insane—and it certainly was logical that she couldn't or wouldn't be led tamely to recovery through my prescribed treatment.

Getting back to Al-Anon's First Step, I was being asked to admit that I was powerless over alcohol (including my alcoholic wife) and that *my* life was unmanageable! I fought that concept. It took time and a dispassionate review of my own actions, but I finally grudgingly admitted to a mental disorder of my own. My management ability that I prized so highly was, in this case, a talent for mismanagement. Apparently I, like Maggie, was a nut, a kook, an insane person.

It was a comfort to learn that I was not alone in my insanity. There were other kooks in Al-Anon, other men and women who admitted their own crazy behavior and were trying to do something about it.

Take Mac, for instance. Mac was a district sales manager who ran his territory with the same concentration, flair and energy that he gave to his golf game: every salesman made his quota in par or better, called on his dealers rain or shine (it never rains on a golf course, right?) and worked on his "short game" of closing techniques in Mac's sales seminars.

Mac, in his mid-forties, was a big man with a golf tan. He was obviously marked for promotion in his company. He loved his wife and children with a deep and honest devotion and had a firm, unshakable faith in God.

2

One evening Mac was winding up a district sales meeting with a late bull session in Conference Room "A" at the local Holiday Inn. It was pushing 2 a.m. He was tired and edgy and hoping that he could wrap it up soon and get to bed.

The company had been very decent about inviting the salesmen's wives to attend the meeting and agreeing to pick up the tab. It helped to involve the wives, Mac thought. His own wife, Vera, had made arrangements to keep the women occupied—bridge games, pool parties, luncheons and tours. Vera had always done that sort of thing very well. Until lately, anyway.

Vera was a few years younger than Mac, tall and shapely, with the natural grace that comes easily to a good athlete. She was equally at home on the golf course or in the swimming pool. Though her own hair was a satiny brown, Vera often found it convenient and fun to wear one of her wardrobe of wigs, particularly after a swim or a game of golf.

This particular night had been a special evening, a cocktail party and dinner, so Vera had opted for a filmy, patterned-silk gown—she called it her "butterfly dress"—and crowned the whole effect with a red-blonde wig. Mac had been mildly critical of her outfit, since she wore only a bikini bra and panties underneath. "Cherry on cheese cake," he said and opined that she was showing more than necessary, at least for a district sales manager's wife on display.

Mac was worried about Vera. Sure, they both drank and held their drinks well, but it seemed that Vera was beginning to hold them too often. Standard breakfast fare, even at home, included a "health drink." Lunch dictated two or three cocktails, and at the sales meetings she downed the Happy Hour martinis with the best of his two-fisted-drinking salesmen.

When he had appeared unexpectedly in the room late this afternoon, he had caught her taking a stiff belt directly from the neck of his bottle of Chivas Regal.

"My feet hurt," she explained weakly.

Mac exploded. "Bullshit! You're drinking like a slob! I'm telling you right now that you're damn well going to cut down and drink like a lady. You straighten yourself out and fast, or I'll lock up the booze—and you, too!"

It had been a rough day, Mac thought. The pressure of the meeting was enough, but added to the scene with Vera, it was too much. He looked up when the door to the conference room burst open. Joe, one of his better salesmen, who had left the party to visit the men's room was visibly upset. "Mac, there's a nekked woman floating face down in the pool!" Joe blurted it out. "I think it's Vera!"

Mac raced down the hallway to the pool, his salesman close behind. Although the overhead and pool lights were extinguished, he could see the dim outline of a blonde head, face down, floating in the dark water. Vera's butterfly dress lay crumpled at the edge of the pool. Without pausing, Mac hit the water in a flat racing dive that would bring him up near Vera's head.

Vera's head, he discovered, was Vera's wig, but Vera was not under it. She was stretched out on a chaise nearby, viewing him with owlish eyes as he climbed dripping from the water.

"You oughta take off your clothes if you wanna go skinny-dipping," she observed. "Now you've ruined your nice blue suit." Vera, minus her butterfly dress and clad only in her wet bra and bikini panties, left little to the imagination. "Hey, all you guys—everybody in the pool for a skinny-dip!" she yelled.

Silently, Mac gathered up her dress and led a protesting Vera back to their room. She was smashed. Still as grimly silent as if he were putting for a birdie on the eighteenth hole, Mac stripped and dried her, pulled down the covers and eased her into bed. He peeled off his own sodden suit, resisting the urge to slap her awake and have it out. She was in no condition to talk, he decided wearily, but, by God, tomorrow she was going to hear from him!

She had a queen-sized hangover the next morning. Mac heard her in the bathroom, being sick, just after she had taken the first sip of a Bloody Mary brought up by room service along with their breakfast. When she returned to the table, red-eyed and blowing her nose, Mac let her have it in his best tough-executive style.

She was a sloppy drinker who had disgraced him and the company in front of his entire sales staff. She didn't even have the decency to stay in the room when she was soused, but had gone to the pool, taken off her clothes and really made an ass out of herself.

Vera straightened defiantly. "But I wasn't drunk, and I didn't go near the pool last night," she protested. "I did have a few drinks with a couple of those boring salesmen's wives, but then I came right to the room and went to bed!"

Mac walked over to the side of the bed, picked up the still-wet wig and the wrinkled, damp dress and shook them at her. "Then who was the dumb broad by the pool that looked like you, sounded like you and was so drunk she couldn't walk?"

"Mac, I couldn't have been. I don't remember anything about the pool—I swear that I went right to our room after bridge ..." Mac was lying, she insisted. If anyone had been skinny-dipping, it was Mac and that gang of drunken bums he called salesmen. She was indignant. He didn't love her, she declared. He was lying through his teeth, and she hated him! Tears streamed down her cheeks, and she blindly raised her drink to her lips and drained the glass.

And good old Mac—confused, sore as hell, and wondering if *he* was the one that was drunk last night—stormed out of the room vowing that this was absolutely the last time he would ever take his goddamned wife to a goddamned sales meeting. The liquor cabinet was definitely going to be locked from here on out, and if she wanted a drink, she'd better damn well get down on her knees and pray for help and stay there until the thought of drinking turned her inside out!

Mac and Vera had a problem. Vera was an alcoholic, now experiencing blackouts, and Mac was going to handle it by locking up the booze, chewing her out, and leaving her at home until she could once again learn to drink like a lady.

Insane? Sick? Of course they were. But when Maggie and I first met them, each denied vehemently that the problem was alcohol.

"I can quit any time I want to!" Vera said, her voice shaking with emotion. "I just drink to forget what he said to me."

"She's not going to ruin my life," Mac told me. "She's going to straighten herself out and shape up or else!"

Nick, unlike Mac, who was still fighting, had pretty well resigned himself to the idea that his wife, Mary, was beyond any hope of redemption. He viewed himself as a modern Job, with a drunken spouse instead of boils on his neck. Even Nick's well-cut suits hung on his thin shoulders with an air of dejection. He had tried everything, he told me, but the hard, inescapable fact was that Mary was killing herself with pills and booze.

Mary didn't see it that way. "It's the pain," she told Maggie, "constant, almost unendurable pain in my stomach. The doctors have tested and tested, and they *say* they can't find anything. They're lying, I know. It's cancer. Sure, I drink. You'd drink, too, if you were dying of cancer!"

Mary was a bright-eyed dynamo packaged in a five-foot frame. Her eyes, however, were a little *too* bright. Her restless hands almost never stopped moving long enough for anyone to see that her fingernails were bitten to the quick. She could have sung at the Met, she confided to Maggie resentfully, if she hadn't listened to Nick and left the conservatory to follow him around the country, while he beat his brains out as a manpower recruiter for a major corporation. Now she did her singing as a choir director, when her health permitted, and fretted about how to get old Miss Lucy out of the choir and into the back of the church, where her off-key soprano wouldn't be so noticeable.

The trouble began, Nick reported, a few years back when they lived in Buffalo. They were active in the church. But they like to "live a little," too. They belonged to a dance club, organized their share of formal dinners, with the right wines, and joined the impromptu Saturday afternoon bashes, "come-on-over-to-our-house-for-a-drink" parties that began early and ended late. Mary always had a good time, but sometimes her hangovers were so horrendous that she couldn't make it to the choir loft on Sunday.

Nick was alarmed. He packed his reluctant wife off to one of those nice, secluded dry-out centers that flourish in New England, explaining to the minister that Mary would miss the next Sunday service and Wednesday night choir practice because she was going away for a few days. "Her nerves," Nick alibied solemnly.

Three days after her return, the children found mother peacefully stretched out on the living-room floor, dead drunk, an empty peach brandy bottle nestled to her cheek.

Nick, as an employment counselor with a nationwide agency, knew the ropes. He consulted a good internist and arranged an appointment for his wife. The report of her examination was not encouraging. Mary should stop drinking, the doctor said. She was very high-strung, had developed a mild stomach disorder due to nervous tension and had a badly inflamed throat that would account for her persistent dry cough. He recommended that Mary take Antabuse daily, a pill that would induce vomiting if she took a drink of alcohol. He wrote out a prescription for pain pills to relieve her stomach, another for tranquilizers to ease her nerves. A good codeine-base cough syrup would help her throat. A bland diet, plenty of rest and exercise and Mary would be as good as new. "Maybe better," the doctor chuckled.

Things got better and stayed better. Nick was a diligent nurse, standing Mary in front of the mirror in the bathroom and making certain that she downed her Antabuse daily. She took her pain pills and her tranquilizers without protest. Nick relaxed as Mary improved, even to the point of letting her take the responsibility of having her prescriptions refilled. Old Miss Lucy had quit the choir in a huff and was now spending her Sundays with the Methodists, thank goodness.

One morning Nick received a phone call from his good friend, the minister of their church. "Nick, something's wrong with Mary. She was sitting right here on our couch, talking about the solo for next Sunday, when her eyes closed and she fell asleep. We just sat there, and in a couple of minutes she roused herself and continued the conversation as if nothing had happened. A few minutes later, she quietly slid to the floor, and we can't wake her.

"We knew she once had a problem with drinking, so we smelled her breath. There's no odor of alcohol. Should we call an ambulance?"

"Please do that. I'll be at the hospital as fast as I can get there."

The emergency-room physician told him that Mary evidently had taken an overdose of some type of drug, her stomach had been pumped, and she was in good condition, a bit incoherent. He could see her in a couple of hours.

Nick went home to wait, and the phone rang. "This is Lieutenant Morrissey at the police station—we've met at church. We have a sticky problem that you'll have to know about. We have evidence that your wife is in violation of the federal narcotics law. She's been buying illegal quantities of certain prescription drugs. When can we get together to talk about it?"

Nick's hand shook as he tried to light his pipe after telling me his story. "Jack, I've put her in hospitals, both kinds—general and mental. I've taken her to clinics for tests, tried psychiatry, and watched her like a hawk. I even took her to Alcoholics Anonymous—nothing works. She's an alcoholic and a drug addict with a police record. She's crazy, and I'm almost crazy myself."

Nick had one thing going for him—he knew that his wife was physically and mentally sick and suspected that he, too, was showing the effects of her illness.

I had much in common with Mac and Nick. I was the product of the paradoxes of alcoholism, a mirror alcoholic with combat fatigue, an unknowing enabler, so filled with guilt that, at one point in the downward spin, a joint suicide pact with my alcoholic wife seemed to be the only solution to our personal hell.

Maggie and I had most of the good things that the world has to offer. We lived in a roomy house in a good suburb, with two cars in a heated garage equipped with door openers. We had gathered a host of good friends and took our vacations in the sunny Caribbean in January and February, when folks were fighting the ice back home. We were proud of our two sons, both grown and married, and of our three grandchildren, happy, well-adjusted youngsters that adored their grandparents, particularly Grandma Maggie.

At plus-fifty, I was a moderately successful exporter of industrial supplies. I was well-traveled and could expound knowingly on the very best places to eat and drink in South America and Europe. In fact, expense-account steaks and good whiskey had made me a little paunchy. A good hair-piece hid my bald spot, and a neat Vandyke beard covered my three chins. I fancied that casual acquaintances mistook me for an international banker, and accordingly I wore well-tailored dark-blue jackets, cloud-gray slacks, light-blue shirts and red-and-blue-striped ties.

My Maggie was an intense, highly charged brunette with no discernible white hair, a youthful figure despite her over-forty age, and a temper with a short fuse. Maggie had more hobbies than she could find time for. She loved art and had a special closet brimming with half-finished canvases, water colors, oils and brushes, and an enormous wicker basket jumbled with sewing, knitting and needlepoint supplies, and a good half-dozen other projects in varying stages of completion. She dressed well. But she hated to throw away out-of-style dresses and shoes, and her wardrobe—in style and out of style—filled three closets. We needed a big house with big closets just for her clothes, I complained.

She could never balance the family checkbook, and our budget was chaotic. I made the money, and she spent just a little more than I made, I told her. Usually, I reduced her to tears when we argued about money. She always lost the arguments—I was so logical and so, so right!

Social drinking had always been important to us. Maggie went on her first drunk when she was fourteen. Drinking made her feel important, sophisticated and worldly, she said. I

9

started when I was sixteen and, though it made me deathly ill, I basked in the thought that drinking proved somehow that I was now a man, accepted as such by my friends and, more importantly, more desirable to the girls in our community. When Maggie and I were married, we learned to drink martinis because they were so "sophisticated." We first limited ourselves to a single drink before dinner, then quickly advanced to the pitcher and a change in proportions from two gins to one vermouth to all-gin with a "whisper" of vermouth. We quarreled more, decided gin was a home-wrecker, and switched to vodka. At least, we believed, it didn't smell on the breath.

We picked up and moved fairly regularly, since I never quite found the job with the understanding boss I could respect and the cooperative staff that would daily demonstrate whole-hearted admiration of my ability. I traveled abroad extensively and was away from home for a month—sometimes two or three months—at a time. Maggie resented, but accepted, my long absences and began to take a few drinks all by herself, just to relieve the boredom and the growing irritation of raising two boys by herself.

One day Maggie discovered that she not only *wanted* a drink but actually *needed* a drink, just to keep going. Although she successfully hid her fears—and the extra alcoholic rations she was now buying—she couldn't conceal the outward manifestations of her drinking. She was shrill and combative, slurred her words and cried easily.

Engrossed in business affairs, I was slow to catch on. But it finally dawned on me that Maggie had a drinking problem. I was righteously indignant. She was making me look bad! If my superiors and associates learned that I couldn't handle my own wife, they might logically assume that I couldn't handle my business responsibilities. The answer, I reasoned, was to consider Maggie's drinking exactly as I would consider a challenge in business. It was simply a matter of management, and I was good at resolving such matters. I went to work on her "bad habit." Certainly I didn't want her to stop drinking

altogether. I enjoyed our ritual of martinis before dinner, wine
with dinner and a brandy or liqueur after dinner. I just wanted
her to learn to drink like a lady. She agreed that this would be
the reasonable, enlightened answer to her problem.

During a period of about eight years, Maggie tried tapering
off, drinking wine and beer only, "controlled drinking," fresh
starts in new locations, medical attention, a return to religion.
She tried going to work, quitting work, volunteer work,
exercise, rest, and psychiatry. Nothing did any good. In
desperation she tried Alcoholics Anonymous, stayed sober for
about two months and returned to drinking, concluding that
AA was great for some people but that she wasn't "that bad."

I managed Maggie carefully, gently, by indirection. She was
not grateful. As her drinking increased, she became deeply
depressed and morose. Finally, she hit upon the reason for her
drinking. Me. My neglect, my shifting of responsibility to her
shoulders, my lack of compassion and my coldness—these, she
felt, were the cause of her trouble. In her resentment and
anger, she struck below the belt.

"You're impotent!" she lashed out, "either that or you're a
latent homosexual!"

My anger dissolved into guilt, humiliation and fear. My
masculine drive crumbled, and I actually did become impotent.
At Maggie's insistence, I signed up for my turn on the
psychiatric couch. I quit my job and took another with a deep
cut in income. I refused to travel for fear that Maggie would,
in her drunkenness, destroy herself.

Maggie tried to meet my worst expectations. She wrote the
traditional suicide note, overdosed with sleeping pills and
went to bed behind a locked door to die. I found her and made
the wild ride with her in the fire department's emergency
vehicle to the hospital. When she was out of danger, I walked
home and wrote *her* a note, suggesting that should she feel
inclined to try to take her life again, she should let me know
and we would go together.

What, exactly, was wrong with Maggie, Mary and Vera?
Other women seemed to drink, have fun and suffer no ill

effects. Was it something in their heredity? Were they simply weak-willed, spineless creatures who had "gone bad," the rotten apples in the barrel? How about parental negligence, something in their upbringing? Maybe, as straight-laced folks put it, Jehovah in his wrath was punishing them for their sins.

Where did Mac, Nick and I go wrong? Mac locked up the booze, took Vera out of circulation and told her to get on her knees and pray. Nick rushed Mary to hospitals, psycho wards, dry-out centers, doctors, lawyers and ministers. When all my efforts failed, I accepted the full load of guilt that I was responsible for Maggie's condition and was ready to pay the supreme penalty of joining her in suicide.

The answers are simple, but our society makes them complicated. Bluntly, our wives were sick—they have a deadly disease. Theirs is an illness that, unless it's properly treated, follows a predictable course that inevitably leads to death. This is the illness of chemical dependency—alcoholism, drug addiction or a combination of both. It can be arrested—not cured, but arrested—and those with the illness held in check can lead normal, happy lives.

Equally as bluntly, Mac, Nick and I—and the families of most chemical dependents—are also sick. We reflect the illness of our practicing alcoholics, learn to play destructive games with them and share their insanity. We're not, however, going to die. Some of us find living with an alcoholic more than we can handle, so we get a divorce or move away. Others share a living death with their practicing alcoholics or drug addicts.

Or, we can do something constructive. We can become informed as to the true nature of chemical dependency, including alcoholism. We can share our experience, strength and hope with others who are facing the same situations. We can learn—and this comes as a shock to most of us—that to help our alcoholics, we must admit that we're helpless: to win, we must surrender: to change them, we must first change ourselves: to save them, we must let them go.

As the Red Queen put it, "It's really quite simple once you get the hang of it."

# 2

# Impossible Things

"I can't believe that!" said Alice.

"Can't you?" the Queen said in a pitying tone, "Try again; draw a long breath, and shut your eyes."

Alice laughed. "There's no use trying," she said; "one can't believe impossible things."

"I dare say you haven't had much practice," said the Queen. "When I was your age I always did it for half an hour a day. Why, sometimes I've believed as many as six impossible things before breakfast! ..."

Nick stood in our doorway thanking Maggie for arranging Mary's admission to Hazelden, a treatment center for alcoholics and drug dependents. Although Nick was by nature a smiling and happy-go-lucky sort with a quick, dry wit, his face now was gray with strain and his body sagged with defeat. His wife was presently bedded down in the local hospital's intensive ward, fighting off the aftereffects of her injudicious blending of cough syrup, peach brandy, a handful of Valium and, Nick believed, a couple of bottles of McCormick's vanilla extract. Mary was a double dipper, addicted to both alcohol and pills.

"I've had her in the alcoholic ward twice, dragged her to the psych hospital three times and stuck her in Sunny River (a popular dry-out center). I've taken her to two psychiatrists and three internists, and spent a week with her sitting across the desk from a marriage counselor."

Nick shook his head wearily. "When I married that woman, there was nothing in the marriage contract about me becoming an authority on alcoholism and drug addiction, but if I have to go many more rounds with her, I can sure as hell set up my own shop!"

No one can guarantee all the answers for every individual affected by chemical dependency. But the questions and answers that follow reflect the experience of professionals who work with recovering alcoholics and their families, and of a lot of old-timers who've been the route and learned how to cope.

### 1. What is chemical dependency?

An illness that, if unchecked, is 100 percent fatal. A person with this disease can be treated, and the disease can be arrested, but not cured. A good comparison is diabetes.

Alcohol is a chemical, the "domesticated drug" served up as beer, booze and wine. And, of course, those lovely addictive pills, often prescribed by the doctors, are chemicals, too. "Chemically dependent" is the descriptive term applied to a drunk, lush, dipsomaniac, sot, souse, hop head, freak, dope fiend, junkie, drug addict. But whether these people use and abuse alcohol in some form or become addicted to tranquilizers, benzedrine or barbiturates or swallow, sniff, smoke or mainline other drugs, their problem is the same—addiction to chemical mind-benders, be they stimulants, depressants, hallucinogens, or what have you.

Dr. Richard O. Heilman, consulting psychiatrist at Hazelden, believes that the illness can better be described than formally defined. The problem, he says, is intoxication, and the "hooker" is the experience of feeling "high." The user gets hooked on this feeling and continues to seek it. Any drug used to achieve this high becomes part of the problem. Exactly what the drug of choice happens to be is of secondary importance. The point is that there is a profound, recurrent urge to become intoxicated. Dr. Heilman states that this urge is stronger than the need to sleep, to eat, to make love or to be socially acceptable. Once learned, the urge cannot be unlearned.

**2. I thought that alcoholics stuck to booze in some form and that the drug addicts stayed with drugs. They switch around, right?**

You can bet they do! Dr. Heilman says that few addicts make use of only one drug during their period of active addiction. When the lady lush discovers that she can get the same high by "eating her booze," she may combine alcohol and pills. That mixture is deadly poison and can lead to death, either intentional or accidental.

**3. Now what's this business about close members of an alcoholic's family being infected, being sick, too?**

One of our friends in Alcoholics Anonymous begins her story with this comparison: "Becoming an alcoholic is something like getting a bad sunburn. You didn't expect to get it, you don't know just how you got it, and you're mighty uncomfortable when you have it!"

That goes for the family as well. We get a very painful case of reflected alcoholic sunburn.

Want a label to pin on your chest? The professionals call us "mirror alcoholics." Another term in use is "co-alcoholic." Some folks call us "dry drunks." Me, I like the term "knurd," which, you will deduce, is "drunk" spelled backwards. Shades of Serutan! "Knurd" has a nice sound, something like the dull thunk of a partly deflated basketball bounced against a wall. So now I'm a recovering knurd, reflecting most of my wife's alcoholic symptoms, except for that recurring urge that Dr. Heilman talks about.

The professionals tell us that it's often easier to spot the alcoholic by observing her spouse and other family members.

A knurd, whether he is aware of it or not (and he's usually unaware), becomes obsessed with his wife's illness, often to the point of paranoia. In his frantic efforts to help, he unconsciously assumes a God-playing role and develops a serious case of "fat ego." Frustrated at every turn, he becomes angry and depressed, assumes guilt and is sometimes suicidal. He's lost his mental health, and it shows. Sick? You'd better believe it. He needs help just as badly as she does.

## 4. What's the difference between blacking out and passing out?

Ethyl alcohol is a depressant, an anesthetic, and if you swill down enough of the stuff, no matter who you are, you will lose consciousness and pass out. Now a blackout, on the other hand, is a very sneaky thing and can be an indicator of alcoholism. (Social drinkers don't have blackouts.) It's a form of temporary amnesia, a loss of memory. It may happen after a few drinks or many drinks and may last for ten minutes or sometimes ten days. Though the alcoholic may get a few flashbacks of what went on, she's not sure and will be in a state of anxiety, wondering who did what to whom at last night's party. When she's blacked out, those around her may think she's okay. She may talk and act as normally as the rest of them. But she's not okay, and she's not normal.

## 5. What's a hallucination?

*Stedman's Medical Dictionary* says it's a wandering of the mind, seeing something that's not there. Any of us might have a hallucination at one time or another. But what about alcoholic hallucinosis? The *Merck Manual of Diagnosis and Therapy (12th Edition)* describes the primary symptoms as auditory illusions and hallucinations which are often accusatory and threatening; the alcoholic is usually frightened. My wife used to hear music coming out of the air conditioners, music that sounded like Bach. She wasn't frightened, just disturbed because she couldn't change the station—she hated Bach!

## 6. What's a convulsion?

The *Merck Manual* says that convulsion symptoms include localized twitching of the muscles, numbness or tingling, visual hallucinations of flashes of light. Loss of consciousness, falling, urinary or fecal incontinence may occur. Sometimes there are stomach pains and a mental fog that may last for several hours. (This definition might also include an epileptic seizure.) Oldtimers in AA warn that the alcoholic who decides to quit drinking "cold turkey" may be subject to a convulsion and could possibly even die as the result. Hospitals and detox centers guard against convulsions through a carefully administered regime to "bring the patient down" under controlled conditions.

## 7. What are DT's?

Pure hell, brother, pure hell. Delirium Tremens include the pink elephants, snakes and spiders and may occur when the severely addicted alcoholic with a high intake begins to "come down." DT's begin with attacks of anxiety, sleeplessness, profuse sweating and depression. There are hallucinations and nocturnal illusions. As the DT's progress, there may be hand tremors, sometimes extending to the head and body. The alcoholic may believe she's back home, leading a band, making a speech. The animal hallucinations are frequent and terrifying. Sometimes the patient feels that the floor is moving, the walls falling or the room spinning. A hospital or detox center can avert most of these symptoms and "bring down" the drunk with only minor discomfort.

## 8. Somebody said I should join an organization called, I think, "All-Or-None." What's the pitch here?

"All-Or-None" is a mighty apt description of Al-Anon Family groups. *All* of us with a drunk in the family need help. *None* of us seems to know how to cope. Together, we can find answers to our problems. We do it in Al-Anon, a world-wide organization made up of the family members of alcoholics and drug-users who are learning more about chemical dependency, how to cope with their mutual problems and to recover from their own illness. It is a form of group therapy, a learning process, one knurd talking to another, a program for self-help. Al-Anon brings the relatives of alcoholics together at regular meetings, teaches the facts about alcoholism as an illness, improves attitudes and emotional health through the study and practice of the suggested "Twelve Steps" adapted from Alcoholics Anonymous.

Most important—it works.

**9. Please—let's get to specifics. There's nothing wrong with me. I just want to know how to make my wife stop drinking.**

I'll reserve comment on whether there's anything wrong with you, old dad, and get on with it. You can accept reality and treat her as a sick woman, which she is. Reality is the fact that she's ill—just as ill as if she had diabetes or a heart condition. But you, my friend, need to shift your mental gears. No one is expected to be perfect and free from upsetting emotions. We are still human, and letting off steam is a very human reaction. You need to be with people who share the same problem and talk it out—let the safety valve blow a bit. You'll find those people in Al-Anon. Don't expect sympathy, which you don't really want, do you? By changing your attitudes you can clear the air at home and create an atmosphere which will encourage—not discourage—your wife to seek help. So stop bugging her!

**10. My kids are driving me up the wall. I know it's because of her drinking, but is there anything I can do?**

Sure. Children mirror their parents' emotions and are highly sensitive to an emotionally disturbed father, as well as a drunken mother. Certainly we can't minimize the chaotic conditions generated by an alcoholic drinking in the home, and home is where most women alcoholics do their thing. They're "closet drinkers." But if father keeps his cool, the effect is far less injurious. If your kids are old enough to understand, give them a quiet run-down on mother's illness. Get them to Alateen meetings. Alateen is for the children of alcoholics, and here your kids will learn to think as individuals, without fear or guilt. They will develop the ability to detach themselves from their parents' problems while retaining their love for them.

## 11. I'm beginning to wonder if I really love my wife, and I feel guilty as hell. Is this unusual?

Take it easy, friend. You're experiencing the same reaction most of us did. Our guilt is so deep-seated that we feel like the proverbial horse's ass. Here's the person we love who, when she's drinking, becomes somebody that we not only dislike, but hate. We think she's responsible for our disgust and shame and wonder if we're losing our self-respect by sticking with her. We reach the point where we have trouble believing that she's even a human being and find ourselves treating her as an animal, or as a child. The resentment and frustration eat away at us, and we blow our stacks, read her the riot act, let it all hang out. We're caught in a whirlpool of emotions, and we strongly suspect that she's dragging us down to her level. Sound familiar?

It's only when we learn to do something about ourselves that we can find a path back to straight, clear thinking. When we learn to sort out our own emotions, when we can make decisions with a mind that's not muddled by false pride or resentment.

I can't decide for you whether or not you love your alcoholic wife. Only you and God, as you understand Him, can make such a decision.

Maybe the following quote from *Fight Against Fear* by Lucy Freeman might give you a better slant:

"Love is acceptance, understanding, tenderness. It does not strangle, grab or possess. It sees the other person not as a god or idol but as a human being possessing the strengths and weaknesses of all human beings. Love does not ask to be served but only to serve. Quiet, gentle, trusting, it is composed of affection and desire without anxiety."

**12. She's spending more on booze than she does on food. I don't make that kind of money, and I'm tempted to put her on an allowance, like one of the kids. Doesn't this make sense?**

It would be very useful if you could strike oil in your back yard! There's no definite answer to this question. Many of us know that the problem of family finances looms as large as mother's capacity for alcohol—which seems to be growing, doesn't it? It has been fairly standard practice for men to turn over most of the budgeting to their wives. We expect them to feed and clothe us, decorate the home, keep the kids looking sharp, have a little spending money left over and make the major decisions concerning our disposable income after taxes, if there's anything left.

When she's drinking, we wonder—with good cause—how much she's spending on the sauce and how much she blows at the deli on convenience foods that even a drunk can warm in the oven. So we get tough, demand to see the cash-register tapes, cut off the credit cards and resentfully take over the essential buying ourselves. Then she gets sore, we fight about it, and she gets drunk again.

Some of my Al-Anon friends say that if we exhibit a little confidence and trust and are willing to put our money where the trust is, we can help our alcoholic face up to reality by returning some of the financial responsibilities to her. She's probably lost most of her self-respect, and a little confidence on your part will help her restore a portion of her shattered self-image. If you do this, you must really keep your hands off, quit breathing down her neck and let her manage her own efforts.

When your wife joins Alcoholics Anonymous, this works even more successfully: Restore communications. Discuss your mutual problems with her, both personal and financial. You might select one special night for this, leaving the rest of the week free of such touchy subjects. Completely surrender the responsibilities which are rightfully hers. Put your faith in her and in your Higher Power that things will turn out all right.

You think that's a big order? You're damned right it is. But it just might be a turning point, so give it an honest shot.

## 13. What's an "enabler"?

Just what it says—one who actually enables the alcoholic to continue her destructive behavior.

## 14. Could I be an enabler?

Maybe you are, chum. Unwittingly, a man may prolong a woman's illness by covering up for her, protecting her from the consequences of her drinking and keeping her wrapped in the cocoon of unreality. If you do any of these things, you're enabling, and you want to bring that to a grinding halt. Sure, it seems to be the natural thing to do—protect her—but the fact of the matter is, your protection is bringing her just a little closer to death. Although it seems cruel, your best bet if you want to really help her is to withdraw your "protection."

If she picks up a DWI (Driving While Intoxicated) citation, let her go to court and face the consequences of losing her license. If she's arrested for public intoxication, let her sweat out a night in jail. If she's in trouble at work, keep out of the fracas. Don't rush out and hire an attorney to "protect her good name." When you pull the rug of support out from under her, you're allowing her to move closer to the day when she'll be ready to do something about her illness—for herself.

## 15. I thought that Alcoholics Anonymous was for gutter bums, those guys with red noses down "under the bridge." You want my wife to join them?

Alcoholics Anonymous members represent an accurate cross section of our society—poor, rich, black, white, professionals and laborers. Women are housewives, students, sales clerks, secretaries, nurses, actresses, doctors, lawyers, teachers and pillars of the church. Here are a couple of definitions. Take your pick:

Some professionals define AA as a "didactic inspirational group program." Dr. Daniel J. Anderson of Hazelden modifies the definition to a more understandable "mutual self-help group of peers."

The following statement of purpose which you'll hear read at AA group meetings says it succinctly:

"Alcoholics Anonymous is a fellowship of men and women who share their experience, strength and hope with each other that they may solve their common problem and help others to recover from alcoholism.

"The only requirement for membership is an honest desire to stop drinking. AA has no dues or fees. It is not allied with any sect, denomination, politics, organization or institution; does not wish to engage in any controversy, neither endorses or opposes any causes. Our primary purpose is to stay sober and help other alcoholics to achieve sobriety."

**16. You say that alcoholism is a deadly disease, which can be arrested. If that's so, do we have to keep our hands off and wait for just the right moment for her to seek help, or can we confront her earlier and arrest the disease sooner? If I knew she had cancer, I'd get her into the hands of competent specialists whether she wanted to go or not!**

Remember that alcoholism isn't purely a physical ailment like cancer—it's a physical, mental and spiritual disease and must be treated accordingly. The women of AA will tell you that the door is always open, and they're ready, willing and able to offer help when your mate asks for it, when she "bottoms out." Some alcoholics may need to experience that helpless, hopeless moment before they can admit their problem and accept help. It's hard to quarrel with AA since it is, by far, the greatest force and has the best track record of any agency designed to aid the hapless drunk. You can't knock success.

Now, there's also a growing belief that the "crisis," which the alcoholic and her friends and family have been trying to avoid, is, in fact, a turning point from dependency to recovery, also that an act of intervention can stop the downward spiral to death earlier in the game.

Vernon E. Johnson, himself a recovered alcoholic, explains in his book, *I'll Quit Tomorrow*, what he believes is a breakthrough method of forcing the alcoholic to recognize her (or his) illness and the imperative need to seek treatment. A similar program is detailed in the Fairfield Community Plan's *How to Help an Alcoholic Who Insists He Doesn't Need Any Help*.

Both methods, which stress the need for outside help and careful preparation, suggest a pre-planned confrontation by persons important to the alcoholic (family members, employers, teachers, lifelong friends). The idea is to present specific evidence to the alcoholic of events which have happened or conditions which exist. The goal is to have her see and accept enough data from reality so that she can understand her need for help. At this point, acceptable alternatives may be offered to her—this hospital, that treatment center, AA—and the alcoholic makes her own decision.

Confrontation can be a delicate business. It's my opinion that anyone planning to try it had better get some good advice and preparation from Al-Anon or from counselors familiar with the process. If you want more information, get the publications mentioned. They are listed in the bibliography at the end of this book.

## 17. What should the attitude of the family be when she does join AA or go to a treatment center?

We're inclined to want to blow bugles, fly flags and demonstrate down Main Street with a 100-piece marching band complete with baton twirlers. Hallelujah—she's sober!

It's best to climb down from that pink cloud and have faith that she's doing her level best. No matter how slow her progress seems to be, be thankful that she's improved. Be understanding, forgive the past, and if you have any misgivings, conceal them.

By all means, *keep your mouth shut and your hands off.* If she's in AA, let her decide when she wants to talk about it and make decisions concerning it. Every AA member needs to work out her program in her own way. If she invites you to attend open AA meetings with her, go. You'll be surprised how much you will enjoy them and the fellowship of a bunch of ex-drunks, men and women alike. And your being with her at these meetings will give her a sense of solidarity, reassurance that you approve of her conduct and activities, that you take pride in her newfound sobriety.

Meanwhile, continue with or start attending Al-Anon meetings and learn as much as you can about the program for yourself. You're recovering, too—you're a knurd, remember?

Don't begrudge or belittle her preoccupation with AA and her work with other still-drinking alcoholics—she'll call it her "Twelfth Step work." In the early stages of recovery, AA members recommend that newcomers attend as many meetings as possible, and you may be elected as chief baby sitter. When she announces, maybe a little defiantly, that her sobriety comes first—relax! Think what it was like when she was drinking and how many other avenues to sobriety (usually under your careful direction) were explored without success.

So if you're no longer tops on her totem pole, enjoy the comforting thought that you no longer have to manage her— she's sober—and maybe you've found your rightful position— that is *after* God and AA. Settle back and be thankful that her preoccupation with AA is healthy, and know that her excess enthusiasm will simmer down and become happiness for you and the family.

### 18. Do I handle her with kid gloves after she finds her initial sobriety?

Don't baby her or humor her, but try a little TLC—tender, loving care. Observe the usual rules of give a little, take a little. Treat her with normal human kindness. Don't indulge in any unusual or excessive giving-in because you're scared silly that she'll go back to hitting the sauce again. If your wife is seriously in the AA program for herself alone, as she should be, it follows that she won't abandon it, no matter what her husband, family or anyone else should say or do.

**19. I suppose now that she's sober, we won't be able to have alcohol in the house or serve it to friends anymore. Is this true?**

Let her call the shots. It's a purely personal problem which must be decided solely by the alcoholic. For a time, she may decide that she doesn't want the stuff around and prefers to skip any social activities where drinking is involved. Okay. That's her decision, and you should respect it without question. However, this attitude often changes after a period of sobriety in AA.

One of the things that bugged my wife after she found sobriety was when our friends who normally passed out the drinks didn't serve them when she was present. Each arrested alcoholic cherishes the privilege of refusing a drink. It reinforces her knowledge that she has an option of drinking or staying sober—and that she has elected to stay sober for this twenty-four hours.

**20. Do I have to quit drinking now that she has?**

This is another personal matter that must be decided by you. Ask her how she feels about it. If she prefers that you don't drink at home or when you're out together, respect her wishes. Again, after several months of sobriety, she'll probably tell you that your drinking, either at home or away from home, is *your* problem to solve as you see fit. She's learned that she is powerless not only over alcohol but also powerless over other people and their actions.

**21. What's this about her maybe going on a "dry drunk"?**

This is an AA phrase to describe the occasions when she's sullen, edgy, morose, bad-tempered or just plain mean over a period of time. It may happen after the first fine flush of sobriety has worn off or later on. (It happens to all of us, alcoholics or not, occasionally.) The "stinkin' thinkin'" that AA talks about may be ascribed to the dry drunk, as well as to the alcoholic. Don't let the dry drunk throw you. Her friends in AA are quick to sense the problem and will help her understand it, help her get her head screwed on straight again.

Here's where you practice that "detachment—with love" that you'll hear about in Al-Anon, and keep yourself busy with your own activities. We knurds can also have our own emotional dry drunks, and many of us have lived for years in a dry-drunk emotional state. That's *our* problem. We find the answers we may need in Al-Anon, where our friends are pretty quick to sense what's happening and help us face up to it.

## 22. How can an alcoholic's mate stop worrying?

None of us was born knowing how to worry. We learned it. Now we need to unlearn. Live the steps of the Al-Anon program, just twenty-four hours at a time. Work on your own plan for daily living. This won't erase the problem that has you uptight, but it will ease the tensions and let you face your fears which started all the worry in the first place. Try it — you'll like it!

## 23. How long does it take to get over being afraid and to develop confidence in her after she finds sobriety?

Well, how long did it take for you to become afraid and lose your confidence in her? It won't take that long, friend. It depends, not on her actions, but on how soon that you, as a mirror alcoholic, a knurd, can sincerely and completely turn your girl and her problems over to God and can concentrate on working out your own problems with the same help.

## 24. What do I do if she starts to drink or use drugs again?

First, resist the urge to kick her squarely in the behind. She's had a relapse, or as the AA's put it, a "slip." It's a deeply emotional experience for most alcoholics, with a return of fear, depression, anxiety and a loss of the self-worth that she's built up during her period of sobriety. AA recognizes that many recovering alcoholics may slip, return to AA, slip again. Relapse, in fact, is characterized as a symptom of the disease.

They tell the alcoholic that regardless of the number of slips, the door to AA is always open, but they also caution her that sometime, after a slip, she might not be able to crawl through it!

If your wife should slip or relapse, you need to practice this newly-learned "detachment—with love" to the very best of your ability. This was brought home to me when I made a trip with my wife to visit an AA friend who had phoned her, near-hysterical and in tears, to tell her that she had just taken a drink after about a month's sobriety. Maggie and I tried to talk with her calmly, practicing the prescribed "detachment—with love," assuring her that she had only relapsed, that any sick person still convalescing might suffer a relapse, that it wasn't that bad.

"Damn you," she shouted, "Don't give me that relapse shit! I'm a drunk and a pig and I hate myself!"

Detaching—with love—sounds easy but works hard. Hear your wife out if she wants to talk about it and cry and tell you about her failure. Then your comment might be along this line:

"Honey, I'm sorry that you slipped. But I've learned that I can't do a damned thing about it. It's your problem. Why don't you call your AA sponsor?"

Many men in Al-Anon say that a slip on the part of their recovering alcoholic seems to ignite their own fuse, resulting in their own version of relapse. If she turns up smashed after weeks, months or even years of sobriety, often we react by blowing our stacks, raising hell, crying and wondering what *we've* said or done to cause her to return to the bottle. Back comes all the old guilt, fear and frustration. Like the relapsed alcoholic, we haven't learned our lesson—that we are power-less over alcohol. So the advice that we so kindly dished out to our doleful drunk applies equally to us. We had better talk it out with a friend in Al-Anon and re-examine the way we are working our program. Attending Al-Anon meetings regularly is the very best insurance we can buy to guard against a personal slip, and to cope with a slip by our alcoholic.

**25. My wife is back from a treatment center and she's a changed person. She seems to radiate peace and serenity. I'd like some of this myself. How do I go about getting it?**

This is the bonus beyond sobriety that some recovering alcoholics find. Some get it rather quickly, and others work at it longer. I've found a certain measure of serenity by doing just about the same things that my wife does. I work the Al-Anon Twelve Steps, as she works the Steps of AA. I attend Al-Anon meetings regularly, and I gain strength and knowledge from the group. I began to develop my own personal philosophy and a daily plan for living. I learned—and am still learning—to "Let Go and Let God," to detach myself emotionally from my alcoholic's problem, with love in my heart and trust in God as I understand him. It's not too tough when you consider that I do this only twenty-four hours at a time, and we can do almost anything for one day, can't we?

**26. Will Al-Anon be of any benefit to me once my alcoholic is sober?**

More than ever, friend, more than ever. There's no guarantee of living "happily ever after" just because she's sober. The initial adjustment to a more normal family life and husband-wife relationship is much easier to come by through the tolerance and understanding gained in Al-Anon. Too, when she stops drinking, she starts growing, in mind and in spirit.

My wife puts it like this: "I've heard that when you start to drink seriously, you stop growing mentally. Since I started when I was fourteen and didn't learn how to stop until I was fifty-two, then it must be true that I'm just a fourteen-year-old in a fifty-two-year-old body! So I still have a lot of 'growing up' to do!"

If she's going to keep growing, I can't assume that things are going to be like they were before. Somehow I need to grow right along with her if I want to preserve our marriage. Besides, if I sweated out the crazy bad times, I want to enjoy the benefits of living with a happy, sober wife. If that takes some work on my part, it's still easier than trying to manage a drunk!

### 27. What's "tough love"?

It's the reverse of enabling, as defined in Question 13. You'll hear much of "tough love" in AA circles. The men and women of AA know that the practicing alcoholic or the woman that slipped is dishonest with herself. These AA's have no compunction in showing her where her thinking is askew, and doing it often in blunt, earthy language.

The AA's can do this, but as the spouse or relative of the woman alcoholic, we can't use the same technique to help her straighten out her thinking. Our brand of "tough love" requires that we let go of the reins of her life and leave her free to accept the consequences of her actions, good or bad. We detach from the situation, but we never quit loving her. Underneath, even if she's still drinking or has slipped, she is the very same woman that we loved so much when we were married. The hardest thing we have to do is to detach, let go, let her face reality, whether she's drinking or sober.

### 28. Now that she's sober, is it all right to talk about the stupid, crazy things she did when she was drunk?

One of my friends had an almost compulsive urge to talk to his wife about the things she did, what she said, and about the mess that she was when drinking. He seemed to enjoy reminding her of how it was and to describe events when others were listening. She was fairly fresh from a treatment center, where she had been taught to bring her resentments out into the open, rather than burying them as she had done in the past, and husband Fritz was beginning to get under her skin.

One night he stopped me on the way into an Al-Anon meeting. He was in a state of near-shock.

"Do you know what she told me last night? She said that if I didn't learn to keep my damn mouth shut about her damn drinking experiences she was going to shove her damn shoe in it!"

That's the answer. When she voluntarily brings up tales from her drinking or pill-popping days, listen. Don't bring up other incidents, either in an effort to be funny or to remind her what a horse's ass she was at a particular time or place. Chances are, she may have been in a blackout and wouldn't remember the event anyway.

Accept her amends. If she's in AA, the Eighth and Ninth Steps of the program suggest that she make a list of all the people that she has harmed; become willing to make amends to them all, and to make direct amends wherever possible, except when to do so would injure them or others. You're probably number one on her list. Accept her amends to you with as much dignity and good grace as you can possibly muster. But remember, the pain of her experience is still very fresh, so let her select the time and place for amends and reminiscences. Otherwise, you may get a shoe down your throat!

**29. She's staying sober with the help of AA, and I'm really proud of her and what she's doing. Is it okay to tell others of her activities?**

Nope. Remember, she's a member of Alcoholics *Anonymous* and you must respect and preserve her anonymity. If she elects to break her anonymity and to discuss her experiences with other than AA people, that's her prerogative. But aside from unburdening yourself to your Al-Anon sponsor or friends in the Al-Anon group, the subject of your spouse's past drinking experiences and present AA activities is a closed one.

**30. What's "Band-aiding"?**

Let's assume your spouse is fresh in the AA program and is having a hell of a time staying sober. The straight talk she's hearing from her sponsor is hard to take, so she's crying on your shoulder. You console her, agree that her sponsor is too tough, and try to make her feel better.

You are guilty of "Band-aiding." You're helping her escape from reality and avoid facing her problems squarely. You may actually be greasing the slide for a slip. Look, you know by now that she's a con artist. She's giving you the "poor me" routine, which is typical.

The same principle holds true in Al-Anon. A new man gets you to one side and spills his tale of woe. In an almost instinctive rush of sympathy, you agree that life has indeed been cruel to him, rationalize away his problems and give him easy answers. Take it easy, brother. Be empathetic, not sympathetic. We're not here to smooth away the problems but to learn how to face up to them and work out solutions with sane judgment. "Tough love"? Yes. "Band-aiding"? No!

### 31. What's so wrong about using minor tranquilizers to help ease the alcoholic through the change from drinking to sobriety?

Sometimes tranquilizers are administered by professionals in a detoxification center. But if she takes them on her own, the alcoholic is playing with fire.

The drug industry certainly didn't do anyone a favor when they came up with the misleading label of "minor tranquilizers." Professionals working in detox centers tell us that these are addictive and highly so when used in excess of the prescribed dosage. What alcoholic could stop with just one drink—stop with just one of anything? Pills are deadly poison to either the practicing or the recovering alcoholic—just as much a passport to death as the old enemy, booze.

My wife has this warning so deeply etched into her brain that she has compiled a list of non-addictive medicines which she can take safely. She let her doctor know that she is a recovering alcoholic and wants no part of any mind-bending drug prescribed for her aches and pains. If the doctor gave her an argument, she would change doctors.

We've seen it happen. A recovering alcoholic is led to a slip as the result of taking a pill under "doctor's orders." Either alcoholics quickly become addicted to the new drug, or, under its influence, lower their defenses and start to drink. That may be enough to set them off and running.

Many recovering alcoholics are dead set against taking potentially addicting drugs at any time except in the most demanding medical situations. The only exception my wife makes to her rule of total abstinence from mind-altering chemicals, is that, during a stay in a hospital, she will take prescribed drugs with the full understanding and agreement of the doctors that she will be withdrawn *in the hospital* from the drug. Is she making a mountain out of a mole hill? She doesn't think so. Use of the mind-benders for her may be a matter of life or death.

**32. My wife is an arrested alcoholic and claims she can't take any medication or use any food with even a minor alcoholic content. Isn't she carrying this abstinence routine to a ridiculous point?**

Not if she's interested in staying alive. She's accepted the fact that her use of alcohol in any form or any quantity may put her back on the merry-go-round.

A friend in AA, a furnace repairman, makes this comparison: "My pilot light is always lit. One drop of alcohol and the main burner may be fired up and roaring. If I'm back on booze, one more drink may mean death for me. I don't know this for sure, but I'm not going to take chances. In my business, you can blow up houses taking chances."

Cough syrups containing alcohol, codeine or other addicting drugs are out for the alcoholic. So are those holiday fruit cakes made with uncooked brandy, so are liquor-centered chocolates. Your wife has learned her lesson well.

**33. I'm sore as hell at our family doctor. He examined my wife and told her that her drinking problem was the result of a nervous condition. He said a few drinks wouldn't hurt, and gave her prescriptions for sleeping pills and tranquilizers. She ended up in the hospital when she tried to kill herself. I want to sue the bastard for malpractice. What do you think?**

I can't give you legal advice. Talk to your attorney. I can tell you that alcoholism was recognized formally as a treatable ailment by the 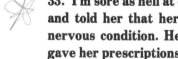American Medical Association in 1955, and of course, there still are doctors practicing who completed their training before that time. Even today in medical schools and hospitals, there doesn't seem to be much instruction in the recognition and treatment of alcoholism. Experience — either professional or personal — has made some doctors more aware than others of the risk of prescribing certain drugs for recovering alcoholics. For an alcoholic, it may be worth finding one of these drug-wary physicians. Authorities do agree that there is no medical cure for alcoholism. That's bad. But the diagnosis and the treatment of alcoholism and other drug addiction are becoming more common and continue to improve. And that's good.

## 34. What's a "gimme prayer"?

First of all, understand that I'm not trying to shove organized religion at you. If you're a professed atheist or agnostic, that's your business. But if you will concede that there could be a Power greater than ourselves, then perhaps you will also concede that a request for help to that Power may be in order.

Many of us will remember from our religious training the statement, "Ask, and it shall be given."

That seems simple enough, so we may wheel out a prayer something like this: "Lord, gimme a nice house, a big car, gimme a vacation in Europe, gimme smart kids, and most important, Lord, gimme a sober wife."

Ever pray like that? If you've been using "gimme prayers", you're mighty disappointed when God doesn't snap to and pour all those blessings you ordered into your lap. When the alcoholic prays loudly and mightily for God to give her sobriety and there's no immediate response, she uses it as another excuse for drinking. God let her down.

So, you say, what kind of a prayer works? For me, there was a clue in the book, *One Day at a Time in Al-Anon.*

It reads: "Prayer is the contact I make with God in my thoughts. It is a Powerful medicine for the spirit. Prayers for guidance are perhaps the most potent of all, providing I keep myself receptive and willing to act according to His inspiration.

"Prayer is simply a reaching out to make contact with a Power greater than ourselves. It is an acknowledgment of our personal helplessness which has been demonstrated to us so often in our efforts to find peace and security."

I believe that if we regularly use a prayer asking for guidance and a prayer expressing our gratitude, we've improved our percentages in enlisting God's help. For a good all-purpose prayer that covers most situations, I can recommend that old standby of AA and Al-Anon—the Serenity Prayer:

"God grant me the serenity to accept the things I cannot change,
Courage to change the things I can, and
Wisdom to know the difference."

# 3

# Poison or Not

"No, I'll look first," she said, "and see whether it's marked 'poison' or not ... if you drink much from a bottle marked 'poison,' it is almost certain to disagree with you sooner or later."

Many books with a serious theme—economics, germ warfare, atomic energy or how to build a compost pile— include a chapter or at least an introduction that deals with the author's qualifications. You know what I mean—he was born in an igloo in Alaska, tended sheep in his tender years, worked his way through college as a Fuller Brush salesman, and took his first degree at the age of nineteen. Then, in rapid succession, he earned his master's and his doctorate and worked as a Research Fellow in economics, germ warfare, etc.

The qualifications for writing a treatise on living with a woman alcoholic is comparatively simple. Being house-broken in an igloo, or acquiring a string of degrees doesn't help at all. First, one's wife, or the woman that you're living with, manages to become an alcoholic all on her own, without your help, but it may not seem that way at the time. The fact that she's an alcoholic sinks in slowly. One day when it's overcast and muggy with no sunshine to give you a false sense of well-being, it becomes painfully clear that a lady social drinker doesn't take a slug directly from the bottle of warm vodka at nine in the morning, except after a snake bite. Nor does she keep a stash of fifths, usually half empty, tucked away in unlikely hiding places throughout the house and a pint or two down in the bottom of her golf bag in the back of the car. These little clues point the way to the conclusion that you-know-who has a very bad habit, which any self-respecting husband will solve for her—or so you think—once he puts his mind to it.

Those are about the only qualifications you need for openers anyway, just enough knowledge to rattle the dice cup and make the beginning moves in the new game you and your wife are going to play, a game called "Alcoholic." Your qualifications pile up steadily as the game goes on—and on. It's one hell of a shock to discover, two years or maybe ten years later, that the name of the game has been changed to "Slow Death," and despite all your training and wisdom, your girl is dying and you can't stop it. Despite all of her years of experience in drinking, wanting to stop and not being able to, she can't do anything about it either.

So gentlemen, meet Maggie and Jack. That's us. I'll relate briefly our qualifications—hers as a souse, and mine as the spouse of a souse. She was an expert at getting smashed out of her mind, and my expertise was in trying to stop her—and failing, time after time.

Maggie. Now in her early fifties, Maggie is a tall, lithe woman that passes even in the daylight for a much younger person, and at night in candlelight, she might appear to be in her thirties. She's poised, Maggie is, and she has a warm smile that lights up her face like the sky at sunset. She is impetuous, warm, sometimes demanding. She's quick to laugh, but her eyes can fill with tears just as quickly. Her head is screwed on straight, and I think she's getting it all together.

When Maggie read that paragraph for the first time, she

said, "You make me sound kinda beautiful without really saying so. How come you never said nice things about me in the BS days when I really needed them?" ("BS" is not what you're thinking, but is our personal shorthand for "Before Sobriety.")

"Because you were a mess."

Not too many years ago, Maggie *was* a mess. There were three deep lines that creased her forehead, lines of discontent. I thought she looked much like her grandmother, who had died of cancer, mouth all turned down like she had just found part of a worm in the apple she was eating. Maggie's eyes were bloodshot, and they brimmed with tears that flowed for no apparent reason. Her features were a little blurred with bloat, her voice husky from too much booze and too many cigarettes. She was nervous and edgy, no matter how many drinks she'd taken to relax.

She was a confessed alcoholic who couldn't see any way out of the corner she was backed into except death. She'd tried that twice, but didn't bring it off.

No, I didn't say many nice things about Maggie then, but I still thought that somewhere in that mess was the girl that I had married.

Someplace, somehow during those first twenty-five years of our marriage, Maggie had crossed the invisible line, moving from her loudly self-proclaimed status of the girl with the hollow leg, the woman that could and did drink most of the men we knew right under the table, to her new and frightening position of the compulsive drinker who needed that morning "health drink" just as much as she needed to breathe. She didn't know when she crossed the line—there was no clear demarcation where, on one side she was a social drinker, on the other, an alcoholic.

One of our friends, a TV personality by trade and an arrested alcoholic by necessity and choice, explained it this way:

"The change from a social drinker to an alcoholic is something like the process of making pickles. Pickle-making, as any first-class home canner will tell you, involves little more than cramming a bunch of cucumbers into a glass jar, covering them with brine and spices, sealing the jar and settling back to wait for nature to take its course. But science cannot tell us at what precise moment those cool cucumbers change into pickles.

"The same perplexing question can be applied to a social drinker's transformation into a compulsive, addicted drinker. There's just no way to pinpoint the precise moment when the cool-cucumber social drinker becomes the pixilated pickle alcoholic."

Maggie was brought up jointly by her parents and grandparents in a good Christian home. I asked her one time why so many members of Alcoholics Anonymous began their stories with a remark about being brought up in a good Christian home.

"I don't really know," Maggie answered, "I suppose it's to show that our parents did all they could to bring us up right, and we did all we could to prove that they didn't."

In those depression days, her parents and grandparents joined forces to save money and then when times got better, never got around to separate residences again. This was great for Maggie, because by playing her doting grandparents against her mother or dad, she usually got her way.

Her way included her first drink when she was nine, just across the border in Mexico, a stop on the way to California.

"I remember that little glass of wine," Maggie recalled, "It did something for me. It made me feel very grown-up and worldly, and that was the way I wanted to be."

Since granddad operated a summer resort complete with beer joint, dance hall and plenty of dark corners, she was able to rediscover that feeling early and often, whenever she could escape from the watchful eyes of her grandparents. She began drinking at twelve and went on her first big drunk when she was fourteen.

"The Labor Day dance marked the end of the summer season, and all of my good friends were very sad. It seemed sophisticated to get drunk and cry a little, so that's what we did. The hangover was important, too—you could tell all the kids who didn't drink about how bad you felt, and they were impressed."

Five years later, she had her first blackout. She recalled leaving a New Year's dance in a borrowed car to find one of her boy friends who, for one reason or another, had to stay home that night. She wanted to wish him "Happy New Year." It seemed very important. Her next recollection was that here she was, driving the car bumpty-bump down the tracks of a busy railroad, all four tires blown out. She backed the car awkwardly to the road intersection, pulled off the tracks and onto the highway. A few minutes later, a freight train thundered along the tracks she had so recently vacated.

Maggie thought she had many valid reasons for drinking. In high school, it was the sophisticated thing to do, and the boys were a little in awe of her. Her father popped her into a fashionable school for young ladies, and she drank because she hated it and there were no boys. She had wanted to go to art school, but lost that battle with her dad. She drank over unhappy love affairs. She also drank over happy love affairs. Maggie continued to like the taste of booze. She liked even more the heightened sense of freedom, the feeling of being somebody and the escape from the dullness of everyday existence, including her job as a doctor's receptionist. She drank to feel better, and she felt better often.

Back in the days of the Volstead Act, her parents made their gin in the bathtub and home brew in the kitchen, but drinking was more in the spirit of thumbing their noses at national prohibition than actually liking the junk that they drank. Her grandparents enjoyed a beer, a glass of wine or a water highball, but drank only lightly to mark a pause in their busy days or to sharpen the taste of their nightly snack of rat cheese and soda crackers. Nobody ever said much about Uncle Hugh, who was a bartender in a cheat joint and who eventually drank himself into an early grave, so the story went.

Maggie was a tomboy, who could swim, dive, play golf and eventually drink as well or better than any of the youngsters that lived or summered on the lake. She was a rebel who resented the sometimes smothering love of her doting grandparents, and the on-again, off-again sharp discipline of her father. She disliked her dependent role in the family and was frustrated when they held her back and kept her in the nest where they could watch over her. Escape, then, was with the help of a Coke or 7-Up laced with gin or whiskey.

I met Maggie the morning that I started to work for her granddad as soda jerk at the dance hall—eight dollars per week plus room and board and tips. I had never worked behind a soda fountain, but I had watched a lot and was hired on the basis of a friend's recommendation.

"Make me a really thick chocolate milkshake," this tanned girl with the great legs and tight bathing suit demanded. I scooped and squirted and whirred the shake, with what I hoped was consummate skill, and poured the creamy mess into a big glass. It was so thick it wouldn't respond to the suction of Maggie's lips to the straw.

"That's just wonderful," she breathed.

I was in love, and that was not good. I needed that summer job badly. I was in college, paying my own way, and the money I could tuck back during the summer would take care of my tuition and books, with maybe a little left over, if I was careful. I couldn't afford, I thought, the luxury of a summer romance, particularly with the granddaughter of the boss himself.

I was the product of a tough little mining town, the son of an easygoing, taciturn father and a mother who was ambitious for her children, but worried about their likely entry into Hell. She believed every word in the Book of Revelation, and my brother, sister and I didn't miss a session of Sunday School, church and the Sunday-night Young People's Meeting. I went because I had to, but I was fair game for the North Side gang who regularly chased me home from school and church.

"THOU SHALT NOT STEAL" was the message my mother was determinedly imprinting on the back of my bare legs with a peach-tree switch—a switch I had cut after having my first two choices rejected as too small for punishment of my heinous crime. I had borrowed a quarter from my mother's purse and spent it for candy, which I had distributed in the hope of making new friends in the North Side gang. Licorice sticks, candy pies in their tiny tins, jawbreakers, red-hots and the three-for-a-nickel candy bars—you could buy a mountain of candy for a quarter in those days. Our neighborhood grocer had ratted on me because no kid bought twenty-five cents' worth of candy with his mother's permission. Obviously, I had swiped the money.

I gritted my teeth and took my switching like the hardened tough that I thought I was. I heard a vivid description of Hell-with-a-capital-H, such as only a mother can describe—lakes of fire with sulphurous smoke, brimstone raining down in torrents, suffocating heat. Today it would sound like a mid-August bus ride to any metropolitan downtown area. But I was going to Hell if I didn't change my thieving ways.

Fortunately, mother didn't know about the plug of Horse-shoe Chewing tobacco hidden behind the garage, lifted from my father's store, which provided me with another entry ticket into the North Side gang. I was tough, chewed tobacco and spit, and donned my first mask, as Peck's Bad Boy. Now *I* could chase *other* kids home from Sunday School!

I discovered girls when I was thirteen and began to remake my mask into that of an irresistible Don Juan. I switched from chewing tobacco to cigarettes and, as I grew, graduated from hard cider to "Jasper Red," a superior product of the area's illicit stills. I affected a worldly knowledge of sex, all gleaned from copies of *Spicy Detective* and like literature, and the raunchy little cartoon booklets of *Jiggs and Maggie*, *Tillie the Toiler* and *Mutt and Jeff*. Complete with pimples, oiled hair and my first suit with a lapeled vest, I was accepted by my peers as a dashing young man about our town of 3,000.

Times were tough in the mid 30's. My parents edicted that I should live at home and attend the local college, preparing myself for a career as a minister of the gospel or more practically, as a school teacher.

Smoking was a grievous sin. "If the good Lord had intended for us to smoke, He would have put a smokestack on the top of our heads!" So thundered the college president at our daily and mandatory sessions in the college chapel. Drinking was the cause of instant expulsion. We might date the girl residents in the college dorm if we returned them safely by 10 p.m., free of course from any telltale lipstick smudges and with all blouse buttons in place.

This was not for me, and I opted for the state university with the hundred dollars that my father contributed to my higher education. I worked as dishwasher, waiter, short-order cook and dormitory cleaner for the National Youth Administration at a pay scale of thirty-five cents per hour.

Striving for the finer things in life, I joined forces with Phil, son of a county judge, in organizing a modest crap game in competition with the local table downtown. We shared a third-floor garret apartment above a beauty parlor, so we shoved our beds in one corner and set up our casino. We collected empty bottles from our more affluent fraternity brothers and refilled them with the cheapest whiskey obtainable. Chips were twenty-five cents (they cost a dollar downtown) and a drink was also priced at a quarter. We ran an honest table, catering to the fraternity crowd, and were an overnight success. We had visions of diversifying by opening a small whorehouse, and Phil had made the necessary arrangements with three girls in the nearby state capitol, once we could find the right location.

We made the strategic error of failing to clear our operation with the local police force, and the downtown dice table manager passed the word to the campus cops. We were quietly picked up and brought before the Dean of Men. Expulsion seemed inevitable, but Phil called his dad, who, as an experienced politician, arranged for mitigation of the expected punishment and we were suspended from classes for three weeks. The Dean further ruled that we should report to each of our professors and explain why we were being suspended, working on the theory that the shame and mortification of such confessions would deter us from further ventures into the field of crime—at least, while we were students.

On the contrary, our professors in the School of Business Administration seemed to applaud and admire our unorthodox business acumen. My professor of marketing rewarded me with a job as his assistant, and I graded examinations and worked on research projects. Who says that rugged individualism doesn't pay off? I quickly developed a thriving business of grade guarantees. I passed the word through the fraternity network that I was in position to assure passing grades in my professor's courses, with fees ranging from ten dollars for an "A" to three dollars for a respectable "C."

By campus standards, I had risen from rags to riches, and I was proud of my enterprise. I needed no one—I could make it and make it good with no help, using my wits to reach success. Tentatively, I tried on the new mask of Horatio Alger, and it felt good. If a fellow had to lie a little, cheat a little, it was all part of the game, wasn't it? It all paid off—if you were just careful not to get caught.

"Jack, you're going to Hell if you don't change your ways," my mother lectured me. I was almost sixteen and sat at the kitchen table, stomach still churning, pale and hung over from my first drunk. It was New Year's eve and, in company with the now older North Side gang, I had purchased my first half-pint of Jasper Red and had drunk it all, sitting in the back seat of someone's car. It didn't agree with me, and I was at home before eleven, tiptoeing quietly up the stairs to my room. When I stretched out on the bed, my stomach turned over and I dashed for the window and expelled my half-pint, along with the hamburger and fried potatoes eaten earlier. The evidence was still there on the roof for my mother to spot and identify when she went out to sweep the light fall of snow from our front sidewalk. Now—for certain—I was going to Hell. My mother said so.

There had to be a religion in which God was more lenient with His backsliders, and during my college years, I explored diligently. The Roman Catholics seemed to have a good thing going with confession and penances (a dozen Hail Mary's and sin no more), but the thought of spilling my black sins into the lap of a priest was frightening. Christian Science attracted me, but there wasn't much latitude for those who liked material things. I checked out the Baptists, Methodists, Presbyterians —even attended a few meetings of Holy Rollers. But none met my idealistic standards. I enrolled in a course in philosophy and rather fancied myself as a hedonist, but that wasn't religion. It seemed a shame, but I would have to become an agnostic. With a little more guts, I could have been an atheist, but I wasn't certain that there was no Supreme Being, and if there was, I sure as hell wouldn't close the door in His face entirely. You never know. I decided to postpone the matter of saving my soul to some indefinite time in the future.

I selected a career on the basis of elimination. Preaching was out, because there was no money in it and obviously no room for a guy that was already halfway to Hell, as my mother said. Teaching was a little better, since a teacher had some status, but the pay was low. I was no athlete and couldn't coach (better pay), and I doubted that I could discipline some of the bigger kids. The sons of miners and farmers tend to come in large sizes. Doctors and dentists did well, but there were years of training and hard work ahead. Besides, I fainted at the sight of blood and quivered at the sound of a dentist's drill. There were too many smarter guys in Law School. That left Business Administration, and I found that I had an affinity for figures, could recognize an asset from a liability at twenty paces, and could cheat my way through courses in economics and corporate finance. Most important, business was where the big money was, and I was going to be rich!

It was going to take me a little longer to get through college because of my false starts in the schools of education, journalism, pre-med and pre-law. I needed that summer job and spent three seasons with Maggie's granddad, rising from soda-jerk to assistant manager. Courting the boss's daughter paid off in many ways.

As assistant manager, I counted the cash at the end of the evening and toted it in a bag to grandpa's cottage and, of course, Maggie always accompanied me. We stopped on convenient shadowy porches of vacant cottages, but never too long, since grandma would come looking for Maggie if we didn't show up in the allotted time. Grandma suspected that nothing good would come of these unauthorized side trips and made it plain that we were to come *straight* home with the money. Maggie and I waited impatiently for her grandparents to finish their nightly cheese and beer and to retire upstairs, probably to listen for any suspect sounds of love-making. Once they were in bed, we dimmed the lights and took over the roomy couch, ever alert to the sound of footsteps descending, which meant that one of the grandparents was en route to the bathroom located adjacent to the living room. They seemed to have very weak kidneys.

As assistant manager, I was in charge of cleaning the women's johns when they overflowed, watching for kids with firecrackers on the dance floor, filling in as waiter when things became hectic. My choice responsibility was to make the rounds of neighboring hotels and restaurants, driving grandpa's big LaSalle, and accompanied by Maggie, posting the big placards that announced our special events at the dance hall.

Maggie and I had a system. We both enjoyed a drink, both were under age, and were agreed that I shouldn't spend my money for booze or beer. I needed that for college. We would enter a resort hotel and stop at the bar, where I would seat Maggie while I left to post my placards in the hotel lobby and elsewhere. Meanwhile, Maggie, sitting alone at a table, would smile alluringly at the men seated at the bar. It never took longer than two minutes before one would move in for the kill.

"How about a drink?" he would ask.

"Why not?" was Maggie's answer.

True to the script, I would return to Maggie's table just when our pigeon was getting warmed up.

"I'd like for you to meet my fiance," Maggie would make the introductions, and I would sit down, frowning as menacingly as possible.

"Well—how about a drink?" was the standard, flustered response. Sometimes we could mooch as many as five or six drinks as we made our hotel rounds.

Then, on the way home, we would park the La Salle behind the barn of a vacant farmhouse, and, safe from grandma's eagle eyes, we would push open the barn door and enter, stretching out on the mounds of musty hay on the floor. Then we counted cobwebs, or did whatever young couples do in old barns.

We were engaged, college style, with Maggie sporting my fraternity pin on her chest. It would be a few years before we were married, since I had to graduate, get that good job and make a lot of money. And then we would live happily ever after. In my daydreams I was the Knight in Shining Armor coming to rescue Maggie from the possessive clutches of her grandmother and to take her away from the irascible and unpredictable tantrums of her short-fused father. It was going to be just like it was in the movies and in the books that I read. I would be rich and famous, with an industrial empire of my own, and Maggie would be at my side, a devoted mother and responsive wife, gracing my home and caring for my curly-haired, loving children.

It wasn't going to work out that way. Galahad in his shining armor was to be Don Quixote tilting at the windmill of alcoholism. My fair lady was already into the early stages of her illness, moving steadily towards addiction. It would take almost thirty years before Maggie's unvoiced plea, "Please help me," would be heard—by a doctor, who happened to be a recovering alcoholic and drug addict, in the emergency room of a city hospital.

You'll find our experiences and those of people like us in the chapters that follow. If you identify with me in some of my efforts to help Maggie either to quit drinking or to learn to "drink like a lady," don't let it blow your mind—you're following a predictable course of action that's common to most husbands of alcoholics.

# 4

# See What This Bottle Does

> "I know something interesting is sure to happen," she said to herself, "whenever I eat or drink anything, so I'll just see what this bottle does. I do hope it'll make me grow large again, for really I'm quite tired of being such a tiny little thing!"

That woman of yours—yes, that one stretched out on the couch, her nylons wrinkled, a little trickle of saliva oozing from her half-opened mouth, the stench of booze rising from her body like vapor from a swamp—what in the hell impels her to get like this?

You've read about drunks, you talked with the fellows at work about your "friend" who drinks too much, and you remembered what you were told when you were still a kid. You've had trouble finding the answer, or the several answers, that seem to make any sense. Here are some of the things you've heard:

"It's in their blood. You dig deep enough and you'll find out that grandpa died of DT's, Aunt Mabel spent part of her life in a sanitarium, and Cousin Willie can't hold a job because he's a drunkard. It's inherited."

"It all goes back to her childhood. I'll bet you that she was an unhappy kid that couldn't get along with her father or her mother. It's all psychological, and she should see a shrink."

"Mark my words, it's God's punishment for her sins."

"You say this woman friend lost her baby? She's drinking to help her forget. Women are like that."

"She probably doesn't have any strength of character. Lots of women are just naturally weak-willed. She could quit if she really buckled down and tried."

"Maybe she's getting even. You know, women will do that when a guy spends more time than she thinks he should at the golf course or down at the bowling alley. Or maybe she found out he's been playing house with some other woman."

"She just doesn't give a damn. Women just don't appreciate what a guy does for them."

"It's this Women's Lib crap."

"She's not getting enough sex."

"She's getting too much sex."

"She's getting it on the side and drinks because she feels guilty."

"How old is she? Maybe she's going through menopause."

"Women need to be dominated. Just cut off her booze and give her a belt in the chops a couple of times and she'll straighten out damn fast."

"Women need God. Make her get on her knees and pray when she wants a drink."

I had read and listened, but I just couldn't quite understand why Maggie couldn't get herself squared away and settle down to a couple of social drinks with me and be content with the mild glow, the way it used to be. Why was she doing this terrible thing to me?

She told me.

Maggie's mother and dad had just pulled out of the driveway after the usual tense and argumentative three-day visit, and I sauntered back to the kitchen for a second cup of coffee to help me unwind. There she stood, head tilted back, taking a long, straight one from the neck of a bottle of warm vodka.

"What in the hell goes on?" I yelled. "Your folks have gone, it's finally quiet around here, so why do you want to drink *now?*"

Tears trickled down her cheeks and she crumpled into the big recliner chair, her "throne" where she spent most of her waking hours.

"I don't *want* to drink now or any other time! Dammit, I *have* to have a drink!"

She had given me an honest answer, and honesty wasn't one of her strong points at this time. She drank because she had to. She was caught in the grip of something so strong, so compulsive, so pervasive that she had no choice. She drank because she was addicted. With the addiction came the mental and the moral degradation, the physical degeneration. She was seriously ill, a sick person caught in the iron grip of chemical addiction.

Maggie was an alcoholic. She didn't intend to become one. I was a mirror alcoholic, a knurd, and I didn't intend to become one either.

Yeah, you say, but how about the other women—the ones who drink, take tranquilizers, use sleeping pills and pain pills and yet don't seem to have this problem. So why did it happen to Maggie or Susie or Jane—*our* girls?

Health authorities tell us that statistically, one out of 13 of us that drink will become an alcoholic (other statistics give this ratio as one in ten). There are about eight to ten million alcoholics in the United States. Estimates say that twenty-five to forty percent of these are women. Nobody knows for sure, since nobody keeps score. It's still common practice in many of our hospitals to admit alcoholic patients with a diagnosis of gastritis, gastroenteritis, cirrhosis or extreme nervousness, so the hospital records don't help much.

I fed these numbers to a new man at our stag Al-Anon meeting. He was concerned about his wife's drinking, but wasn't at all sure that she was an alcoholic. He had, fortunately, retained a portion of his sense of humor and announced at the next meeting that he had worked out a sure-fire system for determining whether or not a woman had crossed the invisible line.

"No trick to it," he explained gravely. "You just jot down the names of twelve of her women friends and list your wife's name last. Then go down the list and ask yourself the question, 'Does this one drink too much?' If you haven't been able to come up with a 'yes' to match against one of the first twelve names, then, statistically, your wife has to be the alcoholic!"

Well, that's one way.

Why do people drink? Dr. David A. Stewart in *Thirst for Freedom* ventures some answers. Most people, Stewart says, drink to feel better, but that oversimplifies the problem. We do a lot of things to feel better—like eating, sleeping, playing, sometimes fighting, even working, making love. Still, there must be a lot of jollies in the jug, and those of us who drink, be we occasional drinkers, social sippers or alcoholics, find something that we like in there. What are some of these attractions? Stewart lists them:

   a.  Alcohol dulls the pain of disagreeable duties, of personal relations.

   b.  It eases tense nerves and tense situations.

   c.  It relieves tiredness.

   d.  It releases those hostile feelings we've held inside.

   e.  We get tired of being adults all the time and, once in a while, like to be childish. Booze breaks the barriers to childhood.

   f.  People seek the approval of others through drinking. The liquor ads imply or proclaim: "Men and women of distinction" drink, and all the "best of people" drink. Alcohol temporarily covers up shyness and inferiority.

Drinking has been around since before the beginnings of recorded history, and most of our societies and our ethnic groups tacitly put the stamp of approval on a custom that seems to help ease the strain of civilized living. There are exceptions, such as the Moslems, who are abjured by the Koran "not to take the first drop" of alcoholic beverages. As a result, there are mighty few maudlin Moslems. (It's a shame that there wasn't something said in the Koran about oil pricing.) Still, if there's a will, there's a way, and some of the modern Moslems have learned to enjoy our more "civilized" pleasures and put a drop from their first drink onto a finger and flip it towards the wall or ceiling, thus assiduously avoiding the "first drop."

When I passed this bit of research to Maggie, she commented, "Now that's what I call alcoholic reasoning!"

Our society today doesn't worry about that first drop, but says that the sensible drinker knows when to stop, that he or she has control over the stuff, is well-disciplined. Therefore, we create a body of law which will punish those who lack this discipline or good sense.

Jerry, a member of our Al-Anon group described his perplexity: "I'll be damned if I can understand her. She knows what booze does to her but she doesn't seem to have enough brains to stop. She can't handle lobster, either. When she eats lobster, she turns a little green and upchucks. She figures that she's just plain allergic to lobster, so she leaves it alone. She doesn't keep open cans of lobster meat tucked in dresser drawers. She doesn't order three lobster cocktails for an appetizer when we go out to dinner. She passes up a two-pound lobster for a main course and never considers lobster Newburg for dessert.

"Liquor works on her the same way—she's allergic to it. She can't handle it, but she won't admit it, won't stop trying. I think she's a little crazy."

Civilized living is disciplined living. We want the order and security that society provides, Stewart says, and are willing to pay for this discipline in the control of our natural impulses. Most of us make the payment with no difficulty. Some of us seem to have no need of drugs, stimulants or pain killers. Others feel a little strain and enjoy a drink or two to smooth the rough edges of life. These are the social drinkers—liquor doesn't grab them any more than a soft drink or a piece of candy would.

Then, says Stewart, there's that large class that may be called problem drinkers. Most aren't alcoholics, at least not yet, but they'll qualify if they continue to drink. They're the ones at your parties that manage to drink a bit too much, get a little too noisy, like to be the life of the party. They are inclined to have a hideous hangover the next morning and want to tell you all about it.

You don't know many of these people? Try this little experiment. Stick to straight ginger ale at the next bash you attend. It gets pretty dull maybe, but you'll be able to spot the problem drinkers without even trying. Another way is to turn on the tape recorder at your next party and run the tape the next morning. You may even wonder if you're the "one in thirteen" when you hear your own voice raised in what you thought was harmony with the impromptu barbershop quartet!

These problem drinkers are the knowledgeable ones who earnestly assure you, "I never take a drink before the sun has crossed the yardarm," and sweat it out until noon. Others say firmly, "I never touch it until sundown." Still others relate the advantages of martinis "on the rocks," insisting that the melting ice weakens the drink to an acceptable level. They have their "controls," and they talk about them a little too often and a little too loudly.

These were my kind of people. As an experienced drinker who could always "handle it," I took my alcoholic temperature each year by staying dry for the month of January. I reasoned that if I could go for thirty days, from the day after New Year's to my birthday on February 1, staying righteously dry, then it logically followed that I had no problem with booze. Besides, I drank enough during the holiday festivities to fill and overflow my January quota with a little to spare.

Maggie always resented the sight of me with my halo on tight, clutching my heavily spiced tomato juice, and proclaiming my virtue to anyone that would listen. I ran through this routine for several years, then started to cheat a little with a drink or two when I was downtown lunching with a customer, or maybe I would knock it off a week early if there was a special party or a dance to attend. Everyone was very glad when my birthday rolled around—particularly me.

Problem drinkers, according to Stewart, find that the price of civilized living seems to have inflated beyond their ability to pay. Trying to keep it under control, they have clashes that shake them up. They're tuned tighter than a violin string. But with a few drinks, they find quick release from all the worries and strains. They turn to booze to make life bearable. They like the way it makes them feel, and particularly for a man, it seems to be the symbol of virility. From this class comes the alcoholic.

How about differences, if any, between the male alcoholic and the female alcoholic? In a broad sense, there are no basic differences. All alcoholics walk on common ground. Or crawl.

Women drunks are less belligerent, you hear. They don't often clobber each other or their gentlemen friends. Instead, they go on crying jags, their mascara runs in dirty streaks down their cheeks, and they sniffle.

Well—not necessarily less belligerent. A man from an exclusive suburb of our nearby city showed up one evening at our stag group meeting, seeking advice for an embarrassing problem. When his wife was carrying a load, she had the habit of pulling the driver from his golf bag and taking practice swings, with his head as the target. She had a poor sense of direction, but it was improving, and what did we suggest?

Facetiously, one of the golfers in the group recommended that he should remove all of the clubs from the bag except the putter. "Everyone, even your wife, knows that you need a soft touch with the putter."

Maggie, always a lady when sober, could become highly aggressive when she was stoked up. We were vacationing at a resort located in mining country, and two couples of us were having dinner at a locally famous country restaurant well known for the quality of the homemade spaghetti, which was their specialty. The other man in our party got into a mild hassle with four miners sitting in the booth adjacent to ours—

he didn't like the language they were using. As a practicing coward, I attempted to pacify the miners and to edge our group out to the safety of our car. The miners followed us and began to jostle my friend, who was physically no match for one, much less four of them.

Maggie and I had made it to the car when she turned, stooped down and took off one of her shoes. The style at the time incorporated a high, tapering heel that narrowed to a needle point. Limping back to the fracas, she shook her shoe in the startled faces of the miners and told them in no uncertain tones, "Now listen, you punks! You get back into the restaurant or I'll punch your eyes out with this!" Angrily she shook her shoe again. They began to move slowly and uncertainly, but not fast enough to satisfy Maggie. She shifted her shoe into her left hand and with her right, delivered a resounding slap to the face of the nearest miner.

Obediently, they retreated, and we climbed into the car and drove away. I shook for ten minutes, but Maggie was unperturbed. "The bastards were *drunk*," she announced gravely, between hiccups.

Stewart lists six qualities common to all alcoholics. All are dependent, sensitive, idealistic, impulsive, intolerant and given to wishful thinking. Booze offers release from grown-up responsibilities, so the drinker reverts to childish ways and dreams. It's not a coincidence that alcoholics resemble helpless babies when they're on the verge of passing out. Most babies get attention from someone.

Still, alcoholics wouldn't differ from all sorts of other neurotics who are "dry," if it weren't for their special kind of sensitivity. Apparently, addictive drinkers have either a constitutional or developed body defect which reacts to alcohol like gasoline to a flame. Boom! Our drunk suddenly explodes after drinking, losing touch with reality and orbits off into her private world of fantasy.

There are other areas of sensitivity, too. Alcoholics are alert to fancied abuse and to ridicule, fearful of being less than they think they are. They're inclined to be grandiose—to tell the tall story, be the big spender, claim the ability to do the impossible. These inclinations show up in various stages of a binge.

One of our male AA friends tells it this way: "I would wander into a bar, order a drink and turn to the guy on the stool next to me for a little conversation.

"Sooner or later he would ask, 'What do you do for a living?' 'I'm an electrician.'

"A couple of drinks later, I would get the same question from another guy, and I would promote myself to a crew chief. As the drinks went down and my circle of new friends expanded, I successively advanced to electrical contractor, vice-president of a national contracting firm, president of an international electrical engineering firm, and finally — with all due modesty — I was Chairman of the Board of General Electric, just passing through town."

The sensitivity of alcoholics is most obvious in their wishful thinking, the elaborate alibi pattern developed over a period of years to protect their fears, rationalize their drinking and account for their defects. Practicing alcoholics are con artists supreme, second to none.

My own con artist had developed arthritis as the result of a bad fall when she had been drinking, and she made the most of her ailment. She hurt, she explained, and everybody knows that a little alcohol deadens pain far better than aspirin, and it was both logical and reasonable for her to take a few drinks on doctor's orders, wasn't it?

This was to become a full-fledged production. When I arrived home in the evening, she would be huddled in a corner of our big recliner, a picture of suffering and pain. She had taken aspirin all day, she would relate, but it just didn't seem to help much. Maybe one little drink would revive her sagging spirits, dull the pain so she could gain enough strength to put something together for dinner. It seemed to be such a minor request, and with my heart full of pity and admiration for her fortitude, I would build her a big brimming vodka-on-the-rocks. She deserved it for such patient suffering.

She never mentioned that she had already worked her way through maybe a quart of sherry and the better part of a fifth of vodka.

Of course, men and women may have different reasons for excessive drinking.

Dr. Stewart refers to Dr. Giorgio Loli, who has studied this matter in depth and makes these special points about the woman alcoholic:

1.  A problem suddenly imposed from the outside may shock her into drinking. For example, a man may lose his job because of drinking, but a woman will drink because she's lost her job.
2.  A woman whose husband's success elevates her into a new social climate becomes insecure, uncertain and anxious and looks for courage in the bottle.
3.  The career woman, faced with the fear of a lonely, childless life, may ease her depression in alcohol.
4.  The threat of such ailments as cancer, a hysterectomy or removal of the ovaries, or going through menopause may trigger heavy drinking. Separation from her children may depress a woman enough to cause addiction.
5.  Men are more likely than women to blame themselves and feel guilty during hangovers. Women are inclined to blame alcohol for their troubles and to minimize their personal responsibilities.

Dr. Stewart thinks that there are other important points which, although perhaps implicit in the above five, need additional clarification.

A woman in the business world, he says, develops a competitive spirit at the expense of something particularly feminine—the role of supporter to her loved one. Competing with him, seeing his shortcomings, she abandons her role as a woman and lover and unwittingly begins to think like a man in competition with another man. The views of several liberated females to the contrary, Stewart believes that a woman is happiest as a partner, not a competitor.

Central in her life is the need to be loved and cherished, he says, not to feel that she is only tolerated or pampered. The hard-boiled mask of many women alcoholics covers an intense feeling of guilt and shame.

The woman alcoholic whose excesses follow illicit intercourse may appear to be completely relieved when she learns that she is neither pregnant nor diseased. But underneath, because of fears instilled during her childhood, reasons Stewart, there's a feeling of guilt about her "sin," and the suspicion that she's "dirty." She turns to alcohol for comfort.

Thank you, Drs. Stewart and Loli. I suspect that some of these ideas will be branded as the products of male insensitivity, should any women's libbers read your conclusions.

One such woman told me that male attitudes of superiority gave her a great alibi for drinking. "I was going to show them," she said, "that a woman can not only work better than a man, she can drink better, hold her liquor better, and if she does get drunk, recover from her hangover faster than any damn man."

I think she also proved that she could become an alcoholic more quickly than a man, too.

Joan Curlee in *Alcoholism and the Empty Nest* suggests that, for women, it is more likely that some quite clearly defined stress or difficulty is associated with the onset of heavy or uncontrolled drinking, compared to a man, who is much more likely to simply "drift" into alcoholism.

Curlee's study covered one hundred consecutive admissions of female patients at a private treatment center in Minnesota, and for twenty-one of these, excessive drinking appeared to relate to problems associated with the middle-age identity crisis sometimes called the "empty nest syndrome." For each woman, the trauma which triggered alcoholism was related to a change in or a challenge to their roles as wives or mothers. They were unusually dependent upon their husbands and/or children for their identity and sense of self-worth. Divorce, death of a husband, a change in the husband's status, children growing up and moving away—these were serious challenges that dealt severe blows to the women's self-esteem and sense of purpose. All of these women retreated into solitary, furtive drinking in their own homes. They became "closet drinkers"— the most typical pattern among women alcoholics.

The study shows that the progression of alcoholism in this group tended to be more rapid than in men, "telescoping" the development of their alcoholic symptoms into a shorter period of time. For men, these symptoms may take years to develop. Within a year or two, sometimes in a manner of months, most of these women moved from their earliest heavy drinking into symptoms characteristic of the later stages of alcoholism, requiring hospitalization or other treatment. They experienced a dramatic loss of control over their drinking.

It would have helped George if he had been able to get his hands on a copy of Curlee's study. He turned up for his first meeting of our stag Al-Anon group because his wife's doctor recommended he attend. His wife, Gwen, had recently been admitted to the hospital with an advanced case of cirrhosis of the liver. George was stunned and bewildered. They had her in the *alcoholic* ward, George told us, and he couldn't believe the doctor's diagnosis of acute alcoholism.

"Why, she hardly drank at all," George said. "We would have one, maybe two drinks together in the evening, and maybe we both drank a little more when we were on vacation. She just can't be an alcoholic!"

She did consume a lot of soft drinks, George admitted. One of the men suggested that maybe his wife just might be spiking those colas with a healthy slug of booze.

"I don't think so," George said firmly, "She's just not that kind of a woman. She would never be sneaky. She's a good honest person—a regular little soldier. When our only son's wife miscarried last year and the doctor said she could never have children, Gwen was disappointed that we would never be grandparents, but she never complained—won't even talk about it."

When our neophyte came to our next meeting, he was still in a state of near shock. "Little soldier" Gwen, now withdrawn from booze, had admitted that during the past year her consumption of vodka had grown from near zero to almost a fifth a day, and — would we believe it? — she had been drinking it in colas, with just enough of the soft drink added to give it color!

George still couldn't understand how it had happened so fast. "She never even acted like she was drunk," he marveled.

Curlee says that excessive drinking also contributed to the decline of self-esteem that had already set in when the patients began to depend on alcohol. They had previously felt that they were getting old and past the time when they were useful in bringing up the kids or helping their husbands; now they had the extra burden of thinking of themselves as "worthless drunks." Since heavy drinking was not a part of their previous lives, they looked with disdain on the drunken woman. Now they were not only old and without value, but also deserved condemnation as weak-willed degenerates, a burden on their families. More drinking was necessary to escape these feelings.

Curlee concludes that none of these women seemed clearly defined in her own right. None seemed to have thought of themselves except in relation to their husbands and family. The question of "Who am I?" is tough at age fifteen; at fifty plus, it seems unanswerable.

I was rather proud of this chapter and gave it to Maggie to read.

"It's okay — I guess," Maggie said when she had finished. "It's important, I think, to know the characteristics of an alcoholic and the differences between men and women alcoholics. But you better warn those knurds out there not to over-intellectualize, and conclude that she can't help it — she's just suffering from the 'empty nest syndrome,' or something.

"I don't know why I'm an alcoholic. You remember my fifty or so reasons that I handed you? They don't matter. If you had disproved every one, I could have come up with fifty more. The point is, I was sick. I needed help."

Very well then, gentlemen. Be warned. The important point to be aware of is that we are dealing with a seriously ill woman. Alcoholism is a fatal disease—100 percent fatal. In most instances, the illness can be arrested—not cured—but stopped in its tracks, much like diabetes.

Bluntly, not all of them are going to make it. Some will be victims of the illness and will die from the physical or the mental effects of addiction. Some may end up in institutions. Be aware of the fact that every time anyone—social drinker or compulsive drunk—takes a drink of alcohol, brain cells are destroyed. The brain can and does restore these cells, repairing the damage. But there's a limit. When the damage is too great, the brain is permanently impaired, and a condition known as "wet brain" occurs. It doesn't happen very often, but it can happen. When it does, an institution seems to be the only answer.

You may hold the key to recovery of your wife, mother, daughter, sister or girl friend. You may help. Or, even with the best of intentions, you may hinder or delay the arrest of her illness. This sickness is so difficult to understand, so pervasive, and the effects on the family so far-reaching, that the generation of positive action at the psychologically right time takes understanding, skill, faith and patience. Your role in her recovery is important, vital and not easy.

Your alcoholic didn't intend to become one when she started drinking, and believe me, you're not responsible for her condition. She is.

But you can help.

# 5

# An Obstacle That Came Between

**"My notion was that you had been**
**(Before she had this fit)**
**An obstacle that came between**
**Him, and ourselves, and it."**

As Maggie's illness progressed, unconsciously she built up her burden of self-hatred to the point where she needed a dumping ground. She took the inevitable step, turning to projection—the process of unloading her feelings on the people around her. As her self-hatred grew, she began to see herself as surrounded by hateful people. Maggie needed a cat to kick, and I was the handiest cat available.

As a very vulnerable and tender-assed cat, I was aware that something was the matter, but I couldn't pinpoint it. Maggie was doing a very good job indeed in transferring her guilt, and I soaked it up like a sponge. My reaction, which may be typically male, was to "fix it"—whatever it was that needed fixing. The hell of it was that everything I tried failed. Like Avis, I tried harder. Unlike Avis, I failed time after time, frantically looking for an answer to a problem I couldn't clearly define, and my feeling of inadequacy began to shrivel away the edges of my fat ego. I hurt!

I was exhibiting many of the same symptoms of emotional deterioration as Maggie. I was one sick cat, a mirror alcoholic, a dry drunk, a thirty-second degree knurd.

Dr. Vernon Johnson in *I'll Quit Tomorrow* says simply that the only difference between an alcoholic and the spouse is that one is physically affected by alcohol; otherwise both have the same symptoms. Like the alcoholic, the spouse loses touch with reality. He begins projecting his guilt and self-hatred back to the spouse, onto his kids and other family members, even toting the load down to the shop for his boss and fellow workers to share.

There's a story told by one of the old-timers in Alcoholics Anonymous about a member who had tried unsuccessfully to help a fellow drunk. This alcoholic had a long track record of sobering up, then returning to active drinking, sobering up again, then slipping again and seemingly was constitutionally unable to make the AA program work for him. One evening this poor soul eased himself into an AA meeting, very obviously much the worse for the wear of a king-size binge. He was shaking, red-eyed, not too clean and stank of booze. His sponsor spotted him and stalked up, surveyed him grimly, then ground out, "They say there's a place for everyone in AA and I've just figured out yours—you're the bad example!"

That was me, too, the classic example of what an alcoholic's husband should *not* do. I was deeply preoccupied with alcohol. I hated the effects of Maggie's uncontrolled drinking, but was developing a sick fascination with what it was doing to her. Of course, I reasoned, it was my duty to straighten her out, so I climbed up on my throne and set about my self-imposed task of playing God. I would "fix it."

Johnson points out that as the people around an alcoholic meet failure after failure, their feelings are predictable. Fear, frustration, shame, inadequacy, guilt, resentment, self-pity — all of these feelings grow, and so do their defenses. They rationalize, they project, they lose touch with reality, and they hurt inside, unable to identify the cause of their pain.

Blossoming into a full-blown knurd takes a bit of time, and I worked diligently to qualify.

There could be compensations in living with a practicing alcoholic if you happen to write soap-opera scripts for television or radio. There is an abundance of material to keep the viewers or listeners glued to the set and eagerly awaiting the next episode. Maggie and I lived this one, which might be aptly titled "As the Worm Turns." Will Jack leave Maggie to her almost-certain slow death and skip out to Mexico, eking out a living selling lottery tickets? Will Maggie, spurned by husband, family and friends, sink to panhandling the cost of a quart of cheap wine and move down under the bridge with the rest of the drunks? Or will there be a miracle? Tune in tomorrow, friends.

I was in my mid-forties, when our world began to crumble a bit around the edges. I was vaguely uneasy about Maggie. She was drinking a little too much, worked a little too hard to be the "life of the party" (her specialties: standing on her head and solo dances), and her hangovers often kept her in bed until nearly noon. I concentrated my efforts on making that first million, but somehow, with house payments to meet, new cars to buy, and taxes, it was hard to hold on to what I made. I had changed jobs several times, trying to find the employer that would appreciate my talents and be willing to pay well for them.

Confident that I could still do it, I took the big plunge and established my own business in export sales management. We tightened the household budget and Maggie went to work as a real estate saleswoman. The business prospered to the extent that I ran afoul of the IRS and was audited regularly. I worried. What would happen if I lost my health and couldn't continue with my travel? What would happen if there was another revolution in Argentina, a new dictator in Venezuela, a depression in Germany? I was smoking too much, and my chest hurt in the morning. Was this the first sign of heart trouble?

An offer to merge my business with that of one of my major clients seemed to hold the answer to all of our problems. I was to set up an international division for my new boss, and I was confident, as I explained to Maggie, that with my big-company experience, education and native shrewdness, I would soon manage to wrest control of the company from the farm-boy founder. The merger involved our relocation to a small community where Maggie would be free of the "bad influences" of those in our circle of friends who, in my opinion, drank too much and were contributing to Maggie's little problem. She would have more time to devote to our sons, particularly our youngest boy, Stan. Stan was having trouble in school, and I didn't approve of some of his friends — mean little devils who seemed to know more about girls than their ages justified. Stan would profit by the clean atmosphere and simple ways of a small country community.

We would "start all over." In Alcoholics Anonymous, this is known as the "Geographic Cure." Our new start would include a series of small, intimate Friday night dinner parties where we might show our new friends the sophistication and impeccable good taste of big-city people. Through Maggie's family ties and my new business connections, we were well introduced and accepted by the "best people," and were invited to join the Country Club. We were "in," no doubt about it.

Somehow, it just didn't work out the way we had planned it. We received and gave invitations, but after the initial flurry of activity, it seemed that the people we had met and wanted to know better simply didn't care for us. But the folks that took us to their collective bosoms were the heavy drinkers at the Country Club, the gang that liked a morning drink on Sunday before brunch.

The country-boy president of our company was, of all things, a teetotaler, a pillar of the church, whose idea of a gourmet feast was fried chicken, cream gravy and plenty of mashed potatoes. Although we stopped in for short visits with the president and his wife and invited them to come for dinner or lunch, there was always some very good and valid reason why they couldn't accept our hospitable offers of a real French meal, "coq au vin" and a "nice little wine."

Rebuffed by the "nice people," we began to socialize more and more with the drunks and near-drunks.

To fill her free time, Maggie took over briefly as the leader of the local Girl Scout troop. These kids pegged us very quickly. One knowledgeable fifteen-year-old took me to one side and whispered confidentially, "You oughta get to know the Moores — you'll really dig them. Last Saturday night I was babysitting across the street from their house, and they were sitting on top of the roof, the whole gang, singing dirty songs!"

Yes indeed, we did become fast friends with the Moores. The parties ebbed and swirled across town, and we were always ready with a case of beer, a few bottles of good wine and a hefty supply of liquor for the Moores and the crowd of drinking buddies that accompanied them.

However, our very best friend was the local liquor dealer. Not only would he deliver day or night and even sneak us a bottle on Sunday, but he extended charge privileges as well as a ten percent discount on case-lot purchases. We bought by the case because every tenth one was free!

Although business boomed and we prospered, all was not rosy at the office. I was frustrated and impatient with our naive management group, who politely turned down my suggestions for changes and improvements. Only Joe, our general sales manager, appreciated what I was trying to do. Joe and his wife were from Chicago, and Joe had formerly been an executive in a major corporation. They were kind and hospitable, but not very generous with their drinks — one before dinner seemed to be the limit. Joe didn't drink at all and told us that he was a recovering alcoholic. He spent most of his free time going to AA meetings and apparently gallivanting around the countryside searching out drunks. Joe was a little odd, we felt. He crimped our style, and we saw less and less of him and his wife, who was all right—she would take a drink.

Maggie had always enjoyed good health, liked nine holes of golf or a swim, and could dance all night. She had a cast-iron stomach and slept ten hours each night if the kids didn't wake her. Now she was beginning to have some physical problems. Shortly after our move, she developed severe stomach cramps, which the doctor diagnosed as overindulgence in coffee. Maggie cut back on the coffee and increased her liquor intake. She wasn't happy, she declared. She was lonely, she was bored, and I was away from home too much. Stan was failing two subjects in high school. She suggested that our sex life left much to be desired, and why didn't I visit a psychiatrist?

Maybe later, I promised her. I really began to look forward to those business trips abroad, where I could get away from her for a few weeks, a month or three months if I was lucky. I spent much of my free time mulling over Maggie's problems— her drinking, her loneliness, her discontent and the bad, bad times she was giving me. She had never had it so good, I thought resentfully. The trouble with her is that I'm spoiling her.

The difficult times came inevitably when her mother and dad came for a visit. They lectured her at length concerning her drinking. "Stick with beer," her father counseled her, "and leave the hard stuff alone."

"Spend more time in church work," her mother advised. "Really get active in the church, and you'll make more friends and won't have time to feel so lonely and unhappy. You'll be too busy to want or need to drink so much."

Maggie appreciated this advice as much as she would have appreciated a suggestion to take up mah-jongg, and, after a day or two, she would be wound up as tight as an alarm clock. One evening after dinner, a meal garnished with solicitous parental guidance, I ducked into the kitchen with Maggie to clean up the mess and to cool her down. I was properly sympathetic and commiserating, when suddenly she picked up the tray of silverware that she had just dried, lifted it above her head and sent it crashing to the floor.

"Damn all of you, why don't you get off my back!"

I caught her as she ran into the hallway leading upstairs for our bedroom, spun her around and slapped her. You're supposed to slap hysterical women, I thought, and she's sure as hell hysterical. I swung a little harder than I had intended to, and Maggie hit the floor, a little trickle of blood running from the corner of her mouth. Her parents had jumped to their feet when they heard her yelling in the kitchen and reached the hallway just in time to see their favorite son-in-law belt their only daughter and floor her.

The silence was deafening. Maggie regained her feet and disappeared to the upstairs bathroom, from which we could hear the sounds of running water punctuated with her sobs. Her folks said nothing—their matching glares told all.

I left via the front door, not bothering to open it but just walking underneath with plenty of room to spare. Still, I rationalized, that slap was justified, she'd had it coming to her for a long time, and now, by God, maybe she would straighten herself up and fly right! I was sick and tired of all the guff she had been handing me, and dammit, I was glad I had finally done something about it.

Maggie did something about it, too. She got herself royally smashed.

Watching her unsteady hands lifting the cup of tea, trembling and spilling a little, hungover to the floor the next morning, I made a decision. She just doesn't know what she's doing to herself, to me and her family, I reasoned. She needs an education on the DANGERS OF DRINKING. Should I tell her? No, it had to come from another woman. She had even mentioned a few weeks back that she wanted to read Patricia Kent's *An American Woman and Alcohol.* Maggie was an avid reader and had great respect for the written word. Without doubt this Kent gal could impress her or scare her or make her realize the error of her ways.

I picked up a copy when I next visited Chicago (it wasn't available in our local library, where I could have borrowed it for free) and spent an evening reading it, carefully underlining the passages which I thought would really get to her. She was always concerned with her personal appearance, so I double-underlined the sentences describing bloat, pasty complexion, tremors, red eyes, the unsteady gait, thick speech and all the other things that might happen if she didn't learn to drink like a lady. This Kent woman made the ridiculous statement that if a woman drank too much and too often she would become an alcoholic and might even die. I thought that she was going a little too far; it might happen to her and those like her, but all Maggie needed was to cut down. Just a little.

I laid the book on her pillow one night, filled with high expectations that she would read it, do something about her drinking, and then things would get back to where they had been. She read it, but we never talked about it. She kept the book on the shelf above our bed for a few weeks, and then it disappeared. Sure, Maggie read the book. She told me later that she read it page by page, cover to cover, even recognized herself in some of the passages Kent had written.

Did it work? Not for Maggie. She resented my purchase of it, even though she had asked for it; she resented reading it, even though she knew, deep down inside, that everything she read was true and applied to her. The end result was that my wife had still another reason to drink.

When there was no discernible reduction in her drinking, I was angry, hurt and very, very frustrated. What in the hell was the matter with her? Was she crazy?

Maggie, drinking, did not play our game by the Marquis of Queensbury rulebook and began hitting below the belt. She drank, she told me, because I didn't love her. Either that, or there was something very seriously wrong with me, physically or mentally. Our sexual activity had become sporadic, waned, flickered, and seemed to be dying. Seriously—didn't I think it was time that I went to see a good specialist who could give me injections or something, or maybe see a psychiatrist?

There was nothing wrong with me, I protested. I was just a little run-down maybe, with a few chest pains sometimes. Perhaps I would quit smoking, get a little more exercise, watch my diet. But those chest pains, manufactured on the spur of the moment, *that* sounded good, I thought. Accordingly, I faked a mild heart attack — not a bad performance even if I do say so — then visited an imaginary doctor, who confirmed the heart attack and insisted I should have complete rest for a while. No sex, particularly. Maggie was properly sympathetic, so I next visited an imaginary psychiatrist, who gave me a clean bill of health. I was normal, no mental problems outside of a little residual hatred of my mother, which just might account for a slowdown or reduction in my sexual drive. But, I glibly explained to Maggie, these things do happen as we age, and she should accept it. Further, the psychiatrist had said she should cut down on her drinking because it made her too amorous.

Drunk or sober, Maggie was able to spot me in a lie, and these latest efforts contributed still another resentment and reason for drinking. I knew I was lying and felt guilty about it, but I wanted her off my back.

Nobody seemed to appreciate me. Our export sales volume grew despite the fact that, in my mind, we manufactured lousy products, failed to meet delivery deadlines and charged too much. The railroads lost my cars, and the steamship lines sailed without my cargo. No one would take action on my suggested improvements. Maggie complained about being lonely and drank more than ever. I was disillusioned and unhappy, convinced that the move had been a great mistake.

Secretly, I drew up a plan to open a new manufacturing plant in the Caribbean Islands and to compete with my employer. On my expense-paid trips, I contacted three friends with some money and manufacturing know-how and convinced them that my scheme was a sure winner. We would each invest a small amount and, with foreign loans and grants, plus tax incentives, we would all be rich within a few years. Enthusiastically, I explained the plan to Maggie, describing our life as it would be in the islands, the perfect sunny days on the beaches, servants to cook and wash and clean the big house we would rent, more time to be together, private schools for Stan—all would be ours. Maggie was hesitant, but game to try anything that might make her a little happier, find her some friends, maybe keep her busier—anything that might help her cut down on her drinking.

Before our plans were complete, the roof fell in. Unknown to my employer, I had been conducting another little business "on the side," using company-paid travel and company time to handle the transactions, and I was quietly salting away a few thousand here and there. It was a good, foolproof scheme, I thought, took very little time, and very few people needed to know about it.

However, my employer did learn of my sideline activities and took a very dim view of them. He fired me. I covered as best I could, dreaming up a long and complicated story, which was greeted with some skepticism, particularly by Maggie. I wanted to get away from the area where the true story was known, so we sold our home, packed our belongings and retreated to our former home town to wait out the subsequent move to the Caribbean. I told Maggie that this temporary move would be great for her, since she would be back with old friends, where she would be happy and could make a new start on holding down her drinking. This time it would be different, I assured her. Maggie went with me gladly—anything to get away from where we were. Maybe she would get active in the church like her mother suggested.

I was dubious about her church kick. As an indifferent agnostic, I questioned a God who rewarded the guys that never had any fun out of life and sent the rest to hell. Sure, I would concede that organized religion seemed to work for some people, but they were the dull, straight-laced, often sanctimonious jerks who seemed to look down their noses at modern men like me. If God was so powerful, how come He permitted Maggie to get in her present state?

During our marriage, I had attended church services with Maggie and the kids, vaguely believing that it was my "duty." I listened and tried, in a half-hearted fashion, to apply these churchly precepts to my own life. I wondered how some church members could bend the rules to their own material advantage, while using the church as a cloak of respectability.

"They're just a bunch of hypocrites," I would protest to my best friend, who was equally convinced that the church was for nowhere, "and I can't *stand* a bunch of cheats and liars, stiff-necked psalm singers who won't practice what they preach!"

Religion in my book was maybe okay for women, and I was all in favor of Maggie giving God a second chance. If the devil had come along and offered to sober up Maggie and keep her that way, he, too, would have had his innings.

Maggie roared back to the church of her childhood with all stops open, her spiritual motor revving up right to the red line. She dusted off her Bible and religious writings, participated in church activities and sought desperately to find her sobriety in God, as she wanted to understand Him. Her sick mind made a series of erratic turns, and she rationalized her failure with "I'm a weak-willed, evil, worthless person, and God doesn't want any part of me. I'm so rotten that I don't *deserve* God's help. Why should He help me?"

Later I learned that Maggie's piece-meal approach to arresting her illness was a common one. The professionals in treating alcoholism size up the problem something like this: alcoholism is a three-fold illness—physical, mental and spiritual—and the sick alcoholic goes charging off for help from only one of the professions. The ailment is physical, but seldom can it be treated by a medical doctor as a purely physical problem. The sickness is mental—but the psychiatrist or psychologist can seldom treat it just as a mental problem. The illness is spiritual—but seldom can it be treated by a minister, priest or rabbi solely as a spiritual problem.

The swoops up were of shorter duration, and the dips down were deeper, on our roller coaster. Take parties. We were good party people, usually the first to arrive and the very last to go. We prepared for these parties with a drink or two before we would leave home, just to "get up a head of steam." On arrival, Maggie would bustle out to the kitchen or wherever the bar was set up and offer her assistance to whomever was pouring the drinks. She gained a lot of ground at the bar, since she could test, taste and pour her own "two fingers" of booze. Two fingers to Maggie was the distance between the first and fourth finger, a much more reasonable measurement than the niggardly little one-ounce shot glass used in concocting a drink for the others. She was never adverse to joining the men for a quick one in the kitchen.

In our rather tight-knit group of close friends, these parties followed a pattern. They began with casual conversation and loud greetings as each couple arrived, clutching a bottle of booze wrapped in a brown paper bag. The conversation would quicken after a couple or three drinks, and the men would cluster at the improvised bar with its motley collection of scotch, gin, rum, bourbon and rye whiskey and our vodka. There was beer in the refrigerator for the one guy who was worried about his drinking. There was an elaborate ice bucket —we did things in style—plus soda, tonic water, a couple of colas, olives, cocktail onions, slices of lime. It was self-service after the first drink poured by the host, and if your bottle happened to be empty, it was okay to pour a drink from a friend's bottle. He was getting a little too drunk to notice anyway.

As the party picked up steam and the sound gained a few decibels, the musicians would swing into action. We were a talented group—with banjo, gut-bucket and me on the mandolin. Sometimes there was a clarinet added, a cymbal played with brushes or sticks, a tin whistle. In some friends' homes there were pianos and electric organs. Our specialties included "My Gal, Sal," "Whispering," "Blue Eyes," "Lazy River," and "Mona." We also did imitations of the Ink Spots and broke ourselves up when the lanky, silver-haired gut-bucket player came in with his quavering falsetto. The ladies had their own quartet or trio, depending on the availability of church-trained sopranos and altos at the party.

When the banjo player broke into "Coney Island Washboard," it was Maggie's signal to go on stage. As a solo dancer, she rotated her pelvis in a series of lascivious grinds and threw bumps equal to the best in burlesque. Once in a while she would do a modified strip, peeling down to bra and panties. The climax of the evening came when Maggie and another talented girl would stand on their heads, back to back, their skirts slowly sliding up to expose two pairs of very shapely legs.

Then came the rallying cry, "All men to the bar!" This was accompanied by a session of dirty stories, often interrupted by Maggie looking for another drink. She would be staggering a bit, her words blurring, as she poured herself a generous slosh of somebody else's booze. Ours was gone by this time.

When the next-to-last couple left, it was time for us to go home, where Maggie would head for the cupboard and one last little nightcap. This was the time when I would cut her down to size — very cool, very dispassionate, very matter of fact. Wasn't she getting a little tired of making such an ass of herself?

"I'm getting more than a little tired of *you!*" Maggie would fling back, and would head off to bed, indignant, bracing herself with the help of the walls of the hall, bound for oblivion.

When Maggie finally did find sobriety, we attended parties with the same people and discovered, much to our surprise, that they had fun but actually drank very little. We had thought all along that everyone was like ourselves — you had to get drunk to have a good party!

Watching the boob-tube after one of our late-night battles, I concluded that maybe Maggie was right — I hadn't been very attentive to her recently, and if I could "turn over a new leaf," maybe she wouldn't drink so much. The next day, I called her from the office and apologized, suggested that we go out for dinner that night. She accepted my apologies with a spell of crying. As I carefully corrected the errors in the correspondence I was to sign, my secretary urged me to knock off a little early. I agreed, reflecting that I might as well, since my business day had been about as productive as if I'd been shelling peas with boxing gloves on.

I hurried home with a seventy-nine-cent bouquet of flowers from the supermarket and found Maggie dressed and waiting for me, make-up on straight, her eyes touched with mascara and eye shadow to conceal the purple circles under them. She wore a black wig that covered her own hair, which had lost its natural luster. She had made a very obvious effort to appear attractive to please me, and I felt a sudden surge of elation and a rush of love for her. I had been neglectful. With more attention from me, she was now trying—trying to control her drinking, to be the woman I had married. This must be the way to handle her!

We drove to one of our favorite restaurants nearby, small and secluded, a spot where the waitresses called us by our first names and brought vodka martinis with the menu. We ordered steaks, and I splurged on a bottle of table wine to celebrate. Everyone knows that you can't get drunk on a couple of glasses of wine, because it's the hard stuff that does the damage, right?

Maggie excused herself several times to visit the john, and I settled back, feeling tolerant and expansive. This had to be the beginning of a new life for us—attentiveness on my part, rationed drinks for my wife, the comfortable routine of friends, parties and social fun-type drinking. Yet, after her fourth trip to the ladies' room, the little telltale signs appeared: a slurring of her words; a tremor in her hands as she held her cigarette; a cutting, critical edge in her conversation. I suspected that she was carrying her grandmother's flask, a little one that held about six ounces, hidden in her handbag. Damn her!

Wearily I agreed to her insistant demand for just one after-dinner drink, a foamy, pale-green Grasshopper. She ordered a second, daring me with her hard eyes to cancel the order. No doubt about it, she was drunk, and I silently edged her out of the restaurant and into the car. Sadly, old "hollow-leg" Maggie just couldn't handle the stuff the way she used to. Time was, she could drink all the men under the table and still navigate, demanding that we find a new party. Now we rode home in uncompanionable silence, thick ugly silence filled with tension and hatred. The garage door rattled up when I pressed the button on the dash, and Maggie preceded me to the kitchen, headed for the refrigerator for ice to cool the big amber nightcap which she sloshed into the glass so methodically. She stirred it absently with her index finger, watching me search the channels on the TV for something, anything that could cut the gloom and the dark, insane rage that filled me to the bursting point.

"Why don't you get the hell out of here and go to bed?" I said, my voice as cold and controlled as a rush of air from the air conditioner. Wordlessly, she left the room and I listened to the sounds of vigorous tooth-brushing, her little dry cough when she lit another cigarette, the flush of the toilet. It was too much, I couldn't take more, I thought, and I bent over with my head in my hands to muffle the dry, bitter sobs that came up from someplace deep inside. I was quiet, but not too quiet, because I wanted her to hear, wanted her to know that she was killing me, wanted her to realize that she was cutting apart the fabric of our marriage. It was all her fault!

There was a child's book on the floor beside my chair, left by our youngest grandchild who was just learning to read. I opened it and stared at the page. "Run, Jack, run! See Jack run?" I observed that Jack was, indeed, running across the page.

I reflected that this was a pretty apt description of me. I was running, but running backwards, *away* from our bedroom. Despite Maggie's scrubbing in the shower, her sedulous tongue-tipping with breath-fresheners, that sick-sweet smell of booze still oozed from the pores of her skin, turning me off like a light. Making love was, at best, a half-assed fumbling that gave neither of us satisfaction or pleasure and, more recently, ended in frustrating, shameful and sickening failure. Maggie needed a lot of sexual attention, and she never let me forget it, insistently demanding when she had been drinking heavily—which was every day, every night. I developed a passionate interest in the late TV movies, became deeply engrossed in the book I was reading or the pile of work that I had brought home from the office. I had to go out for late sessions of poker with the boys. I had dinners with out-of-town guests or forgot the time when I was shooting the fat with a friend. I learned all of the back roads in the area, driving mindlessly, aimlessly through the countryside, waiting for the time when I could be reasonably sure that she would be in bed, drunk or passed out or just asleep, it didn't matter. Just so she wouldn't bother me!

We had twin beds hooked together to make a super-king-sized play pen, and I was advancing arguments which would justify separating those beds or, even better, my moving into another bedroom. My sinuses bothered me, my back hurt, my bladder was acting up, my heart was a little irregular, I was dead-tired at night, needed my rest, and I wasn't getting any younger—it happens to all of us, you have to admit that, don't you? It might even be fun if I would sneak in from the other bedroom and surprise her from time to time.

I had spent an evening driving around, with a stop in a small cemetery, where I gloomily contemplated the tombstones and wondered if there was sex after death. When I did come home, the house, thank God, was dark except for a small light burning in the den. Maggie was thoughtful that way—or maybe, she was just trying to tell me that she was there, waiting for me. I tiptoed down the hall and undressed quickly in the dark, closed the door very softly and brushed my teeth in the john. I slid into bed cautiously, clinging to my side, and hoped that she was dead to the world and I could have one night of peace.

No luck. She's awake, she's drunk and amorous, and despite my best efforts, I'm as limp as a dishrag. Lying there in the dark, Maggie read my pedigree. Not only did I not love her, she was convinced that I was a latent homosexual. Tearfully, she recounted how long and how hard she had tried, graphically reviewed all of my past failures and castrated me as surely as if she had used a knife. Defensively, I laid it right back in her lap. There wasn't anything wrong with me, I told her. It was because of her drinking, the way she smelled, the aggressive way that she acted. Who wanted to make love to a drunk?

I hit a responsive chord and, she flounced from the bed and into our second bathroom (she had a bottle hidden there—I know, because I found it down in the bottom of the closet behind the cleaning supplies) and returned refreshed and strengthened for her next sortie.

"Don't give me that shit! You're queer! And with your pot, your flab, your damned dentures, who gives a damn about making love with you anyway?"

She turned on her side and cried, her head muffled in her pillow, and finally drifted off into a sweaty, snoring, restless sleep. I lay there, board-rigid, brimful of anger, resentment and hate and wondered, "Is she right?"

Did I have homosexual tendencies? I thought not, but those few incidents out of my early years of sexual curiousity and experimentation returned to haunt me. I hadn't gotten much out of those adventures, but maybe—maybe I secretly and unconsciously wanted to be with another man. Was I a fairy, for God's sake? I couldn't be. It was just that I was getting old, I had worked too hard, and I had burned out early, I reassured myself. Maybe something could be done about it. Maybe I could buy some pep pills, take injections or something like that. I would buy a book tomorrow and find out. Consoled, I finally slept, carefully staying on my side of the bed.

I picked up a paperback the next day, a book written by an authoritative psychologist, about male impotency and what a guy could do about it. Successful sex was a matter of mental conditioning, my psychologist said, but physical condition might have a bearing on some cases. Too, there were those hormones that might restore the gleam to the eye of aging satyrs like me.

Encouraged, I made an appointment with our family physician and confided my fears in his receptive ear. He made the expected physical checkup, accompanied with the usual bad jokes a doctor has in store for guys that think they're over the hill. We didn't talk about homosexuality, though. After all, I didn't want our doctor referring me to a shrink.

"Smoke less, start getting some regular exercise, take vitamins and I'll start you on a series of hormone shots," the doctor advised me. "And don't worry about Maggie. She's a high-strung type, starting through menopause, and all women get a little weird about that. She probably does drink a little more than she should, but don't worry—it's all going to straighten out for you."

I hoped so, particularly that straightening out part. It didn't, though. Our bedroom scenes were a series of French farces, with me cast in the role of the aging male who's trying to satisfy his "lustful and demanding" wife. Failure begets failure, and Maggie had a new reason for drinking. She drank just to get herself to a condition where she could sleep. She told me about it, and my self-esteem shriveled like a raisin in the hot sun. That wasn't all that shriveled, either. Sex was just something I read about in dirty books, hoping to get a little reaction from reading about it.

We were fortunate—if a drunk and her husband can ever be fortunate—in that our illnesses seemed to have a limited impact on our family. Our kids were grown and married, our eldest with three children. They lived in the same community and, perhaps wisely, kept their distance from us. Maggie and I were both managers and dispensed heavy parental advice and counsel whenever we could get our sons and daughters-in-law to listen—which wasn't often. I was disappointed in both of our boys. They paid very little heed to the goals I had set for them, and even less heed to my suggested improvements they should make. Dumb kids!

Maybe they weren't so dumb. They were with us often enough to understand much better than I did that their mother was caught up in the grip of something much stronger

An Obstacle That Came Between

than she was. Our eldest, for example, quit drinking entirely. Our younger son who was finding it progressively easier to spend more and more of his time in the local gin mills, kept his visits to a minimum. At least nobody cried, or anyway not much, in the beer joints where he began to find a world more to his liking.

Peter's wife (Peter is our older son) very wisely decided that it would be best to cut down the kids' visits to grandma's house. She knew that Maggie loved her grandchildren dearly and delighted in their presence, but reasoned correctly that Maggie's intake had reached the proportion where she could no longer be trusted with the care of the children.

Maggie knew, and told me resentfully, "She just won't bring the kids over any more because she thinks I won't watch after them and they might get hurt or even killed in the street." Then remorsefully, Maggie said, "She's right. I'm just no good, no good for anything or anyone. I'd be better off dead."

We were fortunate that our grandchildren never realized what was wrong with Grandma Maggie.

My Al-Anon friend, Neil, and his wife, Dottie, with their three children, ranging in age from thirteen down to three, were not so fortunate. Neil had recently been transferred from an eastern state to the company's midwestern plant where he was given greater responsibilities. A tall skinny guy, Neil was quiet and laconic, devoted to his job as quality control manager in a paint company. Their "Sagebrush Green" was faithfully the same color, can after can, or Neil knew the reason why. He was happy with the move, but hoped that, after a few years, they might go back east to corporate head-quarters and he could concoct new paint formulas in new colors that would prove irresistible to buyers the world over.

Dottie wasn't so sure. She was an intellectual, devoted to deep conversaton and self-improvement courses. A lithe, long-limbed girl with honey-blond hair that she knotted loosely at the back, Dottie was the product of comfortably well-off parents from a good Connecticut suburban community. They entertained often and easily and felt that it was part of "growing up" for Dottie to join the party and to drink an occasional beer or two. Her dad worked on the theory that if the kid was taught to drink at home, she would learn her limits and appreciate wine, liquor and beer for what they should be, a pleasant way to relax and unwind, a quick way to loosen up a party. Dottie bought Daddy's theory. Shy and still uncertain of herself, she discovered that a beer or two added a nice rosy glow to the world, made her feel at ease, and folks seemed to like her better.

Her goals were simple. She just wanted to find that one special guy who would want to marry her, father three children, buy her a nice house and take her to Europe once in a while. She dropped out of college after her second year and took a job as a receptionist in the corporate headquarters of a paint and varnish manufacturer. There she met Neil. After a properly long engagement, they were married, and after the mandatory nine months, she had her first daughter. When the transfer was announced, she had a few misgivings about moving to the unknown Midwest, but she dutifully made the move "for Neil's sake."

For thirteen years that marriage progressed without incident, and the family now included three daughters spaced at decent two-year intervals. Dottie now had her diaphragm and wore it faithfully on lovemaking nights, waiting patiently until they could return to the East, where people were "civilized" and the air fare to Europe was a bit cheaper. Neil had developed several new paint hues and a nonpeel process that earned him a personal call from the president of the company and a fat raise. The kids were safely settled in school, making good grades, and their eldest daughter had her first training bra and orthodontal braces, but the routine bored the hell out of Dottie. Housework was a drag. Besides, she still couldn't identify with the young wives she met at PTA and the neighborhood parties.

"They're so *shallow*," she complained to Neil. "They think that art is a framed reproduction of Monet that you pick up at a trading stamp redemption center!"

Both Dottie and Neil had stuck to beer, always keeping a stock of several cold ones in the refrigerator and a case down in the basement. Then there were a few bottles of liquor stored high in the kitchen cabinet, where curious kids wouldn't get at it, plus two bottles of real French wine, kindly contributed by Dottie's dad when he last visited them. Dottie didn't really like the liquor, but the beer helped when she was at loose ends and needed something to take her mind away from the dismal future of another six or seven years in hicksville. Would they *ever* be recalled to the home office, back where her real friends were and New York just a two-hour train ride away? Her dad often sent her a little check with instructions that she was to spend it on herself, which made it so easy to pick up a few extra six-packs of suds at the supermarket for her own private stock. It also helped to keep the count in the refrigerator and the supply in the basement at a consistent level. Not that Neil counted, Dottie reasoned, but it really wouldn't be fair for him to pay for those extra bottles. And she didn't want to give him another excuse to complain about their household expenses.

Neil didn't notice Dottie's increasing plumpness at first. He was preoccupied with the installation of new metering equipment on the mixing vats and, more importantly, the distressing tendency of his prize no-peel paint to drop from the exterior of new-painted houses in large flakes.

Dottie's dress size had gone from size nine to size twelve, and her moods now dipped and soared, ranging from gaiety and elation to sulkiness and depression. Then there were spells of unidentifiable illness, with Dottie bitching at breakfast about "uggy feelings," headaches and lassitude. Neil sent her to the doctor, faintly alarmed that she might have forgotten her diaphragm at some critical time. The lab report was negative, and the doctor suggested vitamins, a short course of tranquilizers for her nervousness and maybe a short trip back east. It was nothing at all serious, he assured Dottie.

Meanwhile, their little angels had turned into little demons, fighting and screaming around the house, their straight A's in school dropping to C's and D's. Dottie punished them for trivial misdemeanors. But more and more, it was, "I'm going to have to tell your father," and Neil was hung with the duty of meting out justice. The kids were quiet when Daddy was home and sat in sullen silence or disappeared to wherever kids go when there's trouble in the air.

Neil arrived one evening to find his youngest daughter playing by herself on the front lawn, still in her school clothes, face and hands grimy and a little cut on her knee. "Mommy's sick again," she announced, proud to be the first with news for Daddy.

Neil hurried to their bedroom, and there was Dottie stretched across the unmade bed, still wearing the robe she donned each morning for the breakfast chores. The bedroom drapes were drawn, and the smell of stale beer competed with the faint aroma of dirty socks. Neil opened the drapes and the windows noisily and gathered up his scattered socks. Dottie rolled over and opened one eye. Groggily she explained that she just didn't feel very well, had a case of the "blahs" and was taking a little nap. She had drunk a beer to help settle her stomach, she said.

"Nobody smells like that after just one beer," Neil reasoned, and dirty socks in hand, stopped by the refrigerator for a fast inventory. There were four cold ones, same count as last night. The case in the basement was about half full, just as he remembered. He tossed his socks in the clothes hamper and poked around haphazardly checking for clean socks. He was short again.

He opened the washing machine to see if maybe she had done socks for him, peered in and discovered that Dottie, never the best housekeeper in the world, had apparently developed a fetish for clean beer bottles—the machine was filled with empties. Neil gathered up an arm load and went upstairs to spill the bottles on the bed. Dottie smiled an innocent smile.

"So what? Okay, I've been drinking a little beer, but it's my beer bought with my money, and it's no skin off your ass!

What's so wrong about a few beers?"

The fight raged loud, long and furious with the neighbors and kids within a half-block radius listening with interest to Dottie's extensive and rich vocabulary as she defended her inalienable right to a beer whenever she damn well felt like drinking one. Dinner was quiet, a quick pick-up affair of bacon and eggs, toast and jelly, all well larded with silence. Julie, their oldest daughter, kicked their youngest under the table, and Neil arbitrated the tears and screams with an order to Julie to go to her room and stay there.

She left obediently but stopped in the doorway to scream, "I hate you, Daddy! And I hate Mommy, too! You're both mean and nasty!"

On Parents' Day, Neil took off from work in the afternoon to visit the kids' classrooms. Dottie didn't feel well, so he went alone. The kids' grades weren't getting any better despite Neil's supervision of their homework, and there had been a note from the junior-high principal about Julie's being caught smoking in the girls' rest room. The teachers were concerned, particularly Patty's third-grade teacher.

"Is there anything wrong at home?" she asked Neil tactfully. "You know, I've had all three of your youngsters in my classes, and your older daughters were so quick, so perceptive and interested. But Patty just sits at her desk, staring off into space, and picking her nose. When I reprimand her, she bursts into tears."

"You damn well better believe there's something wrong," Neil thought. "Her mother's turned into a drunk and a slob — how do you like them apples, teach?" Instead, he told her that Dottie had been ill, nothing very serious, and maybe the kids might be catching the "bug" that always lurks around schoolrooms. He would see to it that they spent more time on homework and do something about Patty's nose-picking, talk to her and get her straightened out.

Neil burned inside, but he covered for his wife, since he just couldn't let any outsiders know about Dottie's bad habit. It couldn't be that she was an alcoholic, because everyone knew that you just couldn't drink enough beer to do much more than get a little buzzed. Meanwhile, the quality control supervisors down at the brewery rigorously controlled the proof of each bottle to assure that there was a content of about one ounce of alcohol in each. Apparently, when Dottie had worked her way through her daily ration of two or more six-packs, she had taken on a load that her blood stream couldn't cope with, but which some inner urge insisted that she needed to retain her sanity.

The kids? They were reacting in their own way to the confusion, the arguments and the mutual condemnations of their parents, but Daddy didn't understand, couldn't grasp the fact that he was projecting his guilt onto the backs of his children in the name of discipline. Nor did he know about the deep hurts inside and the shame of teasing by their friends. Mommy was a snarling, sick stranger who stayed in bed most of the time. Daddy was mean to them. And what's a kid supposed to do?

Neil was rapidly becoming a knurd, with a weird, illogical pattern of conduct, developing the unhappy facility of doing the wrong thing for the right reasons, doing the right thing for the wrong reasons and generally falling flat on his ass no matter what he did. The term is "mental mismanagement."

Watch a mental-mismanagement expert at work. During one of Maggie's parents' visits with us, her dad was shocked to see her preoccupation with alcohol and the mounting evidence of physical deterioration. The two of us went for a ride and after liberal praise for my patience and fortitude in "handling" his daughter, he suggested that it was time that I "lay down the law" and force her to join AA.

"Maybe she *is* an alcoholic, Jack," he said in a shaking voice, "We tried to bring her up right, see that she had a good home and proper training, but maybe it's in her blood." His voice dropped to a whisper, "You don't know that her Uncle Jim — that's on her mother's side — died, we think, of the DT's."

He went on to relate the story of a close friend and business associate who had a problem with drinking and, somehow, AA had made him stop his drinking. Maybe this man who lived nearby us could get Maggie into AA, and they could do whatever it was that they did and get her to stop drinking. As a matter of fact, he had already talked to Frank about Maggie, and Frank was willing to help. He wouldn't do anything, though, until Maggie called him and asked for help.

It sounded good to me. I knew nothing about Alcoholics Anonymous, but if they could help Maggie, they would have their chance. In a dramatic tear-filled scene one evening, I made my pitch for AA.

"Can't you see that you're ruining your life? Can't you see what you're doing to your parents and me? Can't you understand why our own sons don't want to be around you? Give AA a try for our sakes, if nothing else!"

Maggie agreed, and while she poured herself a drink to sustain her, I called Frank and asked for his help.

"Sure, Jack, sure," he answered, his voice warm and reassuring, "but let me talk to Maggie. It's her problem, not yours, not her dad's."

Frank talked perhaps thirty minutes with Maggie and made arrangements for her to attend two meetings. He would meet her at the meetings, pick her up or, if I liked, I could bring her and attend the meetings, too. Feeling that I was the one that had sold her on AA, I was going to deliver Maggie into their hands and see to it that she did whatever they told her to do. I would see that she made the meetings, drunk or sober.

I prepared Maggie for her first AA meeting by making her a good stiff vodka martini. After all, this was going to be her last drink and certainly deserved a small celebration. Maggie's kidneys were bothering her and she made several trips to the bathroom—the one with her stash down behind the cleaning supplies. She arrived at the meeting (not in *our* community, because someone we knew might be there) well in the bag, held my hand and cried through the entire meeting, while I listened intently for the magic formula that would teach her how to cut down on her drinking. Not how to quit, just cut down. That was all she needed, I felt.

Clutching Maggie's dry palm in my sweaty one, we followed Frank dutifully around the room being introduced on a first-name basis to surprisingly well-dressed men and women who looked healthy, laughed and yakked a lot and sipped coffee (choice of decaffeinated or regular) or lemonade. It was mildly irritating to me to be mistaken for the drunk, and I would carefully explain that *I* didn't have a problem, *she* did. Maggie burst into tears with each new introduction. If tears had been eighty-proof, Maggie could have poured drinks for the entire group of forty or so people.

The meeting was disappointingly simple, conducted something like a Boy Scout meeting. A man stood up in response to the leader's request and read a short statement of purpose of Alcoholics Anonymous, followed by another fellow reading the AA Twelve Steps (A Scout is trustworthy, loyal, etc.). The speaker was a young lady, who recounted her experiences in a pattern that we were to know well—her drinking experiences (fascinating!), her use of the AA program to find sobriety, and how things were going now. A little God stuff, the Serenity Prayer and the wrap-up, the Lord's Prayer.

The magic formula eluded us, and we went home for a glass of milk and a restless night because of too much coffee—the regular kind. We had learned only one lesson in Maggie's first AA meeting—drink decaffeinated coffee or lemonade, if they have it. The following night we attended the second meeting, and Maggie was introduced to her first sponsor, a trim, sharply dressed woman, maybe in her late thirties, who looked like a fashion model and was. Maggie didn't like her very much, probably because Doris was sober and happy, while Maggie was still shaking and not at all happy.

I attended many AA meetings with Maggie, fascinated with all of these nice people who had made just terrible messes of their lives but now, through AA, were sober! It seemed that virtually all of them had ridden the roller coaster of alcoholism much further and faster than Maggie. She hadn't been hospitalized, she hadn't seen spiders on the walls, she hadn't been fired from her job, and she hadn't lost her husband. We attended meetings, sat in on late-night bull sessions and listened. Most of all, we compared. With smug superiority, we discussed the personal experiences of those we had met and agreed that Maggie, even in her worst moments, had *never* been *that* bad!

Still, these people were sober, and I bought the AA program, hook, line and sinker. I picked up the jargon quickly, spoke to Maggie wisely of "Easy Does It" and "One Day at a Time," cautiously, carefully explaining it all to Maggie.

"They say that you can take from the program whatever you need," I told my wife earnestly, "so when you get the hang of sobriety, then you can work out *your* program so that you can still have a few drinks. If you are an alcoholic and if it is an illness, you probably have just a light case, and you won't have to stay dry for the rest of your life."

# 6

## An Excellent Plan, No Doubt

"The first thing I've got to do," said Alice to herself, as
she wandered about in the wood, "is to grow to my right
size again; and the second thing is to find my way into
that lovely garden. I think that will be the best plan."

It sounded an excellent plan, no doubt, and very neatly
and simply arranged; the only difficulty was that she had
not the smallest idea how to set about it ...

Maggie tried. For two tense months, she held herself in
check, drinking fruit juices, tomato juice laced with hot sauce
and a twist of lemon (a "Virgin Mary" or a "Bloody Shame" as
we so cutely called it), coffee, colas, milk, tea, even water,
anything to quiet her personal thirst. I held my breath. She
announced her great decision at the next party we attended
and basked in our friends' admiration and comments, "Maggie
you *can't* be an alcoholic! Maybe you drink a little too much,
but don't we all?" Maggie would smile graciously, resigned to
her fate of perpetual dryness forever-and-for-a-day, absently
stirring her sterile ginger ale with her index finger. I held my
breath and slipped away to the bar for a quick drink, so she
wouldn't see me. I didn't want to tempt her.

The parties were dull, and all the joy had gone from the Happy Hour. Maggie was tense, short-tempered and nervous. She attended the AA sessions grimly, determined to stay dry. She was going to quit drinking, if by no other way, by sheer guts and will power.

About three months passed, unhappy, miserable months, and I came home one evening to find Maggie in the kitchen, relaxed and with the faint smell of vodka hanging like a veil over her head, thickly overlaid with the odor of a breath freshener. The great AA experiment had failed, and I didn't have to hold my breath any longer.

"What the hell," I thought, "at least she'll be easier to get along with, and the meals will improve." One thing about Maggie—she was a pretty good cook when she was sober, but when she was drunk, she mixed and measured with gay disregard of recipe proportions, ran the gamut of her spice shelf, and the results were of gourmet quality.

Maybe the meals were better, but Maggie wasn't. She drank lightly at first, but then rapidly reestablished her drinking pattern and seemed to deteriorate physically and mentally. She knew what was happening to her and was getting scared.

"I must be going crazy," she told me one night. "I don't want to drink. I make a drink without even knowing I'm doing it. No sane person would do that!"

"Aha!" my mental tapes spun, the reels clicked, and the answer was printed out for me to read clearly. "MINOR MENTAL DISORDER AND PSYCHIATRIC TREATMENT RECOMMENDED." Maggie's head needed fixing. She was agreeable, but only with the proviso that I would get fixed right along with her. I had some kind of a mental hangup that probably could be traced back to my childhood, some traumatic experience that a shrink could uncover. My impotency would be cured, and when that happened, she wouldn't want to drink and she could be cured, too.

It seemed reasonable to me and, through our family doctor, I arranged for an interview with a psychiatrist that accepted husbands and wives for treatment. Dr. Gordon turned out to be a fatherly, white-haired type, his office dim and cool with the expected couch waiting formidably adjacent to his desk. His visible tools of the trade consisted of a small notebook and a silver pen, plus what must have been an inexhaustible supply of Kleenex. It appeared that his patients cried a lot.

We would start, he told us, with a testing procedure that might give him a clue as to where our problems might lie. This was a multi-page, multiple-choice questionnaire, and we marked the answers with a special pencil. We must be honest, Dr. Gordon told us sternly. Of course, we both cheated, since we wanted him to have a good impression of us. I was particularly careful with the questions regarding sex. He wasn't going to catch me up with those tricky little traps which would indicate that I was a latent homosexual!

At our second session, he sat down with both of us and fanned the pages of a computer printout which showed him a profile of our deviations from the norms. Both of us suffered from severe depression, he said, and we both had suicidal tendencies. I was secretly elated to see that I was even more depressed than Maggie. That depression, I reasoned, was the underlying factor of my failure as a sexual athlete. I was a sick man, and now Maggie would be sorry for all of the nasty things she had said to me.

During the months of treatment that followed, weekly visits at forty dollars per hour, Dr. Gordon peeled back the layers of my memory and my relations with my parents. Had I ever peeked at my mother when she was dressing or undressing? What about my masturbation habits—when did I start, how often did I do it? My experiences with girls—when did I start, how successful was I? How about boys? Had my mother ever dressed me as a little girl? Had I ever "dressed up" in my sister's clothing? He prescribed a series of "mood elevator" pills for me that seemed to help.

Following several months of weekly visits, Dr. Gordon explained my impotency. I was, he said, subconsciously punishing Maggie for her excessive drinking by denying her my sexual favors. I was to relax, remember that she was the same girl that I married, and if I approached her with love and she accepted me with patience, I would slowly regain my sexual powers. It would go slowly, he warned, I wouldn't be a stud bull in the bedroom, but if we persisted, everything would straighten out for me. I sincerely hoped so. I did do better — not well, but better — and I was dismissed as a patient, which cut the psychiatrist's bill in half.

Maggie wasn't faring so well. She kept her guard well up with the kindly doctor, who had suggested early in their sessions that she should quit drinking, or at least cut down, so he might get a better insight into her id or superego, whichever might be out of phase. Maggie armed herself for these weekly encounters by downing the better part of a bottle of fortified sherry. When the doctor would open the session with, "Have you had anything to drink today?", Maggie could respond honestly, "Just a little sherry, doctor."

After all, she reasoned, she was still a lady, and there wasn't anything so very bad about a lady having a nip or two of sherry before what was obviously going to be a trying experience. Maggie wanted to please. She learned quickly that Dr. Gordon was a disciple of Freud and loved to hear her dreams, so she pleased him by manufacturing a new one for his consideration and interpretation each week. She dreamed in color, she told him, and kept him spellbound and busy scribbling in his notebook, with her glowing accounts of her adventures in dreamland. If he tried to steer the conversation around to the subject of her drinking, she burst into tears and reached blindly for the Kleenex box, always conveniently placed at her elbow.

Her treatment neared an end when the doctor announced his plans for retirement. In retrospect, Maggie wondered if he retired because (a) she had filled his notebook with enough dream material to keep him happy and occupied for the remainder of his analytical life, (b) he could no longer buy his Kleenex wholesale, or (c) he was simply tired of playing father confessor to a hopeless drunk. Anyway, within the next few months he would select a younger man, he told her, and arrange to transfer her case (and the forty-dollar hourly fee) to a new set of shoulders.

Psychiatry was failing to fix what was wrong with Maggie. Each session inspired a fresh bout of drinking when she came home, depressed and discouraged. Her mood elevator pills didn't seem to help. There were additional physical problems. As the result of a bad fall—she insisted that she was sober because she never hurt herself when she fell when drinking—spinal arthritis sent her in quest of a specialist that could do something for her severe pain.

A week of physical examinations in the hospital confirmed the arthritis and referral to the "best man in the business." She was frank with the doctor.

"I drink a lot, and I think I'm an alcoholic," she related.

"Better cut down on the drinking," was his prompt recommendation. He then prescribed the chemical wonders, minor tranquilizers to serve as a muscle relaxant. She settled into her new routine, taking three Valium pills daily, Dr. Gordon's mood elevators, plus her daily fifth of vodka and a quart or so of fortified sherry, plus a beer if other supplies in the house were low. She cried with no provocation, her eyes welling with tears, which rolled down her cheeks that she wiped from time to time with a ball of sodden Kleenex. She bought the big boxes at the discount drug stores and our end tables looked like the battlefield of the world's greatest snowball fight. Maggie no longer lived—she simply endured.

One balmy June evening, our usual evening spent in silence with me reading my usual book and Maggie watching me, she came to my chair and kissed me—a long kiss that I tried to shorten because of that insidious, all-pervasive stench of booze from her breath and body. She was going to bed, she announced, and I was glad. When she was asleep, at least she wasn't drinking or chewing me out.

Forty minutes later I decided that I was tired, there was no sound from the bedroom and maybe I could get a good night's sleep if she didn't wake up. The door to our bedroom was closed, and when I tried to enter, I found that it was locked. Goddammit—she didn't have to do that—lock me out of my own bedroom! I called out softly at first, then loudly and angrily.

"Open this damn door, or I'm going to kick it in!" I shouted. No answer. Okay, I thought, if that's the way she wants to play, I'll not only break the door down, but I'll make her call the carpenter tomorrow and she can pay for it out of her own money! My foot hit the door handle squarely, and the wood around it splintered as the lock gave way. I swung the door wide, and there was my wife in bed, a light burning beside her head, eyes closed and a note neatly folded on my pillow. I unfolded it, fumbling, and read that she was taking her life because she was "no good"—no good for herself, no good for me, no good for her family or grandchildren, and this was the simple way out, the best and only way for all of us.

She was breathing shallowly, and I dialed our family physician. He was exhausted from a difficult day with his patients, and my frantic call caught him with his professional demeanor down. "Damn that woman—I *knew* I shouldn't have prescribed those sleeping pills for her!" he shouted. I had reported that her bottle of Seconals had been emptied, but that I hadn't the slightest idea of how many she might have taken or if she had swallowed anything else.

"Will you come over here?" I begged.

"There's not enough time, Jack. Call the fire department for their emergency rescue vehicle."

In minutes, the red truck swung into our driveway, lights flashing, and two fireman toted out my wife on a stretcher. (What will the neighbors think?) I climbed in the truck and rode with Maggie to the hospital. She was whisked away for treatment, and I gave the bored nurse at the desk the required details of name, address, health insurance carrier, date of birth, name of physician and description of the "symptoms."

"She took an overdose of sleeping pills, I think," I told her reluctantly.

"Gastric disturbance," she wrote. Ours was a small-town hospital, discreet and protective. Patients in our town never tried to kill themselves because they were helpless drunks. And besides, suicide attempts meant extra paperwork and special attention. Screwed up the records, too, I thought, as I trudged home, sockless with my heels blistering, tears streaming down my cheeks and my heart overflowing with guilt, anger and shame. Why had she done this to me? Will she make it? Will she try again? It must be my fault—I drove her to suicide. I sat on the curbside and cried. Maybe she *is* better off dead. Maybe we would both be better off in our graves. A twin funeral would probably be cheaper in the long run. Besides, I could think of a dozen ways to die that were far more efficient than a handful of sleeping pills. Let's see—we could have a farewell drink or two, get in the car—the older one, no need to wreck the new car—and I would roll down the interstate, get it up to maybe a hundred, and there was that one place where I could swing over and hit the overhead bridge support. But could our sons collect the insurance? I would have to check the policies.

I settled in front of my typewriter and wrote Maggie a note. I couldn't live without her, I typed, and if she ever decided again that life wasn't worth the effort, she was to let me know and we would "go together." A suicide pact was my solution for our problem, but I was going to manage the production with a smashing finale, right into the grave, where we would lie, side by side, two very wonderful but unfortunate people. It was sad, just like a tear-jerker of a movie.

Dr. Gordon was shocked but not surprised, he said, when I reported Maggie's attempt at death. He strongly recommended—insisted in fact—that Maggie be treated at the very private, very secluded Tudor Hospital for mentally disturbed patients. She needed round-the-clock care in a calm and pleasant atmosphere, where he could give her intensive treatment. Maybe a month or so in the eighty-dollar-per-day haven —they just took the "best people"—would be sufficient, the doctor thought. All I had to do was to sell her on the idea.

The treatment was going to fix her, make her well, stop her drinking, and it would be just like spending a month at an exclusive country club, I told her. It should be a voluntary commitment, but I was wondering how I was going to handle the matter if she resisted. I'd have to get a court order, I supposed. Subdued, sober, but shaky, Maggie was agreeable. She had talked by phone with Dr. Gordon, who assured her that she would definitely not be behind bars, she could take whatever she liked to wear, and it would be almost like taking a vacation at a nice summer resort. A bed was available immediately, and why didn't we get right out there? He would arrange the details of releasing her from the local hospital.

Maggie packed a big bag filled with her finest outfits and a smaller bag with her pills, make-up, and a few pieces of good, but not flashy, jewelry. She might have a few loose screws and be a nut, but she was at least going to be a fashionable, well-dressed nut. We left for Tudor Hospital in mid-morning, stopping enroute for a sandwich and the traditional "last drink" for Maggie. It might as well be a double, Maggie argued, so we had a couple of doubles. She thinks she had a third while I was in the john. Tudor Hospital didn't seem nearly so frightening after our drinks.

From its external appearance the hospital was everything that Dr. Gordon had promised. Decently distant from the city, an old Victorian mansion had been remodeled as the administrative center, and was flanked by two newer buildings of mellowed rosy brick which housed the patients, or was it guests? The complex nestled into the side of a hill with a valley view, the grounds were manicured, the flower beds bloomed brightly, and there was even a charming little pond complete with a flock of ducks. There were no bars at the windows, I pointed out reassuringly.

Registration was quick, efficient. According to the neatly coiffed lady administrator, Maggie would spend a little time in the admissions center, then would be transferred to one of those new buildings for treatment. She would not encounter anyone who was seriously ill. There was one little detail more to attend to, Maggie's signature and mine, authorizing electric shock treatment should Dr. Gordon deem it necessary. Maggie balked. We had read all about electroshock in Mary Jane Ward's book, *The Snake Pit*, and that was just for the hopelessly insane! I told the administrator that shock treatment wouldn't be necessary, since Maggie wasn't really all that sick, and the nice lady smiled and nodded her head, assuring me that we could discuss that later with our doctor. It was nothing for us to be concerned about now, she said, and she would just escort us down to the admissions ward, which was right there in the same building.

Two flights of stairs brought us down to the basement and a serviceable closed door with a window covered with protective wire netting. A knock and the door was opened by a stocky nurse whose arms bulged with muscles more suitable to a bricklayer or Popeye. I stole a quick look into the rooms that rimmed the corridor and saw that there were no bars at the windows—just that heavy wire netting that had not been installed to keep out any troublesome flies. Timorously, I raised the question as to whether we had been brought to the wrong ward, since the administrator had definitely assured us that Maggie was not to be confined.

"Oh, this is not a confinement ward," Big Burly explained, "and anyway, your wife will be here for just a day or two, maybe just a few hours, until we get her settled in and get a case history. She can go outside anytime she wants to, with an attendant, of course. And now, it's 'show and tell time,'" she said playfully.

Maggie's luggage was to be unpacked, her clothing examined, and each item was to be labeled. "Some of our patients try to bring in things that aren't good for them, and once in a while, we get a patient with kleptomania who takes things. It makes it easy if everybody's belongings are labeled —no problem in returning them."

Labeling and inspection was to be carried out by another Amazon who easily could have gathered a patient under each arm if the need arose. She removed each article of clothing from Maggie's two bags, examined it carefully, even fingering the seams, and attached a neat label to each item. Cigarettes, lighter, make-up and jewelry went into a separate basket to be kept in a locked cupboard.

"You're not going to keep my cigarettes," Maggie asked anxiously, "I'm not going to stay if I can't smoke."

"No, we just want to look at them," Big Burly No. 2 answered. She took each cigarette from the package, sniffed them and broke one in half. She replaced them in the package and tossed it to Maggie. "We do keep your lighter. When you want to smoke, you come to the nurse's station and we give you a light."

I wandered down the short corridor for a closer look at Maggie's room. It was a double to be shared with another patient, who was presently outside with an attendant. Probably on a leash, I surmised. The room was furnished in Spartan fashion, with the floor, walls, drapes, furniture and bedspreads in varying shades of brown. Brown linoleum underfoot, neatly made beds with brown striped spreads, brown chair, brown desk, tan wall paper, drapes matching the bedspreads. The decorator must have been a patient with a feces fixation, I thought. The window opened all right, but the heavy wire mesh screen didn't. The door had a lock for privacy —but the lock worked only from the corridor side.

At the end of the corridor, I spotted a TV set in a room furnished with a couch upholstered in sturdy brown imitation leather, two matching lounge chairs and a few wicker chairs, fugitives from a garage sale. This was the "Patients' Lounge," the nurse explained brightly. The set was turned on, tuned to a station that had not yet started its programming, and the screen showed only the geometric tuning pattern. A young man, perhaps in his late teens or early twenties, stared at the screen intently. Seeing me, he began to wail softly, and his crying increased to a high, keening sound. Big Burly No. 1 hurried down the hall and bustled the youngster into his room.

"Now you stay here, and you quit crying!" she instructed him. He stopped immediately. It was obvious that no one disobeyed either of the Burly twins.

"Why don't you go outside and look the place over while we settle Maggie?" the nurse suggested. She unlocked the door, and I climbed the steps from the basement ward, thankful to be in the open air. I admired the craft center with its facilities for basket-weaving and wallet-making, the comfortable lounge chairs scattered under the trees and the neat duck pond.

A dozen or so ducks swam slowly in an orderly circle, leaving the pond from time to time to waddle across the grass, neatly spaced, single file, each duck maintaining a proper interval fore and aft. Perhaps, I fantasized, the ducks were patients also. With proper treatment, daffy ducks might someday return to duck society to live a more normal life. They would learn with the aid of shock treatments not to quack rudely, not to nip at other ducks, to refrain from stuffing their gullets with fermented corn and then go skidding wildly around the barnyard. No more deep dives in the pond to surface under some unsuspecting duck to goose him gaily with a sharp beak. No more duck hangovers, shakes or duck-up-chucking. No duck depressions, no unexplainable duck deaths. If these ducks could do it, so could Maggie!

I returned to the basement ward, knocked, was recognized and admitted. Maggie was now unpacked and labeled, and very quiet. We shared a couple of cigarettes, and I was very quick to light Maggie's before she could comment on the loss of her lighter. We talked in hushed voices, and I reassured her that her stay in the ward would be short, and when she was moved over to one of the treatment buildings, she would find the country-club atmosphere described by Dr. Gordon. Time would pass quickly, and she would be back home before she knew it.. We touched gingerly on the subject of electroshock. I swore by all that was holy that I would never agree to such treatment.

I was making mental reservations, however, and in the back of my mind I was mustering reasons why, if Dr. Gordon thought it essential, Maggie should undergo the series.

Dammit, she just had to be cured of her depression and her insane desire to drink!

It was time to go. Maggie sat silently, tears welling from her eyes, and clung to me. "I'm so afraid!" she said.

Out in the freedom of the grounds, I saluted the ducks as they made their regimented rounds, drove a few miles, stopped and cried. Tears come hard to me. Once home, I settled in Maggie's recliner to think it through. Pictures of her turd-tan room, the wire mesh at the windows, the sound of the young boy whimpering, the Burly sisters, the ducks, flashed through my mind. What would I do when Dr. Gordon inevitably approached me for permission to wire Maggie for electroshock? Would intensive psychiatric treatment help her? In my heart, I felt that the mind-fixers would grow impatient with Maggie's technicolor dreams, and she would be shocked, sedated, tranquilized, and turned back to me docile and obedient — and half-alive.

"Just like those damn ducks," I reasoned. "They're going to make Maggie into a duck-woman. She'll come home dry and maybe she'll never drink again, but she won't be normal, won't be happy. She won't be *Maggie!*"

Hope dies hard in the mind of a knurd. There just had to be a better way than Tudor Hospital and the docile duck treatment. "She's really not that *bad*," I rationalized. "I'm not even sure she's an alcoholic. Drinking is such an ingrained thing with her that it's become a deep-seated habit. But bad habits can be broken and good habits installed in their place if the teacher is patient but firm. I can do it. By God, I can break her habit once and for all if I can get her away from her drinking friends, her doctors and her psychiatrist and the minister. I'll *make* her learn to drink like a lady!"

The next morning I sprang Maggie, over the horrified protests of the hospital staff. I was taking a sick woman out of a hospital, and I was possibly endangering her life! I didn't give a damn. I wanted her back alive, not half-dead, not a mindless vegetable. We were going away, I told Maggie, to a small hotel in the Caribbean where I was known and my wishes would be law. We would limit her drinks to a reasonable, ladylike level, and under my management, she would break her habit and replace it with moderate, social drinking, the way it used to be. When she eased up on the booze, her depression would vanish. When she became a social drinker once again, my sexual hangup would disappear, too, and we could go back to normal living. Maggie gladly would have accompanied me to hell, if it meant escape from Tudor, and would have agreed to drink nothing but salty sea water, if that was the cost of her freedom. Her White Knight had come galloping up on his charger and saved her!

I laid it out carefully to the hotel manager. My wife was not to have one drop of booze, beer or wine unless I personally served it to her. I talked in turn to the bartenders, the waiters, the maids, even the gardener, and extracted solemn vows that "Miz Jack" would be limited to soft drinks or a cup of coffee if she wanted it. I bought loyalty with heavy tips and promises of more to come.

Maggie cheerfully agreed to my rules. She was limited to no more than two drinks daily. She could have them anytime during the day or evening. She could have a beer — just one — at noon when we were at the beach, and then the second one for a sundowner. If she preferred, she could save up and have both of her drinks one after the other, but two drinks daily was the absolute daily quota. Three weeks of control, and she would be a new woman.

Never underestimate the ability of an alcoholic to get a drink when she wants one. As decreed by custom in the Caribbean, my schedule included a siesta in the early afternoon, and Maggie quickly adjusted hers to her advantage. She would stretch out with me at siesta time and wait patiently for me to drift away into an hour's nap, or if I proved restive, she would thoughtfully excuse herself to go outside "to read" and "not to disturb my rest." Once clear of the room and her slumbering keeper, she would hurry to the bar where, with tips much more generous than mine, she was assured of prompt and confidential service. She arranged a conspiracy of silence, explaining that her husband was something of a harmless nut about drinking and they mustn't upset him. She ordered the big double rums (about four ounces) with ginger ale, and could manage to down three of them and would order a fourth, a triple this time, when she figured that I might be rousing from my siesta. Paying cash for her drinks to avoid any evidence on the bar bill, she would return to our room tinkling her triple gaily and announce that she was having her first of the day.

Maggie's perfidious plan worked beautifully for perhaps a week until, flushed with success, she stepped up her siesta sipping and returned one afternoon, floating in a sea of alcohol that I couldn't fail to see and smell. She had put away over a pint of high-proof rum in a period of an hour, and that much, even for old hollowleg, was bound to show.

"You're drunk." It was not an accusation, simply a statement of fact.

"You're damn right. So what?" It was not a defense, simply agreement, and what was I going to do about it?

We stayed for another two weeks, and Maggie tried seriously to control her intake, and with some success. She was never really drunk, nor was she ever completely sober. I was crushed with the failure of my optimistic plan to regulate her drinking, but it didn't seem to matter any more. We didn't talk about it, and it was tacitly understood that she would try not to get too drunk and I would try not to be too unhappy. We simply endured one another.

On our return home, I had made up my mind that Maggie was beyond redemption, and it was my fate to live out our life together with her as a hopeless drunk and with me taking care of her as best I could, until she finally killed herself, either from the effects of drinking or by taking her own life. Possibly I would join her in suicide. It didn't really matter, one way or another.

Now employed in a mediocre job with the important title of District Manager, I refused to take overnight trips for fear that Maggie would kill herself while I was away. I refused a transfer to another city because I felt that Maggie could not make the transition to a new community and make new friends. The president of my company knew my wife was a drunk, because I had told him about her in elaborate detail, relating my troubles while very, very drunk myself. He was extremely decent, and understanding, but also extremely concerned over my lack of new business. He promptly brought in a new district manager, and I was given a secondary desk job, one that did not require travel or transfer. Resent it? I burned with resentment, but what could I do? I was stuck — stuck with a drunk for a wife. I was in a rut with no hope of advancement or more pay, our friends deserting us, our sons avoiding us.

There was only one thing to do, it seemed to me. "If you can't beat them, join them." I might as well settle down and match Maggie drink for drink, and it wouldn't be long before we drank ourselves to death or worked up enough courage to kill ourselves.

It didn't hurt so much this way. I drank double martinis at lunch and goofed off in the afternoon, and joined Maggie in the evening in front of the TV where we absently fingered the ice in our drinks, cursed our parents, criticized our children and mourned for our friends. Maggie cried and I cried and we had another little drink. I retreated further and further from reality and sank deep into my private world of nothingness.

"What do you want for dinner?"

"I don't give a shit."

"What do you want to see on TV?"

"I don't give a shit."

"Want another drink?"

"I don't give a shit — oh, I guess so."

I was whipped, beaten, completely frustrated and beyond any further anger. Maggie wanted to die, and maybe it was a good idea. I just didn't really care any more. I was too numb to care. I didn't give a shit.

# 7

## All Alone Here

"... but, oh dear!" cried Alice with a sudden burst of
tears, "I do wish they would put their heads down! I am so
very tired of being all alone here!"

Recovering alcoholics are thoroughly outgoing people who
love, second only to their sobriety, the pleasure of each others'
company. Conversation seems to take the place in their lives
that drinking once held. They can't seem to get enough of it.
They talk during their meetings, during the social hour following, then get together in a restaurant or somebody's home for
more talk. After that they use the phone. It's said that if
Alexander Graham Bell hadn't invented the telephone, a
recovering alcoholic would have done so.
One evening when Maggie was freshly returned from
Hazelden, the treatment and recovery center where she found
her sobriety, we were invited to Frank's apartment following
an AA meeting for a CCC meeting—coffee, conversation and
conviviality. Frank had been Maggie's initial contact in
Alcoholics Anonymous when she first tried it on for size and
didn't like the fit. I put a question to Frank, a puzzler that I
had been too timid to ask previously.

"Why didn't Maggie make it when she came to AA the first time?"

Frank had a number of years of sobriety under his belt and devoted maybe 90 percent of his free time to AA. I had thought that he might have resented the fact that Maggie had dropped out of AA to drink again and then came back only after a seven-week stay at Hazelden, but on the contrary, he had welcomed her back with open arms.

"I don't know for sure, Jack," Frank said, "but I think that she didn't come to AA that time voluntarily. She was pushed. You'll remember that I had talked to her dad and then talked to you and had a hell of a time getting you off the phone so that I could talk to Maggie. You guys were yelling for help, but Maggie wasn't. She wasn't ready. She hadn't bottomed out. Some of us have a higher point where we're sincerely ready for help and others, like your Maggie, bump along almost to the end of the line before they're ready.

"The secret is to be able to hear them when they call for help. Drunks seem to lose their ability to communicate. I remember one guy that gave me three dozen good reasons why he couldn't stop drinking and another three dozen excuses as to why, if he did want to quit, he couldn't do it now. I heard him out and then asked, 'Ready to go to the hospital?' He grabbed my hand and shook it. 'Sure! What do you think I've been telling you?'"

"But Maggie didn't *want* any help," I protested. "She wanted to cut down, sure, but she didn't want help to stop altogether."

Frank put down his empty pipe. He was trying to quit smoking, and the going was rough. "The trouble with dummies like you is that you wouldn't recognize a yell for help when you heard it. Maggie OD'd three times before someone that *could* understand understood what she was saying. She was screaming in the only way she knew how, 'Help me! Won't somebody please help me?'"

Frank was right. Maggie and I were not communicating. I hadn't learned that the real clue to the puzzle was to be able to *hear what she was not saying.* She still had her guard up even though her unreal world was collapsing, and she was trapped in the shambles of emotional deterioration. She was trying to tell me something, but her words and actions simply didn't make any sense!

Along with one of her letters written from Hazelden, Maggie sent me a copy of an article entitled "Please Hear What I'm Not Saying" by an anonymous author.

"This tells better than anything I've ever read or could ever say just how I really felt, deep inside of me, during my bad time," Maggie wrote.

Maybe it will help you to understand what that woman of yours is feeling and aid you in translating and understanding her cry for help when it comes.

## Please Hear What I'm Not Saying

"Don't be fooled by me. Don't be fooled by the face I wear. For I wear a thousand masks, masks I'm afraid to take off and none of them is me. Pretending is an art that's second nature with me but don't be fooled, for God's sake, don't be fooled. I give the impression that I'm secure, that all is sunny and unruffled with me, within as well as without, that confidence is my name and coolness my game; that the water's calm and I'm in command, and that I need no one. But don't believe me. Please.

"My surface may seem smooth, but my surface is mask. Beneath this lies no complacence. Beneath dwells the real me in confusion, in fear and aloneness. But I hide this, I don't want anybody to know it. I panic at the thought of my weakness and fear being exposed. That's why I frantically create a mask to hide behind, a nonchalant, sophisticated face to help me pretend, to shield me from the glance that knows. But such a glance is precisely my salvation. My only salvation. And I know it. That is, if it's followed by acceptance, if it's followed by love. It's the only thing that will assure me of what I can't assure myself—that I'm worth something.

"But I don't tell you this. I don't dare. I'm afraid to. I'm afraid your glance will not be followed by acceptance and love. I'm afraid you'll think less of me, that you'll laugh at me and your laugh would kill me. I'm afraid that deep down I'm nothing, that I'm no good, and that you will see this and reject me. So I play my game, my desperate game, with a facade of masks. And my life becomes a front.

"I idly chatter to you in the suave tones of surface talk. I tell you everything that is really nothing, and nothing of what's everything, of what's crying within me. So when I go through my routine, do not be fooled by what I'm saying. Please listen carefully and try to hear what I'm not saying, what I'd like to be able to say, what for survival I need to say, but what I can't say.

"I dislike hiding. Honestly! I dislike the superficial game I'm playing, the phony game. I'd really like to be genuine and spontaneous, and me, but you've got to help me. You've got to hold out your hand, even when that's the last thing I seem to want. Only you can wipe away from my eyes the blank stare of breathing death. Only you can call me into aliveness. Each time you're kind and gentle and encouraging, each time you try to understand because you really care, my heart begins to grow wings, very small feeble wings, but wings. With your sensitivity and sympathy and your power of understanding, you can breathe life into me. I want you to know that.

"I want you to know how important you are to me, how you can be the creator of the person that is really me if you choose to. Please choose to. You alone can break down the wall behind which I tremble, you alone can remove my mask. You alone can release me from my shadow world of panic and uncertainty, from my lonely person. Please do not pass me by. Please do not pass me by.

"It will not be easy for you. A long conviction of worthlessness builds strong walls. The nearer you approach me, the blinder I strike back. I fight against the very thing I cry for. But I'm told that love is stronger than walls, and in this lies my hope. Please try to beat down those walls with firm hands, but with gentle hands, because a child is very sensitive. Who am I, you may wonder. I am someone you know very well. For I am every man you meet and every woman that you meet."

(Anonymous)

*You've got to hold out your hand, even when that's the last thing I seem to want.*
*I fight against the very thing that I cry for.*

Reading this, I thought back over the previous eight years, those frantic years when Maggie had fought to conquer her addiction and illness and I had fought to do it for her. I had been fooled by what she said and was unable to hear what she was not saying. I recapped mentally the optimistic, foolish sorties this knight in rusty armor, in reality a Don Quixote on a donkey charging the windmill of alcoholism, had tried, only to fail and fail again.

1. I had moved her to another part of the country for a "new start."
2. I had tried to "knock some sense into her head."
3. I had bought her a book on the dangers of drinking.
4. I had encouraged her to seek an answer to her problem through her church.
5. I had told her to use will power.
6. I had sent her to medical doctors and approved of the tranquilizers and sedatives they had prescribed.
7. I had taken her to a psychiatric hospital.
8. I had tried to teach her to control her drinking.
9. I had covered up for her and fought with her boss when she was fired.
10. I had believed her bullshit alibis for drinking.
11. When all else had failed, I joined her in her drinking and was prepared to join her in a suicide pact.
12. I gave up. I just didn't give a shit what happened.

That's quite a record for the guy who didn't need anyone, a self-made man who could solve his problems and his wife's problems all on his own!

When Maggie came close to "hitting bottom" at the time of her first OD, she was tucking away more than a fifth of vodka daily plus a quart or so (who measured?) of fortified sherry plus the psychiatrist's mood elevators plus three Valium pills plus occasional sleeping pills. She tells me that she was continuously intoxicated for about fourteen months at this time.

The late Professor E. M. Jellinek, one of the founders of the Yale (now Rutgers) Center of Alcohol Studies determined the symptoms and progression of the illness that gripped my Maggie and the men and women like her. He charted forty-three symptoms which describe how, as the alcoholic becomes more dependent on booze, he (or she) has to rationalize, conceal or explain away his behavior, not only to satisfy himself but also to respond to criticism or questions from others. This alibi structure grows more elaborate and grandiose. He moves completely away from the world of reality, but when the true facts of his condition become impossible to explain away, the alibi structure collapses. Now the alcoholic, states Jellinek, "becomes spontaneously accessible to treatment." This parallels the AA concept of "hitting bottom."

When Maggie neared the "bottom," she started calling for help in the only way she could. She overdosed on sleeping pills and left her suicide note. When no one answered her plea, "Won't someone please help me," she tried it again. I roused myself sufficiently out of my lethargy to drive her to the hospital and stood by, waiting to learn if she would live or die. It didn't seem to matter very much which way it would turn out—if she didn't kill herself this time, there would be a next time, and a time after that.

Overdose number three took us to another hospital. Maggie was semi-conscious when I found her, but still the con artist. Our local hospital was very strict about smoking in the rooms. "I don't wanna go back *there*," she mumbled. "It's a dump. The doctors don't know what to do, and the nurses all hate me. Take me to (she named the hospital of her choice). They'll understand what to do."

It turned out that Maggie had made a wise choice of hospitals. Shortly after she was admitted, examined and treatment started, the doctor on duty in the emergency room called me into a private office.

"She's a compulsive drinker—an alcoholic, isn't she?"

Embarrassed and defensive, I admitted that Maggie did drink a little too much and launched into a lengthy story of her physical and mental problems which had, in my considered jugement, led to her series of OD's.

"She'll make it this time," Dr. Tom reassured me. "Fact is, she hasn't taken very many pills, probably less than we might administer to a patient here under certain circumstances. It won't even be necessary to pump her stomach, and you can take her home in a few hours."

He paused. "I think she was trying to tell us something when she took this overdose. Do you think she might be interested in going someplace where she can get some help for her drinking problem—a place where she might do something just for herself?"

I was immediately alert, back in the management business and I made up Maggie's mind at once. "Of course! She'll go anywhere and I'll pay whatever it will cost if somebody can make her quit drinking!"

The doctor broke in, "Just a damn minute. *She* has to make this decision. It's not yours to make. When she gets the pills out of her system and is hopefully, reasonably sober, we'll talk about it."

When Maggie had upchucked, then managed to keep some black coffee down and came back to our world, Dr. Tom sat on the end of her bed and talked to her gently. "I'm an alcoholic, Maggie—a recovering alcoholic. I know how it is with you. Would you like to go someplace where you can get better—a place where I found sobriety? Think about it and, if you want to, come back to the hospital some evening and we'll talk some more."

Maggie eyed him suspiciously. "Are you talking about a 'put-away place'?"

He laughed and assured her that the spot he had in mind was very definitely not a "put-away place," but he did know all about such institutions, both private and public. He had spent some time in them.

Maggie recovered quickly from the effects of her OD and held her drinking to a minimum. She called Dr. Tom, and a few evenings later we sat in his tiny private office listening to his story. He was a "double dipper," he told us, addicted to both alcohol and drugs. Under pressure of work, he had become increasingly dependent on alcohol, then switched to drugs, so handy to a doctor. He spoke of his increasing unfitness as a doctor, his guilt, his preoccupation with chemicals, and of the loss of his practice. He told of his stay in a psycho ward and, when his funds were exhausted, of his commitment to a state institution where he existed—not lived—under heavy sedation. Then, he said, using a term new to us, "the Hand of God," in the form of another doctor, himself an arrested alcoholic, had arranged for his transfer to Hazelden, a recovery center for alcoholics and drug dependents.

He related something of his treatment and how, after some time, he found his sobriety and returned to the outside world, slowly to rebuild his life and career in the medical profession. There were separate facilities for women, he said, and if Maggie truly, at gut level, wanted to get help, he would assist with her admission to Hazelden. There were women in our area, who had been in as bad or worse condition than Maggie, who had returned from Hazelden and were living happy and sober lives. If she wanted to talk to some of them, he would be glad to arrange it. She didn't have to make a decision now but could call him any time, day or night, for help.

Maggie had reached the point described by Dr. Jellinek where she was "spontaneously accessible to treatment." After a short period of hesitation, she called Dr. Tom to tell him that she was ready to go, but could she please talk to one of the women who had been to Hazelden?

"Stay near the phone, Maggie," he answered. "You'll get a call very soon."

Within minutes, the phone rang, and I grabbed it. Maggie was so nervous that I feared she might drop it. I dropped it, picked it up, and it was Connie, a Hazelden graduate, and could she speak to Maggie please? Connie talked for almost an hour, and Maggie listened and cried. The vibes were right, Maggie told me at the end of the conversation. It came right through the wires that Connie was sober, she was happy, she had been a resident of the hell that Maggie knew so well, and that she wanted what Connie had more than anything in the world.

"When can you go?" Connie had asked.

"Would tomorrow be all right?" Maggie responded anxiously.

Connie told Maggie to stay near the phone, and within an hour she called back to report Hazelden would have a bed available in three days! Elated, Maggie and I celebrated in the only way we knew. We had a few drinks.

Connie had not told Maggie to stop drinking, only to drink as little as she thought she could until she reached Hazelden. It was no country club, Connie said, and she would need only comfortable clothes, sweaters, slacks and skirts, jeans if she liked. Remembering the "country club" atmosphere of Tudor Hospital, these suggestions sounded practical and down to earth.

Departure day arrived and I took Maggie to the plane (direct flight, no intermediate stops). I bought her, once again, her "last drink" at one of the handy airport bars. Later, when she was not only sober but honest, she told me that in addition to my drink, she had fortified herself with a few hasty belts before leaving the house, bought two quickies at the airport while I was checking the luggage, drank everything the hostesses would serve on the plane, and arrived gloriously smashed! She was so high, she said, that she could have made the flight to Minneapolis-St. Paul without the benefit of an airplane.

I stood at the gate, just to make sure that she didn't have a change of heart or that there might be mechanical troubles requiring a return to the loading platform. But when that big bird climbed off the runway and turned west, I felt a sudden surge of relief, a wave of elation that washed over me. Winning a million in the state lottery couldn't have made me feel better. I felt so good that it was almost indecent. Someone else was going to look after Maggie now—it was no longer my job. When I joined Al-Anon some time later, I found that they had a term for it: "Let Go and Let God."

"Hey man," I can hear some of you saying in disgust, "is this going to be one of those *religious* books? We thought you said you were an agnostic."

Relax. This is definitely not a treatise on religion, and I'm not trying to convert you to any brand of faith. Your belief or lack of belief in God is entirely your business. The way I feel, and the way Maggie feels, about God as we know him is our business. Both AA and Al-Anon speak of a "Higher Power whom some prefer to call God." The fact that perhaps forty or fifty percent of the men who join these organizations came into the programs as atheists or agnostics and still get along with the concept of a Higher Power indicates that there's room for everybody. In telling my story and something of Maggie's, I just want you to know how I am today, and how I feel. To do this, I talk about God as I understand Him. Okay?

Consider the chain of events that led to Maggie's admission to Hazelden. She survived two attempted suicides and conned me into taking her to a distant hospital where the doctor on duty happened to be a recovering chemical dependent. Despite the best efforts of doctors, psychiatrists, hospital staffs, ministers, miracle drugs and the home treatment of a wacky husband, nothing had helped her. Now, after a talk with an arrested double-dipper and a phone call from a woman Maggie had never met, she was on her way to a treatment center. Unbelievable luck? An improbable coincidence?

"Neither," says Maggie. "This is how God goes about His work." She feels God makes His miracles through people, that people serve as the "Hand of God," as Dr. Tom put it. Webster says that a miracle is "an extraordinary event manifesting a supernatural work of God: an extremely outstanding or unusual event, thing or accomplishment." The miracle of Maggie's sobriety came as the result of Dr. Tom, Connie and the Hazelden staff working as the "Hands of God."

I think that one of the reasons I enjoy attending AA meetings so much is the opportunity to step into and visit with a room full of miracles. Here is a group of men and women who were killing themselves as inevitably as if they were dosing themselves daily with poison (alcohol *was* poison to them) but are now sober, often serene, and happy. These were the "Miracles of Alcoholics Anonymous," miracles not created with a flash of lightning or a roll of thunder, but made through the actions of people. This then, is how we believe God works. Through people.

God must have shuddered a bit and looked the other way for a minute as His people formed a human chain—Dr. Tom, Connie and the airline—and delivered Maggie into the hands of the waiting driver from Hazelden at the Minneapolis-St. Paul airport gate. She was bombed out of her skull, a not-unusual condition for new patients headed for Hazelden. Connie had asked Maggie for an exact description of what she planned to wear for the trip and insisted that she make no last minute changes in her attire. She had relayed this information to the authorities at Hazelden to assure accurate identification by the pick-up driver.

When I made my initial visit to Hazelden, I talked with "Red," one of the drivers, and asked him if he had ever "lost" a new arrival.

"Nope," he told me, "I just look for the drunkest passenger coming off the plane, the one they sorta pour off, check what they're wearing, and that's usually my patient. Someday though, I'm going to pick the wrong drunk, maybe a business man who's just closed a big deal in Chicago, and he's going to get the shock of his life when he discovers where he's ended up!"

Red had collected the drunk that was Maggie with no difficulty and, along with two other passengers, drove the forty-five miles to Hazelden over snowy roads. Maggie remembered very little of the trip. They had stopped en route, she recalled, and Red had invited the new patients into a bar for the customary "last drink—for today." Maggie says she remembers this part of the trip so well because it was the first time in her life that she had ever refused a drink. She was tired, sleepy and close to being out on her feet, so she stayed in the car and slept while the other two patients did the honors for her. She had finally bottomed out, was "sick and tired of being sick and tired," as the AA's put it, and ready to be helped.

Not every alcoholic goes through the experience of shaking hands with the devil before she or he bottoms out. As Frank had explained, there were "high bottoms and low bottoms," and he wasn't referring to the distance from one's posterior to the floor. It would be a lot simpler to understand if that was the meaning of the term. There is a friend of Maggie's who seemed to literally "bottom out." She fell off bar stools. She did most of her drinking in her "home away from home," a neighborhood bar, and as the evening progressed, the regular patrons would place bets as to the minute when Josie would first fall off her perch at the bar. It never took too long—Josie would lift her glass, tilt back her head for the expected sip and slip not too ungracefully to the floor. After settling the bets, her drinking buddies would haul her to her feet, steady her on the bar stool and wait expectantly for her next show. When they could no longer balance her on the bar stool, it was time for Josie to be taken home.

Though Josie's bottom must have been black and blue from her falls, she never let her unsteadiness interfere with her drinking. Her alcoholic "bottoming out" came in quite a different fashion. She had been brought to an AA meeting that Maggie attended regularly, and she explained that she didn't really belong there, that she didn't really drink too much but had these funny "dizzy spells."

The speaker at this particular meeting was an advertising copywriter, and he strung his words together like jewels as he described his efforts to quit the booze through sheer will power. He had decided to take a few days off, stay home and quit drinking "cold turkey." He had been a heavy drinker, and as a result of denying his body its accustomed quota of alcohol, he convulsed.

"First, I noticed that I couldn't quit shaking. My arms shook and then my entire body shook. I began to sweat, and the room turned a brassy yellow, then scarlet red. I couldn't breathe. Every bone in my body felt as if it was being broken, and I was frightened, panic-stricken, certain that I was going to die. I lost consciousness and came to an hour later, in the hospital. My wife had found me and had called an ambulance. I learned that I could have died as the result of the convulsion."

The following week, Maggie talked again with Josie. Josie told how she had listened intently to the speaker's words and how that night she had awakened her roommate, "Hey! Get out to my car quick and get the bottle of whiskey under the cover for the spare tire. I need it right now. I haven't had a drink for over twenty-four hours, and I think I'm going to convulse!"

Josie bottomed out. She was "spontaneously accessible for treatment."

Marge, on the other hand, had a high bottom. She was a strikingly beautiful woman in her early thirties, tanned from ski trips to Aspen in the winter and from hours of small-boat sailing in the summer. Marge had the world in her pocket, except for one small problem. When she had a few drinks at a party, she was wiped out and spent the remainder of the evening stretched out in a guest room, much to the disgust of her husband.

"If I didn't drink, I was okay. I switched to wine, but even then I lost control. I thought maybe it was diabetes, so I went to a clinic for a complete physical check-up. The doctor said that I had hypoglycemia—I was allergic to alcohol. I wasn't an alcoholic, the doctor said, but I shouldn't drink. I could have one glass of wine, but nothing more," Marge said.

Despite the doctor's orders, Marge continued to experiment with alcohol. She would take a few drinks and always had the same reaction—she would either black out and not remember what she did or said or would pass out. She thought about it for a week or so and, despite her husband's protests, she marched into an AA meeting.

"My husband thinks I'm nuts," she told Maggie calmly, "because he says I'm not an alcoholic and I don't need AA. The doctor says I have hypoglycemia. I think that's a cop-out. I don't care if I have hypoglycemia or hydrophobia—I know I like booze, I can't get my mind off drinking and I want a drink right now! I'm an alcoholic, and I know I'll get worse before I get better. If AA can help me, I want that help!"

Mary—you remember Mary, our double-dipper who horrified her minister when she slipped into unconsciousness on his couch—understood the bottoming-out process and honestly believed that she had reached her bottom. After all, good old Nick had steered her through the rounds of the hospitals, the psycho centers, church retreats, dry-out spas, in and out of AA and finally into six weeks of treatment at Hazelden. Mary had convinced everyone—her husband, her friends in AA, the counselors at Hazelden, and even herself—that she wanted sobriety more than anything in the world.

When she returned from Hazelden, Mary continued to complain of sudden, unexpected severe pains in her abdomen. She found a new doctor who was unaware of her alcohol and drug history and, with his help, discovered a pill that was not on the list of mood-altering chemicals which might lower her defenses. The new pill eased the pain and also eased Mary right back into uncontrolled abuse of alcohol and pills. She was adamant in her refusal to return to Hazelden for a re-run to discover what she had missed on her first time through.

Nick had attended Al-Anon meetings and understood the need for detachment. He had also learned that Mary's illness was progressive—that when she returned to alcohol and drugs, she was taking up right where she had left off and was now sliding faster and faster to certain death. He told me of his confrontation with Mary one morning, early in the day when she was still coherent.

"I asked God to help me," Nick related. "I kept my voice down, I tried to keep calm. This was going to be the most important talk I had ever had. I told her, 'Mary, I love you. I remember how I once stood you in front of the medicine chest in the morning and watched you while you downed your Antabuse pill. I remember everything else you tried because I insisted that you do it and you were trying to please me. I know that I tried to play God and run your life for you, Mary, and I understand now that I can't. I won't try to do that any more.

'It's your life to do with as you choose, but I have a life to lead, too. These are the alternatives as I see them. First, we can get a divorce. I love you, and I don't want that. Second, because you'll soon be unable to take care of yourself, there's court commitment to an institution where they can physically control you, keep you sedated if necessary. Remember you're still on parole for violation of narcotics laws. Third, you can go back to Hazelden.'"

This was reality, and Mary had to face it. She chose the re-run at Hazelden. Today, she's sober and happy in her new career as a professional counselor for other chemical dependents.

Dr. Vernon Johnson describes the cry for help when the alcoholic bottoms out as "the mating call of the suffering alcoholic." Unfortunately, it's a very difficult call to identify and a knurd like me is too screwed-up either to hear it or identify it. I guess that's why I needed God to take a hand and to work His miracle with Maggie.

They call Hazelden "The House of Miracles," and Maggie certainly needed one. There she was, her cry for help answered, her bottom reached, now sleeping it off outside a bar in cold, cold Minnesota, but ready for treatment.

Want to see how miracles are performed? Let's join Maggie, shall we?

# 8

## A Chrysalis

"I can't explain myself, I'm afraid sir," said Alice, "because I'm not myself, you see."

"I don't see," said the Caterpillar.

"Well ... when you have to turn into a chrysalis — you will someday, you know — and after that into a butterfly, I should think you'd feel a little queer, wouldn't you?"

Many of the women who have found their sobriety at Hazelden wear a little gold or silver butterfly pinned to a dress or a sweater. They think of their days of compulsive drinking as their "caterpillar period," the fuzzy time when they seemed to be sentenced to an endless, mindless crawling existence, moving in random circles intent only on satisfying an insatiable craving for their chemical of choice. Sooner or later each one wraps herself into a cocoon of unreality and remains as a chrysalis, quiescent, passive and without hope. Then comes the miracle of rebirth and emergence into the real world as a butterfly, still damp, wings quivering, and after a period of rest, the soaring into freedom.

Maggie wasn't thinking poetically about butterflies, except those in her stomach, when she was admitted to Hazelden. She was just plain scared and shaking. Would it be necessary for them to put her into a padded cell or tie her to a bed, wrapped in a strait jacket, while she howled and raged in the throes of a convulsion? What kind of a place was Hazelden, anyway?

The outward appearance is reassuring. The center is located on a sloping hillside dropping to a scenic lake and covering more than one hundred acres. There are no high walls to keep the patients in, but it's a long walk to the village of Center City. Built of stone, glass and brick, the center resembles a modern condominium-type village or, perhaps, a very large holiday resort. The buildings are fully heated and air-conditioned and connected with long passageways. Those passageways are the despair of every new patient, who must daily leave her residence unit, thread the maze to the dining room, the lecture halls, the detox center or the canteen. Maggie felt she was making real progress when she could complete her day without getting lost, and found even more self-assurance when she could give directions to someone who had arrived later than she had.

Inside is where they make the miracles. I'll admit to a strong prejudice in favor of Hazelden and its staff. At least initially, Hazelden is the "Higher Power" of its patients, something they can cling to, respect and hold in faith. Almost every alcoholic—recovering alcoholic, that is—that I've met feels the same way about the place where they found lasting sobriety. It might be the alcoholic ward of a hospital, another treatment center, a particular AA group, or the kitchen of an AA member. These were the turning points, the schoolrooms where they learned about their illness and how to arrest it. Small wonder then, that Maggie and I still think of Hazelden with admiration, respect and not a little awe.

In the over-all picture, Hazelden is one of about 10,000 treatment and rehabilitation centers in the United States. These centers vary widely in facilities and techniques of treatment. They range from the secluded dry-out spa, which detoxifies the alcoholic and turns him loose, to the other end of the scale —a place like Hazelden, with full in-patient facilities. Hazelden and others like it treat the whole person, utilizing an inter-disciplinary team of chemical dependency counselors, physicians, clergymen, psychologists, sociologists and psychiatrists. Everyone—the nurses, the administrative staff, even the janitors and cooks—is involved. Although treatment techniques vary from one center to another, the common element in most of them is group support: the patients help each other.

So far as I know, there is no treatment center that has found the sure cure, the equivalent of the Salk vaccine for polio, and none is in sight. Treatment may range from individualized in-depth therapy to hypnotism, electric shock or drugs such as Antabuse, which makes the taste and smell of alcohol so revolting that a single drink will cause violent vomiting.

One successful center in Seattle, Schick's Shadel Hospital, offers an eleven-day treatment. Each patient, once detoxified, is introduced to "Duffy's Tavern," fitted out as a barroom with a stock of booze to gladden the heart of any drinking alcoholic. The patient is given a shot of a drug that induces vomiting, followed by a glass of her (or his) favorite alcoholic beverage. She sniffs, takes a small sip and swirls it in her mouth. She downs it, has another, but when the drug works—oops! Continuing this procedure during her stay, the patient has it pretty well beaten into her head that drinking means vomiting, and it's just not worth the effort. This, plus mental conditioning under sodium pentathol (the "truth" drug), plus individual counseling and group therapy has done the trick for most patients. Should the graduate feel that she's about to fall off the wagon, she can return for a few days of supportive counseling and conditioning. Hardly a fun place, it offers rough treatment for a killing disease.

There are several "dry out" centers located in or near big cities, often tucked in an inconspicuous corner of the country-side. Here, the emphasis is on short-term treatment; the patient is brought down from her alcoholic high, detoxified through carefully administered dosages of gradually decreasing quantities of alcohol, paraldehyde or a drug such as Valium or Librium. The patient is usually withdrawn from alcohol in two or three days. Other drug addictions may require a withdrawal period of up to three weeks. Our drunk will get lectures on alcoholism and an opportunity to discuss the problem with fellow sufferers. Very probably, members of Alcoholics Anonymous from nearby will hold meetings and talk directly with the patients. The cost may range from thirty to perhaps a hundred dollars per day. It is hoped that the patient will realize the nature of the problem and turn to a long-term sustaining program such as AA.

It's a paradox that leading doctors, the American Hospital Association and the American Medical Association all agree that early hospitalization and treatment are fundamental for recovery and rehabilitation from alcoholism, yet, in some instances, hospital charters written years ago prohibit admission of patients with a diagnosis of alcoholism, either acute or chronic. Fortunately, times are changing, and with increased national publicity and growing public and private support, more hospitals are able to deal with the problem.

General hospital programs range from a five-to-ten-day detoxification and general health program to a complete treatment program with both inpatient and outpatient facilities, which together may require up to two years, for full treatment and aftercare.

I'm pretty well convinced that the best of the general hospital programs is the plan developed at the Johnson Institute in Minneapolis and now successfully employed in a number of hospitals in Minnesota, Louisiana, Wisconsin, Kansas and Nebraska. The oldest program, which opened in 1968, is at St. Mary's Hospital in Minneapolis. The facility has 173 beds in its chemical dependency treatment programs— 120 for adults, 53 for adolescents.

Vern Johnson, a clergyman and a recovered alcoholic now Director of the Johnson Institute, describes the program in his book, *I'll Quit Tomorrow*. The treatment is designed to bring the patient back to reality. There's an average of four weeks of intensive care of the acute symptoms in the hospital and up to two years of aftercare as an outpatient. Johnson's studies show that 52 percent of the patients never drink again after completing the program. The other 48 percent relapse. About half of these that slip return and complete the program successfully and remain dry. That works out to a batting average of about .750 which is mighty good in any league!

Johnson's approach is that therapy for the alcoholic must treat the whole person, who is suffering emotionally, mentally, physically and spiritually. Thus team treatment is indicated — physicians, clergymen, psychologists and psychiatrists, the nurses, the specially trained counselors and even the guy that swabs the floors. Everyone is involved.

Dr. Johnson has a special place in his heart for the knurds in the alcoholic's family and includes them in the act. Participation by the husband or wife of the alcoholic is vital, and during the first days of treatment, the spouse helps fill in the gaps in essential information used to determine the severity of the illness. Later, he'll be called in to confront the patient's defense systems. If her treatment has reached a plateau, she may start playing the rationalization game, and the spouse can remind her of "how it really was." The husband is urged to attend every lecture along with his wife, to read the recommended literature and to attend weekend orientation sessions. He's enrolled in the outpatient "spouse group," where he will learn the goals and dynamics of group life.

Johnson believes that one of the greatest problems of the spouse is repression. The guy has buried his painful memories, choked back his negative feelings, lost touch with himself and his wife's disease and has increasingly exhibited mixed-up emotional and behavioral attitudes towards reality. (The knurd has his head screwed on backwards.) Sometimes, Johnson says, some of these spouses, who have been attending Al-Anon meetings during the bad years, misunderstand the real goals of Al-Anon and believe that repression is the name of the Al-Anon game. He must be made aware of his repression and be given his own set of tools to work on his own emotional distress and mental mismanagement. He must be taught personal insight and how to improve his ability to communicate with others.

Teenagers are not overlooked, and Johnson's program encourages them to join the outpatient group and Alateen, the junior branch of the Al-Anon organization. Another youth group called TK provides something geared to the needs of teenagers. These kids need to recognize their defensive life styles and negative attitudes. Living with a drunk in the family, they suffer guilt, anxiety, fear, shame and a feeling of not being with it. These feelings of aloneness can be brutal, and meeting with other youngsters with the same problem is a tremendous help.

Okay, I think you get the picture. There are all types of recovery centers with long and short programs, some costly, some less expensive. Most of them do what they set out to do. How will your wife select one? Damned if I know, but I hope that she'll consult with the women in Alcoholics Anonymous, the winners that are staying sober, before she makes her decision. There is no *Guide to Treatment Centers* with subjective ratings of "A" or "AA."

Let's get back to Maggie. Was she clapped into the rubber room on arrival, to view the menagerie of pink elephants, snakes and spiders accumulated from the private collections of former patients? Hardly. She was checked into the detox center, where, under the watchful supervision of an RN, she would be "brought down." She was unhappy when asked to turn over any sleeping pills, tranquilizers, mood elevators or other pills prescribed or otherwise obtained. Connie had told her "no pills," but Maggie took them along anyway.

"Look," protested Maggie, "my doctor *prescribed* these! I'm arthritic and I'm in pain. My specialist told me that these Valium pills contain only a minor tranquilizer, act as a muscle relaxant and help the pain. And if you want me to sleep nights, I'm going to need a Seconal or two!"

Nurse Dee smiled at Maggie, "Try it our way. Now did you ever read or hear about anyone that died from lack of sleep? You'll sleep." Then she gave Maggie her first lesson on pills.

No alcoholic, she explained, should ever use any mind-changing drug except under very carefully controlled conditions. The drug could weaken her defenses, setting her up to take the first drink. "For the alcoholic, one drink is too many and one thousand isn't enough." Or, she might find that the mind-altering chemical would give her the same highs that she found in alcohol and she would learn to "eat her booze." Worse yet, she might mix alcohol and pills, a combination that kills.

Maggie was to be withdrawn from both alcohol and Valium. In her case, she was given steadily decreasing doses of Valium for a period of ten days. By careful administration of the dosages, she would be brought down from both alcohol and Valium with minimal physical discomfort and danger of convulsions. "If you convulse, you just might die," Nurse Dee announced brightly, "and we have a very definite rule that no one is to die on the premises. You'll just have to go elsewhere if you want to die."

Maggie would spend the next few days in the medical center to begin her withdrawal regime, give a complete medical case history and take her MMPI (Minnesota Multiphasic Personality Inventory). Any other medication would be administered in the center and only after verification with her family physician.

She was shortly assigned to a residential building, which would be her home during the next seven weeks. The average stay for women was four to five weeks, but Maggie, as she herself says wryly, was a "slow learner."

Presently there are two residential units for women at Hazelden, each accommodating twenty patients, and there is almost always a waiting list for admission. Each unit has a manager, an assistant manager, counselors and assistant counselors and is manned twenty-four hours a day. The immediate staff is backed up by resident and consulting clergyman, psychologists, psychiatrists, medical doctors and sociologists.

One of Maggie's counselors described Hazelden as a temporary home and school for bankrupts. New arrivals are "bankrupt" physically, mentally and spiritually, and each patient is helped to understand her alcoholism or other chemical dependency as well as to develop a more realistic, less self-destructive way of handling her multiple problems. At the core of the program are daily individual and group meetings and discussions. The alcoholic is recognized as a sick person and is encouraged to face up to her illness, to become honest and responsible.

Maggie first shared a room with the "Brown Mouse," a sad-eyed, self-effacing little woman who, according to Maggie, could be lost in a crowd of two. She scurried silently down the long halls, her eyes on the floor searching for something — perhaps her lost sobriety — Maggie thought. The rooms are mostly doubles, roomy well-furnished havens. Each has comfortable chairs, two desks, good beds and a bath shared with the adjacent room. The decor was cheerful, a far cry from the turd-tans of Tudor Hospital. Many of the rooms command a view of the lake or the rolling hills: Maggie said that she really couldn't remember the view from her window, since she was either too busy or too tired to wonder or care much what was going on outside.

Each of the residential buildings has its own large lounge with a stone fireplace, color TV, well-upholstered furniture and, abutting the lounge, a balcony coffee bar with a rectangular table big enough to accommodate a dozen. The unit manager and counselors have offices adjoining the lounge; there was always someone there ready to listen and to keep an eye on the budding female butterflies.

Maggie's first days and nights were a chaotic jumble of uncertainty, fear and confusion. She told me that she had strong suspicions that there were dark, sinister plans and actions designed to trip her up. She was convinced that "they" read her mail (not true) and monitored her phone conversations (also not true).

"They've got to be reading my mail," Maggie insisted in one of her first phone calls to me, "because they know everything that I'm thinking!"

Her counselor explained that one to Maggie. "I'm an alcoholic too, Maggie. Of course I know what you're thinking because I've had the same thoughts and know how you feel inside! I know what you're thinking and you can't con me, lady. I've been where you are!"

She worried, too, that if her behavior was not up to some unexplained standard, they would whisk her away to wherever it was that they hid the "snake pit"—but again without cause. There were no snakes and no snake pits at Hazelden. She was distressed with "work therapy" when she discovered that she was to make her own bed and help the Brown Mouse clean their room. Further, she told me indignantly, she had to set the damn tables in the dining room!

"Cheap labor," Maggie whined.

Maggie learned that the staff members at Hazelden, with few exceptions, were arrested alcoholics or other drug dependents. There's even an AA group made up of staff members. Like the AA's say, "It takes one to know one." There are few degrees offered by colleges or universities in counseling the chemically dependent, so Hazelden has its own one-year training program, drawing candidates primarily from the ranks of its own graduates. In addition to a heavy schedule of instruction, the trainees work as assistants to their more experienced compatriots—"on the job" training. The big problem is keeping them around, since, once trained, they're eagerly recruited by other treatment centers and hospitals.

Although Maggie worked with several counselors, most of her time was spent with Hal, whom she initially hated with a vengeance. Hal was young in Maggie's eyes, about thirty.

"Just a kid," Maggie wailed to me over the phone, "what the hell does he know about how a woman thinks?"

Maggie seemed determined to find the "snake pit" at Hazelden and decided that counselor Hal had just crawled out of it. "He's like a cobra," Maggie wrote. "His eyelids droop down like hoods over his eyes, and he sort of arranges himself in coils behind his desk and *watches* me, just waiting to catch me in a lie. I just hate him!"

The Cobra had been a double dipper, she said—an electrician who drank to excess and then added a Benzadrine habit. He admitted to being a violent man with an uncontrollable temper when he was high, the drunk that offers to fight every man in the bar and ends up by wrecking the joint. When he woke up the next morning behind the door of a cell, he honestly couldn't remember what had happened. Minnesota law recognizes chemical dependency as a serious illness but, practically, disapproves of people who break barroom furniture, glasses and mirrors. The judge gave Hal the choice of a month in the workhouse or a chance for treatment at Hazelden. He chose Hazelden and found, along with his sobriety, that he was a warm, compassionate man with an intense desire to help others. He elected to return to Hazelden, this time as a counselor-trainee. On completion of his training, he remained as a counselor.

I wrote Maggie daily. During the first week there were to be no phone calls in or out, but following this indoctrination period, we talked several times a week. She phoned me from time to time (collect, naturally), and I wondered if the Bell System rubbed its corporate hands in glee when the Center City long-distance calls were totaled up. During the first two weeks, she complained, "I'm not getting enough sleep, only four or five hours. There's no time to rest, and my back hurts. Do you know what the Cobra said when I told him my back was killing me? He just grinned and said, 'So you've got some pain? Be glad, because the pain means you're alive—you do want to live, don't you?'"

Maggie did want to live and, after a week or so, felt that she was making rapid progress. The Cobra wouldn't believe her, she reported. "He says his 'radar' detects that I'm an angry woman and he wants to know why I'm so angry. I tell him that I'm just angry at myself for getting to be a drunk, and he just hoods his eyes and shakes his head."

The days were long and the nights too short, Maggie said.

To prove it, she outlined her daily schedule in a letter:

6:30 Rise and shine! Make bed and "meditate"—which I don't know how to do.

7:30 Thread maze to dining room, help set places, carry food to tables.

8:00 Big breakfast (which I hate) and hurry back to room.

9:15 Through the rat-maze again to lecture hall, take notes. (There are three lectures daily, over sixty in all.)

10:00 Group therapy session back in unit with eight to ten other patients and the Cobra—damn him!

11:30 Back to dining room, set places for lunch, tote food.

12:00 Eat and return to unit, talk a little with the girls in the lounge.

1:00 Trot through maze for another lecture—they last thirty minutes.

2:00 Individual conference with a counselor or psychologist or social worker or clergyman; study required reading material in my room.

5:30 To dining room to set table and haul out food.

6:00 Dinner (food is surprisingly good and I'm hungry), then "free time" until next lecture.

7:30 To lecture hall. Dr. Heilman spoke on "Nature of Drug Dependency." I learned something; I'm not crazy!

8:00 Back to unit for study, writing and session with others in the coffee bar. Watch eleven o'clock news and go to bed.

11:45 Can't sleep, so get up and go back to coffee bar. Talk with three others until one-thirty. Back to bed and I die!

The schedule prevails from Monday through Saturday, with an abbreviated timetable on Sunday. There are only two lectures Sunday, and the patients may have guests in the afternoon. Maggie told me that she had hoped to escape Sunday football, but she could now identify half of the Green Bay Packers by their first names!

She really enjoyed the daily lectures, she said. They covered the history of alcohol and its place in our society: the pervasive nature of chemical dependency—that the addiction is stronger than any natural or learned urge. Alcohol is a depressant, not a stimulant; mind-bending drugs are absolute "no-no's" for the alcoholic. She was introduced to the Twelve Steps of Alcoholics Anonymous and heard them discussed in detail. Clergymen and sociologists spoke on value systems and spiritual bankruptcy. She learned that her first responsibility, above all others, is to maintain her sobriety, that her disease could be arrested but never cured. She was urged to be honest with herself, to be responsible, to meet her personal needs by learning to love and be loved and to maintain a healthy respect for herself as well as others.

Hazelden is equipped with a PA system in the halls and unit lounges and even has a couple of speakers mounted on the roofs of the buildings. Patients and counselors are paged, and the daily lectures are announced with a cryptic "Meeting Time!" On a calm day, the sound sometimes carries clear across the lake below the complex. There's a story supposedly told by a resident on the other side about being approached by some folks staying in a camper nearby.

They asked, "What is that place over there?" pointing to Hazelden. He told them that it was a treatment center for alcoholics. "Do they allow visitors?" they inquired.

The resident replied, "I guess so — why?"

"Well, several times we've heard their loudspeaker announce 'Mating Time,' and we're dying to see just what goes on!"

Maggie was undecided as to how she was going to "handle" the sessions with the "mind fixers" — the psychiatrist, the psychologist, the counselors that were to lead the group sessions. She wanted to be honest, not to con them, as she had Dr. Gordon, by manufacturing dreams in technicolor for them to examine and analyze.

These sessions were different, she wrote. No one was the least interested in the size of her id or superego, her personality blocks or her fixations. Fact was, she said, nobody seemed to give a damn about what went on in the past. They seemed to care only about how she was feeling right now. The past couldn't be changed, they said, but she was going to explore the defenses she had built up over the years, to identify her character defects and to discover herself as a feeling person. There were no well-marked routes to achieve these goals, no one was going to try to change her or "fix" her. As she gained a better understanding of herself, she could then make the changes she believed were necessary, trying them on for size with the help of the staff and her fellow patients. It was up to her.

Maggie tagged her hang-ups as a "can of worms" and determined to take each "worm" out of the can, one at a time, to examine it, straighten it out and then dispose of it. This sounded simple, but it hurt. Later, Maggie described this experience with a quote from Fritz Perls: "To witness one's own death and rebirth is not an easy thing."

Maggie told me in one of her letters, "One thing is for sure. I'm not the same person I was when I came here. I even wonder if I am the same person I ever was. I don't think so. What I hope I am, and think I am, is a mature version of what I was when you first met me — someone I should have become many years ago, but didn't. This experience might be compared to being reborn. I feel that I have given birth to a new Maggie, only instead of being an infant, I'm an adult. I've given birth and have been born at the same time! That's the reason, I think, for such a large degree of pain. I've suffered the pains of labor, of delivery, and then felt the pain of a child trying to find her place in the world. Now I feel that I'm going through the afterpains of delivery and the growing pains of a child. No wonder there have been periods of confusion and suffering!"

When Maggie phoned me, she did the talking, and I served as her safety valve by listening. "They picked on me today! They said I wasn't being honest, that I was lying!" "They," it turned out, were the other women in the therapy group. Another call. "Nobody around here pays any attention to me! I've tried and tried to talk to the Cobra, but he's always too busy, always working with somebody else. I just wish I could find out what they expect me to *do* here!"

# 9

# How To Get Dry Again

**The first question of course was, how to get dry again; they had a consultation about this, and after a few minutes it seemed quite natural to Alice to find herself talking familiarly with them, as if she had known them all her life.**

Maggie's letters from Hazelden told of the caustic, acid tongues, the flaring tempers, the group sessions that seemed to bring forth hurt feelings, explosions, anger, resentments and dark discouragement. Then she wrote of the curious bond, the camaraderie that was being forged between the women in the unit. The pressures and tensions were too much for one woman, and she announced that she was going to "pull the pin." Much earlier in Hazelden's history, a huge map of North America was maintained in the office with a pin placed for each patient, indicating home towns. When someone left without staff approval, he or she "pulled the pin." Maggie said that after the announcement, all of the women surrounded the prospective pin-puller, each of them genuinely concerned, trying to persuade her to hang in there for a least one more day. These women had lived for so long with a belief that no one cared, that they were without value and worthless. Now, when confronted with many who did sincerely show concern, it was often enough to convince them that they could make it.

The staff had told them that almost everyone during their stay would go through the rationalization of, "What am I doing here? I don't belong here—I don't need this place—I'm still not *that* bad!" When a patient is admitted, she agrees only to stay for twenty-four hours. The decision to go or stay is solely the responsibility of the patient—the gates are not locked. There are those who are unable to accept the fact that they are powerless over their chemical of choice, feel that there's still another bubble left in the bottle and leave to "qualify" further.

Becoming an alcoholic is a very democratic process—anybody can be one. Therefore, there's no discrimination as to class, color, creed, occupation or financial status at Hazelden. Patients arrive from all parts of the United States and Canada. And there are imports from Europe, Asia, South and Central America. They're all there for the same reason—chemical dependency. The staff and counselors make it clear that there is no real difference between the alcoholic and the drug dependent. Blacks, whites, Protestants, Catholics, movie stars, housewives, prostitutes, Phi Beta Kappas and illiterates all share the same illness and the same treatment.

"Yeah," you say, "but what were they *really* like?"

Probably no different than your wife or mother or the woman that lives down the street from you. From Maggie's letters, I gleaned enough for these thumbnail sketches.

"The Iceberg"—tall, stacked, platinum hair in a neat French twist. Always—now anyway—immaculate and well-dressed, she's cool, poised, calm and collected. That's all surface—underneath she's lonely and wants desperately to be liked. She's doubly addicted, to booze and Valium. Married and divorced three times. Her last husband kept a tight rein on money, so she supported her habits by prostitution. Her pusher was her pimp. The blowup came when her husband caught on and divorced her. She downed the contents of a bottle of Valium, wasn't discovered until the next morning and hung on the edge of death for five days. She's thirty-two, probably suffered some brain damage, but she's getting the program and should stay sober and clean when she leaves.

"The Clubwoman"—in her fifties, married for thirty years to a successful, busy doctor. She's the product of a good home, wealthy parents, now has five grown-up children and several grandchildren. She belongs to a good country club, has a seven handicap and won most of the matches for the eighteen-holers. She toted a bottle in her bag and never missed the nineteenth hole. She had everything—including an overwhelming need for alcohol. Her recovery may have been set back a bit since her husband has just written that he wants a "dee-vorce"—the unit's term for what seemed to be a very common event in the lives of the caterpillar crowd.

"The Brown Mouse"—very quiet, very shy, still fuzzy in the head, possibly severe brain damage. She's in her late forties, with four children, deserted by her husband and on relief when picked up for shoplifting. Her bag was wine, when and where she could get it. Had a police record and was court-committed. She kind of liked it at Hazelden, regular meals, nice room, and really, what was there for her outside? Her kids are safe in foster homes and don't need her, she figures.

"The Black Pearl" never made it past the third grade. She's the product of a big-city slum, learned to live by her wits. Her chemicals of choice included heroin, methadone and a fruit salad of street drugs. She's a warm and happy person now, highly intelligent, and will probably spend several months at a halfway house, where she'll start night school and learn to cope with the world, little by little. In her early thirties, her ambition is to return to Hazelden, but next time as a counselor trainee.

"The Nurse" is about thirty, an anesthesiologist, a pill-popper. Pills were handy and free if you knew the ropes. They helped her maintain the grinding pace of her work. The oldest of eight children, she wonders about her self-worth and still feels a deep guilt. She's considering a change in vocation, something where the pressures aren't so intense that will still fulfill her need to serve her fellow humans.

"Grandma" is a plump, kindly woman whose fair skin and still-blond hair betray her Scandinavian ancestry. She's sixty-plus, has been in the unit for two weeks and is still wondering why. She's not at all certain that she is an alcoholic. She always worked hard all day, she explained, and liked to settle down nightly with a "few beers" to watch TV and nap a little in her chair. However, friend husband insisted that the "few beers" often totaled a case or more! Maggie thought she was at Hazelden at her husband's insistence and wondered if maybe Grandma wouldn't be back later unless she learns to face reality.

"The Widow" still shows the marks of severe physical deterioration. Her husband died unexpectedly two years ago, and there wasn't enough insurance to take care of her and the six children. She worked in a factory during the daytime and fell into the habit of working the bars at night. Two of the kids, both under fifteen, are in trouble with the juvenile authorities. She has severe liver damage but is very matter of fact about it, talks hopefully about her plans for the future.

"The Kid" hails from a big industrial center and has run the gamut of mind-benders. Her bag included pot, hash, LSD, uppers and downers, and, just to be sure that she wouldn't lose her cool, she never left home without a pint of brandy in her purse. How old is she? Eighteen. She's been addicted for six years. Scrawny and probably undernourished, she goes braless and has a swinging mane of flaming red hair. She smokes a pipe, wears patched jeans with a rip across her butt, sings at the top of her voice in the early morning and shocks some of the ladies with her rich vocabulary. She chews gum and is the pet of all the mothers and grandmothers in the unit until they spot her in a con job—then she gets a few words on the subject of honesty!

"The Graduate" has her doctorate in psychology and a logical answer for every question, including why she drank.

Her husband didn't like her answers on the drinking and looked elsewhere for his feminine companionship. She had another reason for drinking, but couldn't convince the judge when her husband asked for a "dee-vorce." By choice, the four kids went with daddy. There are a couple of bright spots; her ex-husband has been attending Al-Anon meetings and the kids are in an Alateen group. The Graduate hopes that when she leaves Hazelden, they can give marriage another try.

"The Southern Belle" comes complete with a sugar-coated drawl and a family plantation. Fifty years ago her family would have locked her in the back bedroom and sent in her meals along with a fifth of bourbon. She told Maggie, "Honey, youah going to keep me sobah when ah get out o' heah. I'll remembah what a mess you were when you came in, and that will shuah kill any urge ah might ever have for even one little ole drink!"

"Teach" is a lean, dignified woman who heads a junior high school several hundred miles away. She was a closet drinker, who spent her days battling her teaching staff and thinking about the first evening drink waiting for her in her apartment. The first one helped her relax, but the twenty-first, as inevitable as next day's hangover, left her sprawling helpless on the floor or, if she was lucky, in bed. She took a leave of absence to come to Hazelden, explaining to her super-intendent that she was "going to a clinic for corrective surgery." As her first step in honesty, she phoned her super-intendent to tell him where she was and why she was there. He told her, "Good for you! We've been worried about your drinking, but didn't know what to say or do. Hurry back!"

What are the odds on these butterfly ladies staying sober? Hazelden says that of those who are patients for the first time and stay to complete the course of treatment, about fifty per-cent will not drink or use drugs again. For those who don't make it and return for a re-run, about fifty percent will learn what they missed during their initial stay and will stay sober. There's a third and fourth chance, maybe more, for those who leave, try and fail, but who have a genuine desire for sobriety.

Connie, Maggie's sponsor, made three trips before she got the message.

As an important part of their treatment, the ladies (and, of course, the gentlemen in their quarters at the other end of the complex) are required to complete the first five Steps of the AA Twelve Step Program to the satisfaction of the Hazelden staff.

FIRST STEP. "We admitted that we were powerless over alcohol—that our lives had become unmanageable."

SECOND STEP. "Came to believe that a Power greater than ourselves could restore us to sanity."

THIRD STEP. "Made a decision to turn our will and our lives over to the care of God as we understood Him."

FOURTH STEP. "Made a searching and fearless moral inventory of ourselves."

FIFTH STEP. "Admitted to God, to ourselves, and to another human being the exact nature of our wrongs."*

No problem with these, Maggie told me proudly. She had breezed, she felt, through the First Step, hesitated momentarily with Step Two, and spent long hours of introspection with the third. She decided that she had bought it and presented herself to the Cobra. She had the first three Steps under control, she announced, and, please, could she get on with the Fourth Step?

Staff approval was required, the Cobra told her, and he was reluctant to recommend it. "Maggie, I'm still getting those beeps on my radar," he told her. "I have the feeling that, inwardly, you're still a very angry person. What makes you so angry?"

Maggie was frustrated and resentful. She wasn't angry! The Cobra's radar needed an overhaul and realignment, she decided. If she was angry, it was just because of his male stubbornness and his "I'm infallible" attitude. She told him so, and he hooded his eyes and smiled at her.

"Think about it some more," he suggested.

She could find no answer. Meanwhile, the days paraded past her and the deadline, set in her mind for completion of her

*The entire Twelve Steps are given on pages 170 and 171.

treatment, was rapidly approaching. She was determined to be home for Christmas.

"It was self-will," she told me later. She had been back playing her old game of management, making her decision as to when she would be ready to leave, and her acceptance of the first three Steps was superficial.

Maggie surrendered. She reached the honest and realistic conclusion that it didn't matter if she spent Christmas singing carols at Hazelden, if she celebrated New Year's with the uncapping of still another cola, or even if she found herself coloring Easter eggs with a new group of women, hiding them on Hazelden's freshly green lawns. She would stay there until the Cobra and the staff agreed that she had found whatever it was that she needed for lasting sobriety.

She surrendered. Dr. Harry M. Tiebout discusses this process in "Surrender Versus Compliance in Therapy With Special Reference to Alcoholism." Surrender, he says, is essential to wholehearted acceptance. The key word is in the first of the AA Twelve Steps, "We admitted that we were powerless over alcohol—that our lives had become unmanageable." The second word, "admitted," is a blood brother of acceptance. Relapses in AA, says Tiebout, are the result of one not truly accepting his alcoholism. Many reach a state of mind where they accept rather than reject or resist; they go along, they cooperate. Since a person can't force himself to accept anything wholeheartedly, the acceptance is too often half-hearted, mere lip service. There has to be more—a deep feeling, a conviction.

Very often, Tiebout points out, compliance, basically a partial acceptance or a partial surrender, tosses out a road block in the surrender process. Compliance means agreeing, going along with the game, but it is not necessarily enthusiastic, whole-hearted assent and approval. Since compliance is a form of acceptance, every time the individual is faced with the need to accept something, s/he falls back on compliance, believing that s/he has accepted. Since s/he has no real capacity to accept, s/he's soon swinging in the other direction. Since compliance says "yes" on the outside but "no" inside, it contributes to a sense of guilt and inferiority. Only when a real surrender occurs is compliance knocked out of the picture and the individual freed for a series of wholehearted responses.

Tiebout doesn't suggest the magic formula, but notes that through the AA experience, compliance can often be permanently replaced with surrender to wholehearted acceptance.

In talking about her surrender, Maggie said that then and only then, she could open her mind and her heart to clear reason. She recognized her anger and could trace it to her dependence for so many years on others—her parents, her grandparents, then her husband. She felt that she had no choice in the matter and deeply resented the unbending rigidity of the dependent role in which she was cast. Damn right she was angry!

But, she reasoned, dependence was an *optional* role. She had a choice. She had the option of freely electing such dependence or rejecting it. She could change her choice whenever she liked. While at Hazelden, she could elect to be dependent on the Cobra and the staff. When she came home, she could elect to be dependent on me.

"I've elected to be dependent on you for the next twenty-four hours," Maggie may tell me now. The system works two ways, I respond. I can accept her dependence or I can reject it. We can agree as equals that we need each other, but only for twenty-four hours at a time.

It's a strange and wonderful thing which works for us. We each feel a sense of freedom, that we're no longer bound together but freely elect the pleasure of each other's company.

But back at Hazelden, the Cobra's radar was clear, and Maggie began work on her Fourth Step Inventory. This was to be a simple listing of her assets and liabilities and her moral assets and liabilities. It wasn't to be a confession in any religious sense, but a factual and objective list. The counselors stressed detail. Actual experiences—several of them—were to be written in each of the inventory areas. Maggie was to give it plenty of time, thought and effort and to develop a balanced inventory with nothing omitted. No one was going to read her inventory except Maggie, and if she wanted to destroy it afterwards, she could—and did.

In addition, she was to prepare a Daily Plan for Living. She knew where she had been, knew where she was now and could face the future with confidence. She had her own set of tools for maintaining her sobriety, so how would she use them on a day-by-day basis?

My wife is an excellent cook, drunk or sober. She might be so drunk that she couldn't count her fingers, but she could still cook up a storm and serve a meal fit for a gourmet. Possibly she couldn't eat it herself, might not be able to duplicate a dish she had prepared, but she was and is a great cook. Alcoholics have an addictive personality, we learn, and one of Maggie's addictions was cookbooks. She gathered cookbooks as some women collect jewelry, antiques or miniature owls, and our bookshelves overflowed with cookbooks, domestic and foreign. Of course, she also collected jewelry, antique glass and miniature owls. As I said, the alcoholic has an addictive personality.

When she went to work on her Daily Plan for Living, it came out in the form of a new version of one of her favorite recipes. The difference is that she needs to be sober to prepare this one properly. Spaghetti lovers, please note:

**Here's what's cooking:** Recipe for Life          **Serves:** God

**Recipe from the kitchen of:** Maggie

**Ingredients:**

| | |
|---|---|
| 1/2 cup oil, for the base | (Use daily prayer and meditation) |
| 2 cups onions for flavor | (Use work) |
| 2 cans tomato paste for body | (Use the AA program) |

| | |
|---|---|
| Add pinches of salt, pepper, sugar, sweet basil, oregano and garlic | (Use generous helpings of divine virtues and little virtues) |
| Add chicken, veal, pork or beef for variety and change of flavor | (Use recreation and hobbies) |
| To cook, simmer gently | (Use plenty of peaceful rest) |
| Serve with pasta | (Serve with love of God and one's fellow man) |

Maggie guarantees no heartburn from the original recipe and no soulburn from her modified version. I'll vouch for that.

Armed with her inventory and her Plan for Living, she had her appointment with a staff clergyman—known irreverently at Hazelden as the "Garbage Collector." She would now orally admit to herself, to the clergyman, and to God, the exact nature of her wrongs, and indeed, dump the garbage of the past onto the shoulders of the clergyman. Having dumped her garbage, she could now begin to forgive herself, bolster her self-respect and actually begin to learn to like herself.

So, after seven weeks, just three days before Christmas, Maggie "graduated." The Cobra was her good friend, Hal, now that his radar was clear, and the new butterfly was ready to stretch her wings in the world of reality. She brought a new set of tools along with her, tools that would help her maintain a happy sobriety. All she had to do, she was told, was to use them daily.

Not all of the Hazelden graduates come home directly. Because of death, separations, divorce or estrangement from family, some are homeless. Others might require a longer stay in the treatment center, and sometimes, a return to the outside world on a gradual, controlled basis.

These people may go to a halfway house, a temporary home where they will have the benefit of friends and counseling when needed. They'll get regular, balanced meals, the opportunity to participate in group sessions and, often, in-house AA meetings. If desirable, they will be helped to find a job, but for several weeks or months, they will return to the halfway house at the end of a work day.

Hazelden operates two such halfway houses, and there are others. These may be organized by treatment centers or hospitals, private citizens, churches, or charitable foundations. Labor unions also have been instrumental in providing funds for these temporary homes, and many owe their existence to the efforts of electricians, plumbers and carpenters who do the necessary remodeling and maintenance work without pay. Some halfway houses are operated under county contracts for service.

Government in general—federal, state, county and city—is becoming more sensitive to the chemically dependent person's illness and the dangers he creates for himself and others. Since 1970 when the United States Congress demonstrated Washington's changed attitude by passing an alcohol abuse and alcoholism act, a score of states have enacted laws that remove drunkenness (although not drunken driving) from the criminal statutes. In these states, drunks are not jailed. Other places are provided to receive them. These are called Local Alcoholism Reception Centers (LARC) or Detoxification Centers where the alkies are detoxified. Some are then passed along to treatment centers or to hospitals if physical condition warrants. Many of them graduate to halfway houses and continue treatment as outpatients. Since LARC makes a strenuous effort to reach the alcoholic early in the game, the centers usually can improve the physical condition, earning ability and family situation of their residents.

Led by Iowa's former Senator Harold Hughes, himself a rehabilitated alcoholic, the federal government has begun an extensive program to combat alcoholism through research, education and funding of local programs. Starting with 70 million dollars in 1971, federal spending for the cause reached 194 million in 1974. Eighty-five percent of this amount was allocated to treatment and rehabilitation centers and halfway houses, many of which would, no doubt, still be only token efforts without federal funding.

Though I was reasonably confident that Maggie had really "got it" at Hazelden, I had the nagging doubt that maybe she wouldn't be sober when she stepped off the plane (direct flight, drinks served, one dollar each back in tourist). I knew that her sponsor, Connie, arrived home just as smashed as the day she left. She hadn't even made it past the bar in the Twin Cities airport. Her sponsor had been able to convince her that she should make the return trip to Hazelden. But what about Maggie? If she arrived sober, would she stay sober? For how long? How was it going to be, living with an arrested alcoholic? Of course, I was swimming in a pool of happiness to have her back—I had missed her cooking. I was very tired of TV dinners eaten alone in front of the set, the pick-up meals of scrambled eggs and bacon and hamburgers from the fast-food, carry-out restaurants.

She had changed, visibly. Her eyes were clear, hands steady, and she wore a radiant smile, one that must have started from her heart and filtered up and out to spread over her entire face. I think that maybe even her fingers and toes were smiling the day she came home. Beyond that, she wore a new sense of dignity and poise, a calmness. She seemed to have grown up. There was something else—an indefinable aura that surrounded her that signaled peace, serenity and happiness.

There shouldn't have been very much for us to say to one another since we had seemingly said it all, courtesy of the Bell system. I was a little shy, a little nervous, when I settled her in her favorite chair.

"Do you want a drink?" slipped out, automatically. We had *always* has a drink to celebrate any occasion. Good Lord, I thought, panic stricken, I've blown the whole ball game. What if she says yes, that she wanted a big double vodka martini on the rocks?

"Yes," Maggie replied promptly, "I'd like an iced tea, please. And thanks for asking me. Keep asking me, because I like to have the freedom of choice!"

Relieved, I mixed the instant tea and iced it. Though we had virtually lost the art of conversation during Maggie's drinking days, the practice on the phone had helped me. There were things I still wondered about.

"Did you ever discover what made you an alcoholic?" I asked.

"I drank too much."

"What's the secret of staying sober?"

"Don't take the first drink."

"Do you think you'll never touch a drink for the rest of your life?"

"I don't know. I have a choice, and I choose to stay sober just for twenty-four hours at a time."

Was she kidding me? These answers she was giving me were too obvious, too easy. She had to be holding something back.

"Maggie, just what *did* you discover at Hazelden?" I asked more insistently.

"I learned to KISS," she replied softly.

"Kiss? You *knew* how to kiss before you left! What in the hell are you talking about?"

Maggie put down her iced tea and smiled at me. "KISS," she said, "means 'Keep It Simple, Stupid!' And I love you—today."

Okay—Maggie had told me what she had learned and what she hoped our future might hold for us today and tomorrow.

Love and KISSES—one day at a time.

# 10

## Tweedledum

"I generally hit everything I can see — when I get really excited," said Tweedledee.

"And I hit everything within reach," cried Tweedledum, "whether I can see it or not!"

I suppose I should apologize for not keeping this story in a more exact time sequence. I'm sorry, but we're going to back up a bit. This time, I'm the one who's riding the plane to the Twin Cities, enroute to Hazelden in response to a phone call summoning me for a "Family Interview." Maggie had now been a patient for four weeks.

Early in her treatment, I had received a lengthy questionnaire from Hazelden, which gave me the opportunity to describe Maggie's illness as I had seen it, right from a box seat. I could add any additional comments I might have. For a page and a half of single-spaced typing, I bared my soul, groaned "mea culpa" and laid it all out — my guilt and remorse. Through my neglect and my sexual unresponsiveness, Maggie had become an alcoholic. I had to be guilty, since Maggie had told me so. Not once, but hundreds of times. I confessed to Hazelden that I was an asshole of the first degree.

I leaned back against the seat headrest, so neatly covered with a paper doily, and watched the bleak winter landscape of Wisconsin slide by. I still held the remains of a "double" martini on the rocks, two of those little bottles of premixed drinks, two poor, weak things that cost a buck each, including the plastic glass and two ice cubes. Still, it helped ease my fears and apprehensions of the pending interview at Hazelden. I was going to catch hell for turning Maggie into an alcoholic, no doubt about it. I ordered the second double and let the comforting warmth of the drink calm my fears.

After all, I had done everything that I could and surely I deserved some credit for that. Even her folks had told me how much they had appreciated my patience in staying with their drunken daughter, sticking it out when I could have divorced her. Business friends and even some of my personal friends complimented me on my forebearance, sympathized with me and admired the crown of thorns that I wore so gracefully. I was a pretty great guy, they told me, and maybe someday Maggie would learn to *appreciate* all I had gone through for her. Maybe I was the exception, the one husband out of a hundred who stuck it out, the man who took the bitter with the sweet and kept his wife out of trouble no matter what. Didn't I deserve a pat on the back for that? Damn right I did!

I relaxed, closed my eyes and thought of the "Family Interview." Probably I would be escorted right into the office of Dr. Dan Anderson, Hazelden's Director, the real VIP treatment.

"Jack," he would say, hanging a brotherly arm across my shoulders, "I wish the husband of every alcoholic woman could know you and emulate your example. Putting it simply, you saved Maggie's life. Without your help, she would have never made it to Hazelden.

"Sure, you're probably right about your responsibility for her condition, but don't forget, she is a woman with a woman's weaknesses. But you tried, Jack, you did everything a man could be expected to do, and on balance, you did an amazing job of holding her together, and I congratulate you!

"Maggie is going to need a lot of guidance in the future, and here's what I want you to do." Dan (we would be on a first-name basis by now) would then spell out the ground rules which I would enforce with tact and sympathy, but without deviation. I would keep her nose to the grindstone, her feet on the ground, her eye on the target, her back to the wheel and her hands off the bottle. A difficult task, Dan would tell me, but he was confident that I could do it. With me at the helm and following Dan's chart, Maggie would be forever protected against the evils of alcohol and we would sail a steady course through the stormy seas of life towards the sunset.

Unfortunately, Dr. Anderson had not received his copy of the script. He didn't even meet me at the airport!

Following my reunion with Maggie, counselor Hal, cobra eyes wide open and radar ticking merrily, I supposed, ushered the two of us into his office. It was Hazelden's hope, he told us, that every spouse could spend a little time with the staff, tour the physical plant and ask any questions that came to mind. He patted Maggie's file folder, that no doubt included my response to the questionnaire, and told us that during the alcoholic's uncontrolled drinking period, many members of the family, particularly the spouse, might develop deep resentments and this would be a good time to get mine out in the open for examination. What bugged me?

To begin with, I thought, how come I'm not up with Dr. Anderson, or Dr. Heilman, the consulting staff psychiatrist? Heilman and I could talk a little shop. I could tell him about my sessions with Dr. Gordon and he could take a look at my id, time permitting.

I kept this resentment back from Hal and told him that I really had no particular resentments to bring out, no fireworks to shoot off. He didn't ask about any guilt I might have stored away, so I saved those for my expected meeting with Anderson or Heilman. Maggie had nothing new to contribute, simply saying that Hal already had been personally introduced to her can of worms. Hal discussed Maggie's treatment. She was progressing, but he could give us no definite information as to when treatment might be concluded. We would meet later in the day for another interview, and in the meantime, I could be with Maggie, meet the other patients in the unit, join them for lunch, and attend the afternoon lecture.

I met Teach, The Iceberg and the rest. They were pleasant women, informally dressed, very much at ease and gracious. The Brown Mouse had graduated, and Maggie had a new roommate. The Southern Belle had graduated, too, and was back on the old plantation, sober and happy, she had written. There was nothing to distinguish these women from any other group. They could have been the members of Maggie's bridge club, gathered for a couple of hours of cards and conversation.

We had an hour or so of privacy in Maggie's room, with the Kid, red hair swinging and bubble gum popping, assuring us that she would stand guard at the end of the hall to see that we were not disturbed.

The afternoon session with Hal was definitely not conducted in accord with my script. Neither Anderson or Heilman made the meeting. Unavoidably detained, I concluded. Hal probed gently into our marriage relationship, and I opened the floodgates, spilling out my lengthy confession of guilt, the epic saga of my trials with Maggie and subsequent martyrdom. Hal listened, seldom interrupting my story.

Winding it up, I leaned forward across Hal's desk and told him earnestly, "Look, all I want to do is to keep Maggie sober and somehow make up to her for all the years of pain and suffering that I've given to her. That's why I'm here. Now please tell me what to do to help her."

He sat silently for a moment, no doubt checking his radar for blips. I hoped he was not going to give me the "angry person" routine that was delaying Maggie's return home. "Jack, let's get a few things straight," he began. "When Maggie leaves here, she'll have the necessary tools in good working order to maintain her sobriety. She won't need you to run her life and to keep her sober. Remember that.

"But," he continued, "there is something that you can do to help her, and that is to do something about yourself. Maggie has conned you for years, and if you'll think about it, you'll see that you've been conning yourself. You may not buy this concept right now, but you need some help with your own emotions. Do you know anything about Al-Anon and have you attended any meetings?"

I allowed as how I had read about Al-Anon in the material Hazelden had mailed to me, but I hadn't gotten around to attending a meeting as yet. Sure, I would go if it would do any good.

"But is it necessary now?" I asked. "I do understand that Al-Anon is for the families of alcoholics, but since Maggie isn't going to be drinking when she gets home, what's the point in me joining up at this stage of the game?"

Hal pointed out that Maggie would always be an alcoholic, a person with an incurable disease, but that the disease had been arrested in her case. Still, the problems that arose during her drinking days, as well as any problems that may have existed before, all these problems were still there, waiting for us. Maggie was learning how to face her problems honestly and realistically, but could I do the same? If I wanted to give our marriage a fair shake for survival, Hal said, there was much that I had to learn, not for Maggie but for myself. She had changed and would continue to change, and it was now up to me to do some changing and some growing, too.

"The fact that you've had psychiatric help hasn't solved all of your problems," Hal said. "They won't just automatically disappear because Maggie is sober. There will be changes in your relationship, new problems to solve. The most important thing in life to Maggie is her sobriety. It's going to be up there in the number-one spot, ahead of you and ahead of your family and hers. You must understand why. You'll need help in restoring communications with her. You may need to take a closer look at your personal goals and your pattern of living.

"You can learn how to do this in Al-Anon. You need to learn when to keep your mouth shut, how to keep off Maggie's back and what kind of a person you are underneath the masks you're wearing. Al-Anon people can teach you."

Dismayed, I beat a hasty retreat and controlled my anger. What in the hell was this young punk trying to tell me to do? He had to be dead wrong—his radar was sadly out of whack. He might know all about alcoholism, he might understand Maggie and her can of worms, but he sure as shit didn't understand me. There was nothing wrong with me! If I was free of resentment when I came into the interview, I certainly wasn't now. Dumb kid!

I gave it more thought on the flight back home, even refusing the drink that the hostess offered. It was just possible, I conceded, that there might be more to this Al-Anon jazz than I had thought. Maybe my attendance was a form of insurance that Maggie would stay sober. Or, perhaps I could inspire some of the less-fortunate men whose wives were still drinking. There wasn't anything wrong with me, and if for no other reason, I would go to the damn meetings just to prove that Hal was wrong!

Grimly, I checked the Yellow Pages and then the regular phone directory, when I was safe in my own home, and dialed the Al-Anon number. A warm voice told me that there was a meeting just a few miles from where I lived and I would be very welcome to attend. That was a little too close, I thought, but I screwed up my courage, assumed the air of bluff good fellowship that worked so well in Kiwanis and Rotary, and slipped into the meeting which was held in the basement of the city hall building in a neighboring village. I was reassured to find that I didn't know a soul. I was less reassured to find that I was the only male in attendance. Oh, well, maybe only men were the drunks out this way.

"Hi—I'm Hazel," one of the women came across the room with an outstretched hand. She introduced me to the ten or so women aged from mid-twenties to late sixties. They handed me a cup of coffee in a paper cup, and the meeting was under way. One of the women told the group her story—how it was in the past, how she had been helped in Al-Anon, how it was with her now. It was a very simple, very straightforward story, a matter-of-fact recitation with no tears, no complaints, no criticism of her husband, who must have been a first class son-of-a-bitch when he was drinking. She ran in a bunch of old saws like "Easy Does It," "One Day at a Time" and "First Things First."

The meeting closed with us standing in a circle, holding hands and repeating the Lord's Prayer. I felt a little foolish. I did listen to the closing remark made by the lady that chaired the meeting.

"Give us a chance to help you. You may not understand how we can benefit you at first, but do attend at least six meetings before you reach any decision. Keep coming back!"

"Not me, lady," I reflected when I was settled in front of the TV at home. I wasn't coming back. Did they really expect me to get up and tell them about how I felt, to relate our sex problems when Maggie was drinking and about our suicide pact? I simply couldn't do it, and if I did, what could a bunch of women tell me that would help? Then, there was all of this talk about God. They spoke of their "Higher Power" or "God as I understand Him" just as easily and naturally as if He had been sitting in on the session. Nobody was going to convert me, not at this late date! And that hand-holding while we stood in a circle reciting the Lord's Prayer ... I was proud of the fact that I could still remember the words, but that was church stuff. Maybe there was another group somewhere that ran their show a little differently.

I phoned Mrs. Warm Voice at Al-Anon again, and she suggested that maybe I might feel more comfortable with an all-male group. I agreed that this might be an excellent idea, and she gave me the address and meeting date of the stag group. It was to be held somewhere in a large downtown hospital, and I was to check with the guard at the back entrance.

"The Al-Anon meeting?" the guard said, "Just go straight down the corridor, take a right at the coffee machine, take the first left you come to and follow that corridor almost to the end. The door oughta be open."

The door was locked. Maybe I had the wrong door, and I tried others until I found one that did open. I stepped inside, but discovered that I was at the base of a staircase that stretched, dimly lit, upward to other floors. Turning, I found that the door I had just entered opened only in one direction. I couldn't get out, so resourcefully I climbed from floor to floor, trying each door, peering into busy hospital corridors, but all of the doors were locked. Fortunately, the sixth-floor door worked in both directions. I peeked out to be sure no one was watching, then slipped into the corridor and, trying very hard to look like a busy doctor making his rounds, I hurried to the elevator and punched the "B" button, hoping for an unobserved descent to the basement and the guard's desk.

He seemed a bit surprised to see me again, but patiently rose, led me through the winding corridors, pointed to a door and said, "In there." He marched back in the direction of his desk to wait for the next dummy who couldn't follow simple directions. I watched him for a moment and tried the door which was still locked. Maybe the next door? It opened to the stairwell and I stepped back hastily before I was trapped for the second time. I didn't have the guts to go back to the guard again and leaned against the wall, hoping that someone might show up and redirect me. Shortly I spotted a man hurrying down the hall, laden with a coffee pot and a huge brown sack under his arm.

"I'm a little lost," I announced.

"So was I," he responded with a grin, "I'll bet you're looking for the Al-Anon meeting. We specialize in men who are 'a little lost.'"

He introduced himself as Louie, and he was the secretary, he said. He wore a neat gray business suit and bore a startling resemblence to a Bassett hound, complete with sad brown eyes, a drooping face and a pair of big ears that seemed to sag. "The secretary has to make the coffee and clean up afterwards," Louie told me. We chatted for a few minutes, and I learned that he had joined the group a couple of years ago, was an accountant and had spent his free time measuring the level in the whiskey bottle, ferreting out his wife's hidden stash of additional booze and pouring the stuff down the drain. I liked Louie immediately and resisted the temptation to scratch him behind the ears. He no longer looked for his wife's stash, he said, and had quit marking the level on the booze in the kitchen cabinet.

Several other men drifted into the room and introduced themselves, still just first names. Some were older than I, some younger. Some were well dressed, others less dapper. They had wives, mothers or sisters, some still drinking, some now sober. I felt at ease with these guys, but hoped that they didn't go in for that "God" stuff and hand-holding.

When Harry arrived, he moved tables and chairs into place and distributed clean ash trays. He was the chairman for the meeting, he explained, and these were the chairman's regular duties. Harry was a bustling, cheery guy, an insurance salesman with a wife that had been sober in AA for two years, he said. When I told him about my first meeting with the Al-Anon ladies, Harry grinned.

"I know how you felt," Harry said, "the same thing happened to me. I did go back for a few weeks, long enough to realize that these Al-Anon ladies knew more about alcoholism and how to live with an alcoholic than I did. More importantly, I found that I was feeling better, that I had a little more confidence in myself and didn't blow my stack every time I came home to find Lil drunk.

"Lil didn't understand it when I stopped nagging her and just walked away when she was cocked and primed for a good fight. She was suspicious of my motives. 'I know all about your Al-Anon thing,' she'd yell, 'and I know that you're going to those meetings to meet women who hate their husbands like you hate me, and you're going to divorce *me* to marry one of *them!*'"

Since I was a newcomer, Harry slanted the meeting in my direction. As an insurance man, he said, he spent much of his time explaining to wary prospects just what his policy would do and what it wouldn't do for them. In insurance language, the Al-Anon policy didn't cover the alcoholic—it wouldn't make her stop drinking or keep her dry. The direct benefits of the policy went to the policyholder—the man in Al-Anon.

The benefits included a thorough grounding in the facts of alcoholism as an illness and something about the methods of treatment. As insurance is a mutual sharing of risks, Al-Anon is a mutual sharing of problems and learning to cope with them. The pay-off—the major policy benefit—was a change in the members' attitudes and personalities. Tensions in the home would be reduced, and through a change in attitude of the non-addicted parent, the understanding and behavior of the chldren would be improved.

The Al-Anon policy had limitations, Harry warned. There's no specific advice on family finances, separation and divorce, sex, legal matters, medical, psychatric or clerical aid. Instead, members *suggest* only what's helped them in their own situations and *refer* the alcoholic's relatives to professional sources of help when the need is indicated. As in Alcoholics Anonymous, only first names are used to protect the anonymity of the alcoholic and the Al-Anon member. There's no gossip, just concentration on principles, not personalities. There is no intrusion on the religious beliefs—or lack of them—of members. Al-Anon is spiritual, not religious, and the term "Higher Power," as used in the Twelve Steps, may be interpreted as each member wishes. Finally, Al-Anon doesn't believe that the *only* solution to the alcoholic's problem lies in affiliation with AA.

I bought Harry's policy, and made my way weekly through the hospital labyrinth confidently, staying clear of the door to the stairwell. I worked up sufficient courage to attend other group meetings, made up principally of women with a sprinkling of men. It wasn't as tough as I originally believed and I found that the "weaker sex" often prove themselves stronger than many men in the face of living with a practicing alcoholic. They don't seem to cut and run so often.

I learned from the literature that Al-Anon, in concept, is nearly as old as Alcoholics Anonymous. In AA's pioneering days from 1935 to 1941, close relatives of recovering alcoholics realized that they could handle their own personal problems by applying the same principles that helped their alcoholic menfolk. It was the wives of these early AA members who told each other of the help in the Twelve Steps and how this help improved things at home even after the alcoholic mate found sobriety.

In 1954, this loosely-knit concept found cohesion in the incorporation of Al-Anon Family Group Headquarters, Inc., a non-profit organization. Twenty years later there were over nine thousand groups in the United States, Canada and in sixty-four foreign countries. Many of these groups have progressed with the times and welcome the families of the drug addict as well as the spouse of a souse. More and more men are finding Al-Anon. It's not that we're getting smarter, but as the number of women alcoholics increase, more and more men are looking for answers.

Maggie referred to her treatment at Hazelden as a course labeled "Life I." Passing the course was a matter of life or death. A return to drinking was a one-way ticket to death, unless the drinking could be halted again. I had enrolled in the same course in the Al-Anon night school. It might take me longer to master the theory and practice, but I was using about the same textbook as Maggie had. There wasn't the same sense of urgency, since if our wives or husbands continued to drink, *we* weren't going to die. It took me a little time to realize that this might be the problem—we might *not* die. Unless we took some constructive action, we were going to live in a private hell of our making.

I transferred my allegience to a new stag group which met much closer to home. I was still much more comfortable with a gang of men and felt that I could open up more freely. New Al-Anon groups are organized without fanfare. The structure of Al-Anon is loose—there's no charter, no book of bylaws, no initiation, no membership fee. Each group runs its own show, "passing the hat" to cover the necessary expenses, such as rental of a meeting room, coffee and doughnuts, purchase of

Al-Anon literature for free distribution, and a party now and then. Minimal contributions maintain a district office, staffed by volunteers, and a national headquarters in New York, which publishes over forty books and pamphlets and a monthly newsletter, answers direct inquiries and provides a public relations and educational center. Each group governs itself, using as a guideline, "The Twelve Traditions of Al-Anon."

Our new group started off with three members, and within six months, grew to ten regulars and another ten to fifteen who floated in and out as the mood, or the need, struck them. We didn't keep an attendance record, no formal roster or listing of members for reporting to headquarters. We met on the third floor of an accommodating church annex, and another group composed entirely of women met in the basement at the same time. This was a great arrangement, since we joined the ladies for coffee and whatever goodies they might have baked or purchased. We held joint meetings monthly or whenever either group had an unusually good speaker from the outside.

I've never been a joiner, and my experiences with Kiwanis, Rotary, Lions and fraternal organization bored the hell out of me. Of course they did—I joined them because it was the "right" thing to do; it made me look good and gave me a chance to get away from home. Since I contributed nothing but my presence, I received nothing but maybe a good meal and a place to buy a cheap drink. The difference in Al-Anon is that we're all there for the same purpose—to consider our mutual problems and do something about them that's more constructive than what we've done in the past.

The make-up of our group was about what you might expect if you sliced a cross section of American life. Some were loudmouths, bores, cocky and conceited asses—and I didn't like them. As time went by, my attitudes changed, as did theirs. They said I wasn't *quite* as loudmouthed, cocky, etc., as I had been!

Pull up a chair and sit in on a session. We met in one of the children's Sunday school rooms, and the furniture wasn't sized to six-footers. Tables had been pushed together to form a hollow square and the perimeter was occupied by a dozen or so men ranging from their twenties to late sixties. Dress was informal with sweaters, slacks and sport shirts predominating, maybe an occasional business suit worn by the guy who came directly from work. Maybe there were a few soup stains on the pants of the man who just finished cooking dinner for the family while mother "slept it off" on the couch.

Mac was chairman for the month. His wife, Vera, was the gal with the penchant for skinny-dipping in hotel pools. Mac was an avid golfer with a scratch handicap, and Vera drank, she told him, because he was more interested in his backswing than in her and his kids. Vera had made the usual round of hospitals and church retreats and made a few passes at AA. Then Maggie had sponsored Vera at Hazelden, and I had invited Mac to Al-Anon. He was a devout Christian, had little difficulty in accepting the precepts of Al-Anon and quickly became a solid support for our fledgling stag group.

It was a good thing. One of his sons ran into trouble with an LSD experiment and with street drugs peddled at school. Vera was badly shaken and succumbed to the magic of a "nerve pill" prescribed by a friendly doctor, which helped her, she thought, handle her son's problem. The mind-bender lowered her defenses, so she took that first little drink and was off to the races.

Al-Anon suggested that, rather than repressing anger and resentment, the non-addicted spouse should find a physical outlet to "work it off." Bowling, gardening, tennis, chopping weeds and long walks all help. As the result of Vera's drinking and his son's drug problem, Mac claimed to have added thirty yards to his distance from the golf tee.

"I would look down at that little white ball," Mac said, "and imagine that it was filled with a mix of booze, bennies and LSD. I would remember to bring the club back slowly, and then—I WOULD CLOBBER THE SHIT OUT OF IT!"

Mac had selected "self-pity" as the subject for his meeting and read several passages from Al-Anon's chief textbook, *One Day at a Time*, relating to this common problem. He spoke briefly of his own "pity parties" and how he tried to deal with them. He opened the meeting for discussion, and Sully, who made his living as a school psychologist, unraveling the knots in the minds of teenagers, piped up first.

"Tonight, my wife said that if I came to this meeting, she was going to get drunk. I told her, 'Okay, I'll stay home,' and went into the den to do some work. I sat there, feeling sorrier and sorrier for myself. Dammit, I couldn't even leave the house now! How long could I take this?

"Then I thought of the phrase from the Serenity Prayer, 'change the things I can.' I could change something—I could come to this meeting. My wife was probably going to get loaded if I stayed home, and she threatened to get drunk if I went to the meeting. So I came."

Sully had been able to deal with the traumas of teenagers, but his training, experience and reference works didn't help him solve his wife's problem. He felt that there was an answer somewhere in the books that lined the four walls of his den. After his first Al-Anon meeting, he had explained his theory to a few of us sharing coffee and homemade cake. Sully was convinced that his wife had a "father fixation."

"Father fixation, my ass," one of the guys retorted, "Sully, she has a grandfather fixation—Old Granddad!"

Sam had a comment on the subject of self-pity. He was a newcomer, had made only a few meetings and spoke hesitantly and apologetically. "When you're feeling sorry for yourself, you just don't have the time for anything else. I know. I think maybe I hold a world's record for a marathon pity party, and I worked myself into near paralysis. I couldn't work, couldn't think, couldn't act. Some of you guys saw me when I came in here—I was whipped. Now that I've been able to understand what I was doing, I've put priorities on my problems, and things are better—not great, but better."

Sam was indeed a sorry sack when he shambled in the door of our meeting for the first time. His wife had just "sorta gone crazy" when he chopped off her booze. She had convulsed. Fortunately, Sam was there to call an ambulance for a fast ride to the hospital. His wife was still in the detox center, and a social worker at the hospital had recommended Al-Anon. Life had treated him badly, he said. He was past sixty, and his job was being phased out. His pension wouldn't keep him in cigarettes, and he couldn't find another job. Then, to top it off, his wife drank herself blind with the grocery money, now he had a big hospital bill, and neither of his sons would come near the house. He needed a prostate operation, and his teeth were loose. He didn't believe that his wife was sick, she was just plain ornery and mean, he said. He was disgusted with her, bitter and depressed. He was just an old, worn-out man, and nobody gave a damn about him, nobody cared.

We cared, we told Sam. He listened to us relate similar experiences and how we had coped with them. We talked about the illness of alcoholism, and, slowly, Sam began to recognize that his wife was sick, not just mean and ornery. He found another job, nothing great, but they wouldn't starve. The people he had worked with gave him a surprise farewell party, complete with presents, a wall plaque telling of their appreciation and personal assurances of affection. It was a source of deep satisfaction to all of us to see the changes take place in Sam's attitude and appearance.

When Sam finished his comment on the subject of self-pity, Nick had something to add. You will remember Nick—his wife, Mary, made a bee-line to the minister's couch—or floor—when she was loaded. Nick is a tall guy, good-looking, in his late forties, thin, but out of shape. He claimed that his only exercise for years was in picking Mary up from the floor and carting her to their bedroom or to a hospital.

"I think I can top Sam's record for pity parties—mine lasted for over nine years. I was past feeling sorry for myself. I was a martyr, complete with hair shirt and crown of thorns, and tied to the ground for the ants to eat. I remember spending a lunch hour crying on a client's shoulder (Nick was a personnel consultant) and giving him the lurid details of living with a double-dipper. My client was properly sympathetic and said, 'Nick, I know it's really been tough — you have the patience of Job!'

"I hadn't read about Job for many years, so I dug out our family Bible and read his story. I wondered that if, like Job, God was testing me. Maybe God had another bull session with Satan and described me as one of his best boys — a guy who feared Him and shunned evil. Then Satan, cunning devil that he was, made a deal, and God gave him the nod to hang a few disasters on me, just to see how I would hold up and to prove that God had overqualified me.

"You remember what happened to Job: he lost his herd of sheep; someone made off with his donkeys, sold his camels to a cigarette company; his children died; and he was afflicted with a miserable case of boils. I figured that Satan had kept up with the times and had hatched up a shiny new disaster that would beat the hell out of Job's — he had hung a swinging wife around my neck — a wife that swung from booze to pills, pills to booze, and if the day was a little dull, she scrambled them together. *That* friends, is disaster!

"I gritted my teeth and stayed in there, feeling very noble, with my disaster stretched out at my feet — literally. I was waiting for the payoff. After all, God had rewarded Job with 14,000 sheep, 6,000 camels, 1,000 teams of oxen, 1,000 female donkeys, seven more sons and three more daughters, according to the Bible. I would settle for a smaller payoff — a new sports car, a bigger house with no mortgage, the presidency of my company, a rich son-in-law and the grand prize of a wife that was sober and clean.

"It didn't work out that way," Nick continued, "though I was patient and persevering, Mary added to her diet four new pills and a 40-proof cough syrup and developed a yen for vanilla extract. I would have gladly traded her for a case of boils and thrown in all the camels in Arabia! *That's* when I came to Al-Anon and I *am* getting my pay-off—Mary's in AA and staying sober."

Mac grinned, "You've made Al-Anon history, Nick. If there are no further comments and no new business, let's pass the hat and wind it up."

One of the newer men suggested that it might be in order to have a sign or two pointing up the stairs, something to help first-timers find the meetings. He had gotten lost, he said, and spent several minutes wandering through the choir loft. Remembering my own experience in the hospital downtown, I suggested that perhaps it was part of the program to have Al-Anon meetings tucked away in hard-to-find places. We needed to be reminded that we did need help in finding our way, that we were lost in more ways than one. Then, once we could find our way around the building, we could have the satisfaction of leading the newcomer through the right door. "It is very symbolic," I said.

"Could be," Mac smiled, "but we have a little saying in Al-Anon, 'Keep it Simple,' so, Jack, make us a couple of signs."

A year or so later, I had the opportunity to help organize another new stag group. We met in a Catholic school, and to reach the meeting room, one entered the back door (the front door was locked at the end of the school day), went down a short flight of steps, left into the basement corridor, up another flight of steps, then right down the hall to the teachers' lounge. It wasn't easy, and prior to the first few meetings, I hovered anxiously at the door to do my good deed. Sure enough, a stranger entered and hesitated, obviously uncertain. "Pardon me," he asked. "I'm a little lost. Can you tell me how to ..."

I interrupted, "I know. You're looking for the stag Al-Anon meeting. We specialize in men that are a 'little lost'."

He stared at me, puzzled. "You do? That's interesting. But I'm looking for the gym. My kid is playing in a basketball game here."

Many of our meetings were devoted to discussion of the Twelve Steps, the core of the Al-Anon program. These suggested Steps have been adopted from the program of Alcoholics Anonymous. Al-Anon's little book, *Alcoholism — the Family Disease*, explains the purpose succinctly: "In a broad sense, the Steps are a spiritual philosophy with some of the elements of the Golden Rule, the Ten Commandments, the Sermon on the Mount and the centuries-old teaching of Oriental philosophers. In their simple words, the Twelve Steps encompass a magnificent body of ideas whose study will be rewarded by the enrichment of our characters and personalities, a deeper understanding of our relationship to our fellow man and a sustaining confidence and serenity that will help us to live more fully each day."

The AA's sum up the Twelve Step Program's success even more succinctly: "It works."

Here are the Twelve Steps. A little later, we'll catch another stag group meeting and watch the knurds nick away at them:

FIRST STEP: "We admitted we were powerless over alcohol—that our lives had become unmanageable."

SECOND STEP: "Came to believe that a power greater than ourselves could restore us to sanity."

THIRD STEP: "Made a decision to turn our will and our lives over to the care of God as we understood Him."

FOURTH STEP: "Made a searching and fearless moral inventory of ourselves."

FIFTH STEP: "Admitted to God, to ourselves and to another human being the exact nature of our wrongs."

SIXTH STEP: "Were entirely ready to have God remove all these defects of character."

SEVENTH STEP: "Humbly asked Him to remove our shortcomings."

EIGHTH STEP: "Made a list of all persons we had harmed and became willing to make amends to them all."

NINTH STEP: "Made direct amends to such people whenever possible, except when to do so would injure them or others."

TENTH STEP: "Continued to take personal inventory and when we were wrong, promptly admitted it."

ELEVENTH STEP: "Sought through prayer and meditation to improve our conscious contact with God as we understand Him praying only for knowledge of His will for us and the power to carry that out."

TWELFTH STEP: "Having had a spiritual awakening as the result of these steps, we tried to carry this message to others and to practice these principles in all our affairs."

These were all very impressive, I concluded after my first reading. Was there anything here that could benefit me? I reviewed my reasons for coming to Al-Anon: I was going to prove to myself that the Cobra was wrong—I didn't need it. However, if it was a form of insurance that Maggie didn't relapse to compulsive drinking, it would be worthwhile. If she did drink again, maybe I could learn how to stop her. I wanted to get our marriage back to normal, back to the way it was before Maggie drank compulsively. Perhaps somebody would tell me how to do it.

The Cobra had said that I was sick, too, and in need of a personal recovery program, and if I wanted to preserve our marriage, I needed to change and grow, just as Maggie had. I did want to preserve our marriage. If Al-Anon could give me a clue, I'd stick around until I had some answers. I still thought the Cobra was wrong, though.

I learned the disheartening fact that the divorce and separation rate among alcoholics and their spouses is much, much higher than the rate of our society in general. There is no national figure, but the unofficial odds are quoted at four to one that the marriage will fail. Eighty percent of marriages involving alcoholics, drinking or sober, go on the rocks. I could accept that damn few of us, unless we're pretty kinky, enjoy living with a drunk. It's easier to divorce her, separate or just walk out. But the scary thing is that the rate of divorce and separation among *arrested* alcoholics soars well above the norm.

Several years before alcoholism was to become a major problem for Maggie and me, we had watched our good friend Al lose his battle with the bottle. Wife Ann suffered in silence, just enduring, holding the family together, we felt, for the sake of their sons and as a matter of stiff-necked pride. Al finally bumped bottom and turned to AA. He found sobriety and gradually worked his way back to the world of the sane. Formerly a sodden and abusive drunk who could no longer hold a job or keep up mortgage payments on his home, Al became a quiet and gentle man, gradually making a new life in a new job. Their financial burdens eased, there was a new home and some money tucked away to help the kids through college.

We were surprised when, after three years of his sobriety, Al and Ann were quietly divorced. We hadn't seen much of them since Al was sober. We had moved away, and our only contact had been a letter to Maggie from Al, offering help with her problem, which was evident to another alcoholic. Maggie had politely rejected Al's offer, explaining that she could "quit anytime she wanted to."

It was only after we were into AA and Al-Anon, making our own adjustments and hearing how others had succeeded or failed, that we could understand. It was possible and even likely that Ann assumed that since Al no longer drank, things would return to "normal." She would expect him to "make up" to her all of the slights, the money worries and "disgrace" that she had endured. She would resent bitterly her position in a number-two slot secondary to his sobriety. She would fail to realize that his zealous attendance at AA meetings, his willingness to crawl out of bed at two in the morning to talk with some drunk for hours on end were more important to Al than breathing. Lacking understanding and common goals, the marriage failed. They couldn't buck the odds.

It was now my turn to serve as chairman for our stag group. I hurried through the details of my important chores—arranging the tables, placing the kid-sized chairs around the perimeter, digging out the ash trays. Now we were ready.

The easiest way to handle a meeting was to induce someone in Al-Anon to speak to the group, and I had called Harry from the downtown stag group.

"This is Harry," I announced. "He's going to talk about something that interests all of us — insurance."

"Jack has blown my anonymity by revealing my profession," Harry announced. "To learn my last name, all you need to do is to check the phone directory and you'll find me listed as a partner in that well-known firm, 'Tom, Dick and you-know-who!' I'm here to tell you about insurance — not drinking insurance, which isn't available yet, but a form of health insurance."

Some of the new men were getting a little restive, squirming on their midget chairs. Now they knew what stag Al-Anon was all about — we got together each week and sold each other our particular products!

Harry had changed his story a bit, I realized, as he continued. "My policy covers mental health. It will cost you very little in money — just whatever you want to pay. It does require that you spend some time complying with the agreements in the body of the policy, but you can modify it to suit your particular requirements. It's written by a Company that lets you participate in the profits. You'll receive dividends, and the more time you give to the Company, the greater the dividends which are paid out in the currency of peace and serenity. The name of this policy is 'Honesty' and everybody knows that 'Honesty is the Best Policy.'"

There were a few groans, and Harry continued, "My policy has twelve clauses, twelve conditions of insurance. In most policies, these conditions are described as the 'fine print' and salesmen gloss over them, concentrating on the benefits. Our clauses are printed in large letters, so that even Eddie here can read them with no difficulty.

Eddie was another "old timer" and legally blind. He wore thick glasses and could recognize anything big, such as tables and chairs, but had a hell of a time hitting the ash tray with his cigarette butt. He was a little guy with a shock of graying hair, maybe about 40. Because of his limited sight, he held his head erect, straining to see, much like a bird-dog pointing a covey of quail. His wife, Ethyl, was also legally blind. As their eyesight had dimmed, they discovered that things looked a little brighter after a drink or two. Or three. Or more. Ethyl crossed the invisible line between social drinking and compulsive drinking first and had demonstrated, to the satisfaction of bartenders, police and social workers, the true meaning of the term, "blind drunk." After several short terms in the workhouse and six hospitalizations, Ethyl was addicted not only to alcohol, but tranquilizers and had also acquired a taste for paraldehyde, the drug once used to bring down the drunks in the charity wards.

They had discovered AA and Al-Anon almost simultaneously, and now they were addicted to meetings, spending their free time making the rounds of AA and Al-Anon groups, traveling by bus and hitching rides. They joked about their blindness, shrugged off the fact that they had little money, and generally were content.

"I have one of your policies already, Harry," Eddie retorted, "but I'll sign up for another one if it will help you make your quota."

"Okay, Eddie, I'll write it up later," Harry went on. "Now as I said, the name of the policy is 'Honesty,' and the clauses in the big print are called the 'Twelve Steps.' Tonight, we'll talk about the first three of them. Most of you men have read the Twelve Steps and have your own ideas as to how they work, how you use them. Maybe you even have a question or two. This is an open session, and interrupt me any time you feel the urge."

He picked up a little blue book, *One Day at a Time in Al-Anon*, and read, "We admitted that we were powerless over alcohol and that our lives had become unmanageable."

"This one goes down hard for many of us. We figure that there's nothing very wrong with us, but that our wife or daughter, whoever in the family that has the problem, *she's* the one that's powerless over alcohol and it's *her* life that's so unmanageable. Now, if you'll think about it honestly, I believe you will conclude that, despite your best efforts to reform her, you've failed—completely, utterly, miserably failed. Right? Then you'll agree that you're powerless over the *alcoholic*. Dig a little deeper. Is there anything you can do personally to control, legislate, regulate or exert any lasting influence over alcohol? If you can't, then you're powerless.

"You can buy the first half of this Step—maybe reluctantly —but you bounce right out of your chair when you're asked to admit that *your* life is unmanageable. Me, I thought that I was doing a remarkably fine job of running my life, considering the handicap of a drunken wife. I still made a decent living, no thanks to anyone but myself. I did all right, even with the extra burden hanging on my back. Still, if I was doing so well, how come I was so unhappy, so depressed? I was honest, I had to admit that I had been bullshitting myself. Why did I go off half-cocked at the office, why couldn't I find a job where I really liked my boss and respected my associates? If I was such a great manager, then how come my kids constantly got themselves in a pack of trouble and disappointed me? Was I a victim of circumstances, or had I been spending my time building a dream castle where I lived as king?

"Step One is an act of surrender. It hurt like hell to own up to it, but I had to admit that I had never faced the world of reality head on. I had struck out trying for my one big goal, my dream of financial security, plenty of money for all the material things. I was afraid, I was insecure, I was frustrated. I took plenty of time, examined myself like an auditor going over a set of books and concluded that I was a failure under present management. I just didn't know how to run my show."

Paul interrupted. He was our "brain," an electronics engineer, an executive in a major research and development outfit, cleared for access to the "Most Secret" files on their government-sponsored projects. He was often quoted in the press with respect, a recognized authority. Paul was maybe a little eccentric, a Civil War buff who wrinkled his nose like a rabbit when quoting entire pages from history books. Despite his abilities, he hadn't been able to invent the electronic gadget or find the answer in his photographic memory to keep his wife sober. He had been attending our meetings for a couple of months.

"I may never get beyond this First Step. Right now, it's enough to understand that not only am I powerless over alcohol, I'm powerless over my wife, powerless over the men I work with, powerless over my kids. I have responsibilities to them but no power over them. The one person I'm not powerless over is myself. I can do something about me. I'm not very sure about how I'm going to do it, and that's why I'm here. Now consider General Lee, for instance ..."

He was winding up for another historical analogy, but subsided when someone suggested that, for starters on "how to do it," he should shut up and listen.

"Just hang in there, Paul," Harry advised, "once you've truly accepted the First Step—surrendered wholeheartedly—the next two steps follow in logical progression. The Second Step looks like a real back-breaker. 'Came to realize that a Power greater than ourselves could restore us to sanity.' I was reminded of my first swimming lessons. There I was, a skinny kid, shaking and blue with cold. The instructor had finally convinced me that I wouldn't drown if I put my head under water. Then, he told me to stretch out in the water and float! He slid one arm under me to give me confidence and, by golly, I floated! Once I learned I had to trust the instructor, the rest came easier.

"Now, I had accepted that I couldn't beat booze and wasn't doing too great in running my own show. In the Second Step, I'm asked to believe that I'm a nut, I'm insane, and that some nebulous Higher Power can square me away! I looked up the definition of insanity in Webster. 'Unsoundness or derangement of the mind, implying unfitness to manage one's own affairs.' Hell, I had already admitted that in the First Step!"

Nick broke in: "I thought I could manage Mary's problems with booze and pills along the same lines as I managed the characters that came to me looking for a job. Once I learned to quit 'playing God,' things got better. I have this fantasy of strolling the streets and stopping the first person I meet and saying, 'Good Morning! My name is God and who are you?' Or, 'Hey, I'm God—anything I can do for you today?' Or, 'I'm God—wanna see a miracle?' If I had actually done that, after about the first three 'visitations,' the men in the white coats with the butterfly nets would have had me salted down in the rubber room. Insane? Damn right I was."

"Thanks, Nick," Harry commented drily, "it's always nice to hear from a retiree—a guy that's quit 'playing God.' This business of God hangs up a lot of us.

"Fellows, we're not *required* to believe anything, just to keep an open mind. I know that some of us won't believe in God, others can't, and still others, who think they do believe, have no faith that He can swing a miracle our way. But we can keep an open mind."

Fritz waved his hand vigorously. He was a pragmatic, hard-headed Dutchman who had always believed that the woman's place was in the home, that his word was final and his wish, her command. Ruddy-faced and still crew-cut, Fritz was in his late 40s and owned a busy screw-machine shop with about fifty employees. All he wanted from his wife, Maureen, he had told me, was that she make a good home, entertain his folks and hers once a week, keep the kids clean and quiet, entertain his business guests and crew his sailboat on sunny weekends. Maureen saw it differently and took a lover. He was a secret lover, came from Canada and wore a uniform—a brown bottle. Fritz took a very dim view of Maureen's lover, particularly when he began to find his uniforms hidden around the house. Maureen had been Maggie's first referral to Hazelden.

"I need a rest and a place to think things out," she had said. Maggie giggled when she told me about it. Maureen didn't find Hazelden very restful, but she did find her sobriety.

Fritz finally caught Harry's eye. "Now about this Higher Power business," he began, "some of you know that my wife and I are agnostics. We attend a church, but the folks there are pretty relaxed about God. We do believe in a natural order of things, but not in God as we've heard about Him. Maureen had a rough time accepting the concept of a Higher Power when she was working on the Second Step at Hazelden."

"She said that her counselor told her, 'Okay, Maureen—try this. 'Act as if' God exists. When you 'act as if,' pray to God, ask Him for help, ask Him for guidance.' Maureen tried it, and it worked for her. She still does it, and she does get help. She still doesn't believe in God, but she believes in 'Act as If.'"

Harry concluded his remarks on the Second Step: "Look— the Higher Power that I'm talking about is a spiritual idea. Use whatever term you like—God, Our Father, Holy Spirit, Friend, or Maureen's 'Act as If.' Some of you may accept the idea that maybe this stag group is a Higher Power. The fact that we can surrender to the First Step means that we're getting a spiritual idea, and then things begin to happen.

"Step Three in this 'Learn to Swim' program is where we make up our mind to trust the Instructor when He tells us that the water is going to hold us up when we relax. Then we learn to float and finally, to use our arms and legs. Step Three asks if we're ready to detach from the alcoholic situation. It reads, 'Made a decision to turn our will and lives over to the care of God as we understand Him.'

"It sounds like we're supposed to give up our independence and that's in direct opposition to our masculine pride, our upbringing, our self-importance, our old attitudes of male dominance in marriage. 'Tain't so. It's a fact that the more we're willing to depend on a Higher Power, the more independent we are. It follows that dependence, as Al-Anon will have us practice it, is really a means of getting true independence of the spirit.

"As males, we fight this. When it comes to emotional independence, we reserve the right to independent action. Sure, we listen, but we still want to call the shots the way we see them. We don't need help. But, if we don't need help, how come we're here? To listen to Jack's dirty stories?"

# 11

# Words of One Letter

"Of course you know your 'A B C's'?" said the Red Queen.

"To be sure I do," said Alice.

"So do I," the Red Queen whispered: "We'll often say them over together, dear. And I'll tell you a secret — I can read words of one letter! Isn't that grand? However, don't be discouraged. You'll come to it in time."

Sully tells this story about his wife, and I have to believe it because Sully is in the Al-Anon program and is trying to be honest.

Clara had determinedly resisted his best efforts to "fix" her with Freud, jolt her with Jung or to grab her with Gestalt. He pulled down a reference work on other types of therapy and stumbled across a few lines covering Alcoholics Anonymous. It was recognized by the professionals.

Sully marked the place with his finger and went into the living room where Clara was stretched out on the couch, idly contemplating the ceiling.

"Listen to this, honey. This book says that Alcoholics Anonymous is 'a didactic inspirational group program for the treatment of alcoholism.' I'll put that into words you can understand. Since 'didactic' means 'teaching,' I would presume that there are regular classes taught by these people in how to control or to stop drinking. 'Inspirational' is hardly a scientific term, but psychologists recognize that a patient may need to rise above one's self to have hope of being cured. 'Group' refers to the handling of several patients simultaneously by the analyst rather than individual treatment sessions.

"We didn't get into this type of therapy in school, and I've never heard a paper on it at any of the seminars. But I think you ought to try it. I'll handle your enrollment for the classes if you like, and pay the fees. I can maybe get a professional discount."

Clara had listened, her eyes now contemplating her navel. "Read me the definition again."

"A didactic, inspirational group program."

"'Scuse me a minute," Clara said. She hurried into the kitchen, and Sully listened to the banging of cabinet doors, the sound of the refrigerator being opened and closed, the whir of the blender, and shortly Clara returned to the living room bearing two stemmed glasses brimming with a pale amber liquid and topped with foam.

"Here," said Clara sweetly, "Try my new cocktail. I call it the 'di-daiquiri.' When I can work my way through a group of di-daiquiris, I'll be inspired to teach you what a pompous know-it-all smart-ass you really are!"

Sully swears it's true.

When Maggie came home from Hazelden, we spent the first seventy-two hours with each other, but on the evening of the fourth day, she disappeared into the bedroom and returned dressed for the street. "I'm going to an AA meeting," she announced brightly, "Want to come with me?"

I figured this was going to happen, sooner or later. The guys in the stag group had warned me that I might even see less of her than I had in the past, but knowing that she was at an AA meeting would beat the hell out of watching her drinking herself to death. I was lucky to have had three days with her alone. We talked about her need for AA. She pulled out a battered green stenographer's notebook filled with her notes taken at the Hazelden lectures and thumbed through it rapidly.

"Here it is—one of Heilman's lectures. Did I tell you what a doll he is? I think at least half of the women at Hazelden were a little in love with him. Anyway, he said that the urge to drink would come and go, but time would decrease the urge and the frequency of it. But once in a while it would pop up again, a thirst, a tickle right behind the eyeballs. He told us to keep this urge on a conscious level, and that regular participation in AA meetings and activities will help us remember how it was and accept that the disease is only arrested—not cured.

"Heilman also told us that we would be most vulnerable when we felt particularly good. Holidays, such as Christmas, Thanksgiving, birthdays, special days—these were the prime times when we might get tipped over and take that first drink.

"Now these last three days have been very special to me, and you've taken care of at least one of my urges, but I think it's time I went to a meeting and let AA take care of my eyeball tickle. Okay?"

AA, says the Christopher D. Smithers Foundation, is very good with eyeball tickles. A private charitable organization concerned solely with alcoholism as a disease, they say this in their booklet, *Arresting Alcoholism:*

"Within the past quarter of a century, AA has proven the greatest constructive influence for good among alcoholics that the world has ever known. Yet AA's most successful members would be the first to say that they are not certain just how AA works, 'but it works.'"

The Foundation estimates that all other known methods of treatment—medicine, psychiatry, group therapy, hypnosis, etc.—account for about thirty percent of the arrestments of this illness—that is, alcoholics who have stopped drinking with a minimum of two years of sobriety. Perhaps another ten percent have stopped "doing it on their own." AA then, accounts for the remaining sixty percent of arrestment and recovery from alcoholism.

Expressed in AA shorthand, the inference is obvious: "Stick with the winners."

Since it was Sunday night—no football or golf on TV—I elected to attend the meeting with Maggie. I had gone to several AA meetings with her during her first encounter with AA—hell, I thought I *had* to take her just to be sure that she ended up in the right place! Our town had a secret asset that was never described in the Chamber of Commerce brochure: there were four AA groups meeting weekly with plans cooking for a fifth. Should Maggie tire of the home-town fare, she had a choice of about 360 weekly meetings within the county. She could find them in union halls, church basements, factory conference rooms, city buildings, schools, or in a store-front building downtown. There were morning meetings, noontime meetings, afternoon study groups, evening meetings, and even midnight meetings for AA's working the second shift. Institutional groups met in prisons, reformatories and workhouses. "No smoking groups" catered to those that were trying to kick the nicotine habit.

We arrived thirty minutes early, since one thing about Maggie hadn't changed with sobriety—she was always among the first to arrive at a party and the last to leave. It sounded like a party when we pushed open the door, a heavy buzz of conversation from other early arrivals, a few fellows clustered near the door to welcome oldtimers and newcomers alike, the sound of laughter. It could have been a cocktail party, but for one significant difference—it offered a choice of coffee, tea or lemonade instead of beer, booze or a glass of wine.

Maggie was having a little trouble remembering names as we made the rounds, but no one seemed to mind, and they introduced themselves, first names only, and Maggie apologized for her memory loss.

"Brain damage," Maggie would say, her standard remark

when she forgot a name, forgot her cigarettes or failed to close a zipper.

Scotty and Ike seemed particularly glad to see my wife. They had been her unofficial sponsors during her first shot at AA, two kind guys who would sit patiently at one end of the phone, listening to Maggie alternately try to con them or cry for help. Scotty, in his early sixties, still spoke with the burr that was a clue to his homeland, where they have that lovely peat which adds an expensive flavor to tasteless alcohol. He listened, waited and told Maggie of his own experience in accepting AA, how he would hurry from a meeting to his car for a quick drink from the bottle hidden under the front seat.

Ike was a retiree who lived for AA and golf in that order. A trim, slim man with a golf-hat tan, he was an ex-schoolteacher and an ex-drunk, a closet drinker, who could produce a reason for taking a drink as efficiently and quickly as he could polish off the pints carefully stashed away from the prying eyes of his wife.

"If my students had done their homework, I'd have a few drinks just to celebrate," Ike said. "If they were bugging me, which was more often than not, I'd drink because they were driving me up the wall. If it rained, I drank to keep from catching a cold. If the day was sunny, I drank to avoid a sunburn." Ike understood Maggie and her alibis.

Scotty and Ike were old-timers in Alcoholics Anonymous, an organization that began in 1935 with a chance meeting of a doctor (Dr. Bob), who drank too much and a stockbroker (Bill W.), with the same problem. These men had tried the "cure," tried to quit on their own. Together, they developed the principles on which AA is founded—the Twelve Steps—and put them into practice. They stayed sober and began to "carry the message" to other willing candidates that they found in hospitals, bars, on the streets, in cheap hotels and flophouses and in jail. Often these men were brought into Dr. Bob's home and nursed back to mental and physical health by the doctor and his wife.

There are still a few of the "old oldtimers" around. We heard one of them speak, telling of drinking a mixture of kerosene and buttermilk (the predecessor of sniffing glue or gasoline?) and being taken from an Akron, Ohio, hospital to Dr. Bob's house. "He would ask me to read just one page from the 'Big Book,' still under revision, the story of how a man might learn to stay sober. I had trouble getting through even one page daily. My mind and body were almost paralyzed, and it took several months just to be able to concentrate for even ten minutes."

The word was out. Now there was something—a program —for the hopeless drunk, that recognized his problem as a disease, that didn't require "taking the pledge" or even belief in God, but could help him get better. It was a simple program for complicated people and it worked. The Twelve Traditions came a little later, the simple statements that govern Alcoholics Anonymous. They wisely bypassed the usual organizational structure, with authority delegated down an established line. There was to be no national president, no officers, no "ramrods" in AA. Alcoholics, the founders reasoned, were a pretty rebellious bunch, and a tightly organized structure wouldn't work. Each new group was to run its own show. They would stick strictly to the business of helping one another get sober and stay sober. There would be no efforts to influence legislation, no "deals," no grants of money given or accepted. There was to be anonymity, for their mutual protection as well as to emphasize the need for personal humility.

AA grew because of the Twelfth Step, which requires that the members "carry the message to others." Members don't consider themselves as missionaries. Scotty once explained to Maggie, "AA is a selfish program. It's essential to my sobriety that I make Twelfth Step calls. To keep it, I have to give it away, so I'm doing it for me."

Founders Dr. Bob and Bill W. spelled out how it works in a chapter of *Alcoholics Anonymous*, the *Big Book*. Still, many professionals, doctors, psychologists, social workers and the clergy can't seem to pin it down. How *does* it work? I asked a few AA members:

"Ike, what was it in AA that did it for you?"

Ike paused to think: "Jack, I can only speak for myself—it was 'Easy Does It.'"

Then Scotty. Scotty told me, "Well, speaking only for myself, it was 'Let Go and Let God.'"

Then Annie. She was a big woman, with dyed black hair, a grandmother who bulged a bit around the seams of her white silk dress. She might have been a retired madame or an aging tug-boat operator. Annie was very serious when she said, "I don't know about the others, but speaking for myself, it was 'Keep It Simple.'"

*Now* do you understand?

The Sunday night meeting began with Ike reading the Twelve Steps of AA and Scotty reading the Twelve Traditions. The chairman (secondary duty: help clean up the place after the meeting) announced that there was a double bill featuring Al and Doris, married, both alcoholics, both in AA.

"My name is Doris and I'm an alcoholic." Doris is tall and slender, her skin is beautiful and glowing, and her close-cropped hair is tinted silver. She's forty-ish, looks thirty, walks like a fashion model, which she is. In a low voice, she tells her story quickly and concisely. Two drunks living together were something like a pair of scorpions in a bottle, she said. She and Al had drunk together, partied together, fought together and, together, watched their marriage trickle down the drain. There was a separation and a suit for divorce. She had reached bottom in the alcoholic ward of a hospital and learned about AA from another woman, a nurse. She had joined both AA and Al-Anon, since Al continued to drink. She learned to detach from Al's illness, and they decided to give their marriage another chance. "Detaching with love" came hard, Doris said, because Al was a particularly unlovely fellow when he was drunk! But when she pulled the rug from under him, letting him accept the consequences of his insanity, he had turned to AA for answers.

"I'm Al and I don't have to tell you that I'm an alcoholic—Doris has done that for me." His uncontrolled drinking, Al told us, had led him into the bankruptcy court and to the front door of the divorce court. When Doris had first joined AA, he had taken malicious delight in needling her, drinking in front of her, ridiculing her efforts. But when she quit playing games with him, refusing to do battle, no longer covering for him and telling him simply that drinking was "his problem," he "got sick and tired of being sick and tired." As a cynic who knew all of the answers, acceptance of the AA program had not been easy. He had joined an AA closed men's group, where he had been cut down to size, stripped of his defenses and taught something about honest self-appraisal. Then he could turn to Doris for support rather than for a sparring match. Things were better, definitely better, Al said. He had lost his business and was now selling cars. That wasn't the easiest way to make a living, Al thought, if a guy tried to use the principles of AA in his business life. "An *honest* car salesman?"

Maggie remembered Doris well. She had served briefly as one of Maggie's sponsors during her first try with AA, and Maggie had disliked her with a passion. Under that smooth surface, Doris was tough. She couldn't be conned because she, too, was a past master of the lie, the alibi, the manipulation. Maggie mourned that Doris was too hard, too mean and didn't understand her. Subsequently, she rejected her help.

When the twin talks were finished and the chairman asked for comments, Maggie was first to her feet. "Thank you for reminding me how it was, Doris. When I first heard your story, I compared. Sure I was a mess, I was bad, but not as big a mess or not as bad as you had been. I hadn't lost my husband or been hospitalized, so who were you to tell me how to stay sober? Tonight I didn't compare—I identified."

A big hulk of a man unfolded himself from his chair to comment. This was Bert, ex-pug, ex-barroom bouncer, ex-sailor and ex-drunk. His face carried the marks of his barroom brawls as well as his losing battles with booze. His nose was flattened, and he had a livid knife scar running diagonally across one cheek. He was certainly not a man to meet at night on a dark street.

"Thanks, Doris, for telling how great it is to look out of a window and really see—to see green leaves, a bird on a tree branch or the shape of a cloud—it's really wonderful, isn't it? And to see inside of people, to know them and to love them— that's an experience that comes only with sobriety. It's beautiful!"

"Thank you, Bert," Doris smiled, "and I think you're beautiful, too!"

Bert sat down quickly, red-faced. He had been sober for over five years but still flustered easily. When he was drinking, he would have back-handed any dame that would have dared to call him "beautiful"!

The meeting moved rapidly to a close. A coffee tin with a slit cut in the top passed from hand to hand, each person dropping a coin or folding a bill and sliding it into the container. Everyone gave whatever they liked—nothing at all if they were strapped. The secretary read announcements of coming meetings in the area. There was to be a tenth anniversary celebration by a nearby group. Another was featuring a "first lead," the first telling of his or her story by a member, perhaps in his eighth month or at the end of a year of sobriety. The meeting ended with an invitation to enjoy the traditional "coffee and ..." session which would include the inevitable coffee, sometimes tea, soft drinks, plus doughnuts, sandwich makings and maybe a cake commemorating a member's year of sobriety. It was a relief for a tender-ass like me to stand up. For some reason, AA meetings always had the hardest seats in the world, usually folding chairs selected for their stackability and durability but never for comfort.

Maggie headed for a clutch of women surrounding a "new gal," attending the meeting for the first time in the tow of her sponsor. Generally, Maggie had explained to me, a new member was asked to attend as many meetings as possible for perhaps two or three months, and many sponsors saw to it that they were safely transported to and from the meetings.

Later, the "new gal" could begin to balance these meetings with family responsibilities. Maggie settled into a routine of three or four meetings weekly or more when she felt that she "needed one."

I lined up with the folks waiting for refreshments. Tonight, there were two homemade cakes. I took two pieces, reflecting that I was a recovering mirror-alcoholic, a knurd that needed the nourishment and could always skip lunch tomorrow. Ahead of me were Ollie, the group's chairman for the month, and Chuck, serving his six-month term as treasurer. Ollie was a distinguished looking gentleman wearing a checked sports jacket, pale blue shirt and dark tie, well-tailored trousers and gleaming black loafers. He looked like a successful banker (which he was) and a pillar of the church (which he wasn't). He would never be typecast as an alcoholic (which he was).

Chuck wore a sport shirt open at the throat, a soft green button-down-the-front mohair sweater, tan slacks and polished brown loafers. He looked like a successful corporation executive who had just finished eighteen holes of golf and had won ten bucks. This was true. It was also true that nine years ago he had been fired from his job for excessive drinking.

I remembered Chuck and Ollie well because of a mistake they had made. During Maggie's first brush with AA and our initial appearance at this group's meeting, these fellows had assumed that I was the one with a problem. It was a perfectly natural error on their part, since I had the earmarks of a drunk trying to do something about his problem. I was a little furtive, a little nervous, and had an air of grim determination. I bulged at the waist and could count three chins. When they had introduced themselves, I hurriedly pointed in Maggie's direction. "She's the one with the problem," I said. "I don't need help."

Tonight, they greeted me loudly, "Hey Jack, you're looking much better. Staying sober?"

I assured them gravely that, indeed, I was much better and that, yes, I was sober and feeling happy. We chatted until the line moved forward and Chuck and Ollie were busy with the coffee and cake. The man behind me nudged me.

"I'm Bill, and this is my first time visiting this group," he said. "How long have you been in the program?"

"Not very long," I hedged.

"I thought maybe you and those guys ahead of you were old-timers—you all seem so happy and relaxed. It's hard to tell, isn't it?"

Inside, I felt a warm glow of pride. I *was* happy and relaxed, I felt at home, and this fine gentleman had just paid me the supreme compliment of thinking that I was a recovering alcoholic, and an "oldtimer" at that! I was pleased and flattered to be mistaken for an ex-drunk, a member of AA.

Maggie pried me away from the cake and led me back to the group around the newcomer. She introduced me to Harriet, now in her second twenty-four hours of sobriety, still puffy-faced, hands trembling and smelling faintly of booze redistilled through the pores of her skin. She was flanked by her sponsor and a stern-faced man who was a little furtive and nervous but with an air of grim determination. Her husband, no doubt. We shook hands and he asked. "You an alcoholic like the rest of this bunch?"

"I'm not sure about me, but I'm married to one and I think I know how you feel. Let's get away from here and talk about it," I responded.

We moved to a less-crowded section of the room and the storm broke, his words tumbling out, peppering me like a gust of rain mixed with hail. "You could *never* know how I feel! Let me tell you, friend, I've been through hell with that damned woman! I've told her that this is absolutely her last chance—she either straightens herself out or we have had it!" There was more. She had disgraced him in front of his boss and his wife at the company picnic, she had alienated their friends, and their daughter was becoming a juvenile delinquent because of hating her mother. He had spent thousands on doctor bills, hospital bills, psychiatrist's bills. She had totaled the car and was a liar and a thief—she had stolen money right out of his billfold to buy booze!

I listened admiringly. If resentments were ten dollar bills, he could have paid cash for Kuwait and had enough left for a substantial down payment on Iran. I *did* know how he felt, and remembered my own guilt, confusion and anger. We talked for a bit, and I suggested that maybe he would like to meet a group of men who had similar problems. He wasn't sure, he said, but agreed that I would pick him up the next night for a guided tour—down the stairs, up the stairs, past the choir loft and into his first Al-Anon meeting.

Not all of my recruiting drives with prospects I met at AA meetings turned out well. Merritt was, no doubt, my most outstanding failure and an unabashed critic of Al-Anon. Merritt and wife, Jane, were both on-again, off-again alcoholics who couldn't seem to stay sober. They couldn't seem to stand success; if Jane was sober, Merritt was on a two-week bender. When he sobered up, Jane had a slip. Merritt approached me one Sunday night at the AA meeting—it was his turn to be sober—and asked me confidentially, "Do you think it would be OK if I could go to a few meetings of this stag group you talk about? You know that Jane is an alcoholic, and I need some help in learning how to cope. That woman is going to drive me to drink if she keeps going the way she's headed now!"

They lived nearby, and I picked him up one evening to take him to his first Al-Anon meeting. He didn't have much to contribute, but he listened intently. I had visions of Merritt gaining detachment, understanding and patience, visions of the two of them finding a lasting sobriety with a gentle nudge from Al-Anon. On the way home, Merritt remained silent. I asked if I might pick him up the following week and went through the "give us six meetings before you make up your mind" routine.

He thought about it. Finally he spoke, slowly and a little reluctantly, "Jack, I don't think so. I hate to say this to you, but some of those guys at that meeting—man, they're really SICK! I think I'd better stick with AA."

Oh well—win a few, lose a few.

I enjoyed AA meetings, looked forward to attending them in Maggie's company, and came away with a good feeling of peace and happiness in my heart. I felt faintly uneasy at first, wondering if I wasn't wearing another mask, parading myself as a recovering alcoholic to those that didn't know me, until I talked to Ev one evening. Ev was in his late fifties with an air of childlike innocence in his eyes, which were covered with thick-lensed glasses. Someone usually helped him into the room, and he moved slowly and painfully to a chair in the corner. Everyone came up to Ev and chatted for a few minutes, and I had assumed that he was an oldtimer, perhaps a victim of bootleg gin, the bottle that you tilted to check for fusel oil, which reportedly crippled you for life if you drank it. I asked Ev how he came to AA.

"I'm not an alcoholic, Jack," Ev confessed. "There's nothing said in the Big Book or elsewhere that you have to be a drunk to join—just that you 'have a sincere desire to stop drinking.' I suspected that if I continued to drink I might have a problem some day. But I come here because I like the people here and I think they like me. This is home, and I go away from here feeling better. It does something for my self-respect."

It began to look as though Alcoholics Anonymous had something for not only the sick alcoholic but also for a recovering knurd like me and a man like Ev who might have been a borderline alcoholic. It worked.

Dr. Dan Anderson explained, in non-technical language, something more of the workings of AA in his taped lecture, "The Revolution in Psychotherapy." Group therapy, he says, has been around for thirty or forty years. AA is difficult for the professional psychologist, psychiatrist or social worker to understand because it doesn't speak their language. Group therapy techniques have directed that the trained professional delve into the patient's past, seeking answers in his or her early life, where the problem was presumed to lie. The emphasis was on the past.

Anderson related that a clinical psychologist, Dr. O. Hobart Maurer, had dug a little deeper into the phenomenon of AA and discovered that here was a different concept — AA said to forget the past, do something about changing yourself right now, today, learn honesty and responsibility and the future will take care of itself. This concept was a 180-degree swing for the professional, almost like starting at the tail end and forgetting about the beginning.

AA dropped the doctor-patient relationship of traditional group therapy and introduced a new idea — that people, meeting as equals, all with the same problem of chronic alcoholism, could benefit one another. The less authority and organizational structure the better. Although AA is a teaching program, each member is both a teacher and a student: he's a sponsor and he is sponsored. He tells his story and listens to others tell theirs. In a group of peers, a member finds it easier to talk honestly and freely, to let down his guard and to reveal his inner self. He is in contact with others who, by example, demonstrate that it is possible to feel better, to act honestly and responsibly.

Through these regular contacts, there is a change of values. As these values change, the participants find a peace, an easiness, something the professionals call mental health. Alcoholics Anonymous then, says Dr. Anderson, is a mutual self-help peer group. It works and works well, but no one except the alcoholics can tell exactly why it works.

AA is the practical granddaddy of many similar self-help groups, Dr. Maurer reported, with over 240 in existence. A later count by Dr. John Drakeford ran the total to over 300. Al-Anon for the families of the chemically dependent and Alateen for the children of alcoholics are early examples.

A few others mentioned by Dr. Anderson include TOPS, Overeater Anonymous and Weight Watchers for those with a weight problem; Better Health, Emotions Anonymous, Stutterers Anonymous, Recovery Inc., Parents Anonymous, Families Anonymous (specifically for those in a family in which one member has a drug abuse problem) and Widow-to-

Widow. These organizations draw liberally from the AA Twelve Steps, changing the key words to make more specific reference to the problem. For example, changing "... powerless over alcohol," to read "... powerless over emotions."

This then is Alcoholics Anonymous. My Maggie—now a believer in the AA tenet, "KISS" (Keep It Simple, Stupid)— offers this borrowed simplification of what AA members do:

1. Have Faith
2. Clean House
3. Keep Active.

# 12

## Curiouser and Curiouser

**"Curiouser and curiouser!" cried Alice, "Now I'm opening out like the largest telescope that ever was!"**

"Tell me something about the care and feeding of freshly-hatched butterflies," I challenged the men in our stag group, "Hazelden's shipping me one in a week or so."

This was shortly after Maggie had phoned me excitedly, telling me that she was now working on her Fourth Step inventory. On its completion, she would share it with a clergyman—give her Fifth Step—and then would be coming home!

I had attended several Al-Anon meetings and gained two bits of wisdom. First, ask for help, something I hadn't done since I had begged my boss to come up with something, anything short of amputation, to keep me free of the draft in WWII. That was a bust, since I had been drafted anyway. Second, I had learned that the men in Al-Anon had preserved or retained their sense of humor and weren't above a bit of bullshit. Their suggestions were fast and facetious:

"Burn or bury your dirty socks—they say in AA that 'stinkin' thinkin' leads to drinkin'.'"

"If it's snowing when you get her home, careful with your skis—taking them off is the *second* thing you'll do."

"Hide the key to TLC—The Liquor Cabinet".

Louis-the-Beagle interrupted the flow of advice, "Jack, we really can't tell you what to do—all we know is what worked or didn't work for ourselves. There are guidelines in Al-Anon, and for me, it was the logic of 'First Things First.' My wife had been mighty sick as an alcoholic, and when she found sobriety, it just stood to reason that she was going to go through a period of convalescence. So TLC—'Tender Loving Care'—made sense. Now then—you've been attending enough of these meetings to concede that you've been more than a little sick yourself. So doesn't it follow that you're going to go through convalescence, too, and maybe the first thing to think about is what you're going to do for yourself."

"Louie, you're a helluva coach," I protested, "My wife has been ill and is coming home to complete her recovery. Now you're saying that I should give her a peck on the cheek and get back to the big job of worrying about poor, mixed-up me?"

"I don't think that's what he had in mind, Jack," Harry interjected, "He's telling you that, once you start getting your own head screwed on straight, the atmosphere in your house will change and make it easier for Maggie to continue her recovery. I wish we could chart it all out for you—do this, don't do that—but like I keep telling you, this group is an association of retired management consultants who have given up running the universe and managing our wives. The password is 'Powerless'—remember?"

"Look, there must be a clue someplace," I argued, "You don't expect me to make a list of 'what she did' and come racing in here every week to find out how you guys handled a similar situation, do you?"

Bart sat there puffing on a dry pipe, listening. In his late forties, Bart was a taciturn man of infinite patience. He needed the patience, since he worked all day for a West Coast company that was under the impression that he was in the Pacific time zone and kept him on the phone until eight or nine in the evening. Bart's wife, Jan, was a Hazelden graduate, now a professional chemical dependency counselor at a nearby Veteran's Administration hospital.

Bart carefully balanced his pipe on the edge of an ash tray. "Jack, I think I know what's hanging you up. There are guidelines and signposts that will help. Maybe the first of your 'First Things First' is a little homework. You know folks in AA, so why don't you borrow a copy of the *Big Book* from one of them and read the chapter, 'To Wives.' You'll find that the ideas apply equally to husbands. The other chapter to read is 'The Family Afterwards,' which relates to necessary attitudes for a successful readjustment to life on the part of both the alcoholic and her family.

"You have a copy of *One Day at a Time in Al-Anon,* don't you? The index at the back of the book is classified by subject matter. Read the references listed under 'Sobriety.' These are the suggestions and ideas that have worked for others and may work for you. If you want to start with a primer, this is as basic as breathing.

"Next, get yourself a copy of *The Dilemma of the Alcoholic Marriage.* There's one over there on that table," Bart said, pointing to the display of Al-Anon literature. "Before I read it, I thought I was in a trap, not a dilemma. There's some good straight talk on sexual relationships and some advice on communication that beats IT&T's best publications.

"These were my beginner's textbooks, and there are plenty more when you want to broaden your views. Look over the Al-Anon publication list."

I followed Bart's suggestion obediently and picked up my primers, wondering if I should also grab a clean handkerchief to wipe my nose when teacher said to. Here I was, fifty-plus, on my way to kindergarten to learn my ABC's! "A is for Apple." "B is for Boy, C—for Cat" and on down the line to "S." "S—is for Sex?"

I've always been an avid and omnivorous reader. As a kid, I discovered the public library when I was ten and worked my way, shelf by shelf, through every book available, except those volumes jealously guarded by the librarian in the "locked case." Unfortunately, I could seldom remember anything I had read. I was the only kid in the third grade that carried a crib to the multiplication tables. I mastered the art of printing in miniscule letters and spent hours laboriously transcribing the conjugation of French verbs and important dates in American history onto tiny slips of paper that I rolled into neat cylinders, to smuggle into classrooms, hidden between my fingers.

Nothing has changed, and I found it necessary to jot down the suggestions I found in my basic references from AA and Al-Anon books. Idly, I sorted them into some kind of order, then alphabetically by subject. Let's see—"A is for"—what else? "A is for AA and Al-Anon." Good start. The organization was easy except for "X" and "Z," but, by fudging a little, I came up with my primer:

**"A"—is for AA and Al-Anon:** She's going to spend more time in AA activities than I had imagined and it may be pretty easy to resent it. There's real danger here that I'll try to use her sobriety to find new reasons to feel sorry for poor lil' ol' me. Solution: Use Al-Anon contacts and meetings for understanding.

**"B"—is for Body Language:** I'll need to understand and watch body language just as carefully as words. Attitudes come through. Though I mouth the right words, any anger, resentment, contempt or "holier than thou" attitudes come through to belie the words. An alcoholic is a very sensitive person, drunk or sober, and don't forget it! Al-Anon says: "No Band-aiding in thought, word or action."

**"C"—is for Confidence:** You gotta believe! If I have confidence in her newfound sobriety, it's going to help her maintain it and keep me on an even keel. No hovering like a mother hen with her first chick—just trust her.

**"D"—is for Danger Signals:** Red flags are going to fly and rockets burst in mid-air for both of us. Watch for impatience, self-pity, resentments. Recommended: Daily Inventory Sheet for self-discipline, AA and Al-Anon contacts — (others may see what we may be missing). Big bugaboo for me is danger of reliving the past!

**"E" — is for Easy Does It:** Relax — both mentally and physically. Tension can be an enemy to both of us. A relaxed atmosphere, uncritical acceptance that neither of us is perfect or ever will be, will let us live naturally, openly and honestly with one another.

**"F" — is for Family:** Sure, there will be family problems even though she's sober. They won't go away all by themselves. The big difference is that now we should be able to talk about them without getting into a free-for-all. We can examine them and look for solutions with the help of our Higher Power. Solving family problems can draw us together, help us grow.

**"G" — is for Growing:** If she's working her AA program, she's accepted the fact that she's an alcoholic, and now she is growing, spiritually and emotionally. Just how this will affect me depends largely on how I adjust to it. My role in our new relationship is to overcome my shortcomings so that we can grow together. Our growth may not be at the same rate, but this is no Olympic competition with gold and silver medals. We won't even get a halo and wings. The growing never stops unless we get lazy and let it.

**"H" — is for Habits:** The adjustment from active drinking to sobriety will require a change in many mental and some physical habits. She knows what habits she has to break; the new habits she must make a part of her life. Could be that I have to make some mental adjustments too. For example, if I had taken over some of her responsibilities during her drinking days, such as taking care of the kids, getting meals, cleaning house, buying the necessities, these roles need to be reversed. Maybe not 100 percent reversed, since marriage should be sharing, including some of the routine chores of running a household. I won't expect too much too soon. (See "E" and "G.") And if I've gone gung-ho on golf, taken up tennis or am batty over bowling, I'd better ease up, include her in or find a sport or hobby that we can enjoy together from time to time.

**"I"—is for Illusions:** It's an illusion, dad, to believe that now she's sober, all of my problems are solved, all is rosy and things will get back to "normal." Sobriety is only the first step. It's an illusion to think that we can forget all about how bad it was, sweep it under the rug or bury it in the closet. What we need to do is to work together to overcome those emotional conflicts in ourselves that are still alive and kicking. (See "R".)

**"J"—is for Joint Relationships:** My gal recognizes that sobriety is only the beginning of her growth and that she needs to sustain and encourage that growth in AA. Me, I'll need help in adjusting to the problems of our new joint relationship, in learning how to meet these new responsibilities with love and dignity. If we both concede that we were not too well put together, it makes sense that we both need the help of a personal growth program—AA for her, Al-Anon for me.

**"K"—is to Know the Difference:** Shake hands with the Serenity Prayer which says it nicely and concisely:

"God grant me the serenity to accept the things I cannot change, The courage to change the things I can, And the wisdom to know the difference."

I can't change her—I tried and I proved it. I can change me. I can change many of the things about me. I will need to remind myself from time to time that I do need God's help for shaking out the "can-do's" from the "can't-do's."

**"L"—is for Learning and Listening:** I'll learn not to perch my wife on a pedestal again. I tried it, and she didn't like it. If I set the standards and she doesn't live up to them now that she's sober, I'll be frustrated and angry. She'll resent my management. I need to learn to leave her to God and her friends in AA. I won't look for perfection in other people, including my wife and family, until I attain it myself. That's some time from now. I need to learn to listen to her, really listen when it's my turn to be on the receiving end of a resentment. She's learning not to hold them inside. I'll learn to keep my cool and hear her out and to remember that one good resentment does not deserve another!

**"M"—is for Martyr:** Consider this one: Did I, down underneath, rather enjoy my role as a martyr? Did I really like her dependence and all those soothing words my friends poured out when I was crying on their shoulders? If this is the case, there are troubles in River City. I'll resent a sobriety where she's insisting on accepting her own responsibilities and asserting her independence. Our communication will break down quickly and if we don't talk together, we can't make it together. Solution: Al-Anon has a great trade-in program for hair shirts.

**"N"—is for No Demands:** Give her the data without telling her what *I* think the answer is. Leave the choice up to her; if she wants to do something about it, fine. If she doesn't, it's still her problem, and the door is left open for communication. The AA's talk about "self-will." It's going to be tough not to issue ultimatums and flat-out directives, but it's essential that I refrain from imposing my will. I'll recognize her as an equal in this marriage partnership and knock off the "father knows best" attitude.

**"O"—is for One Day at a Time:** That's the way she is keeping sober and the way she will live. If I want to share her life, I'll go the same route. I can only live right now, this minute. I can't do anything about yesterday, and tomorrow isn't here yet. I won't bring up the past, but if she wants to talk about it, I'll listen. I won't worry about her sobriety tomorrow, because tomorrow isn't now, and her sobriety is her problem, not mine.

**"P"—is for Pedigree Reading:** There are two areas marked "Eggs—walk at your own risk." It's easy to slide from the subject at hand into verbal speculation about her Aunt Mabel's unfortunate sherry-sipping and the inheritance of alcoholism—the old "tainted blood" routine. If I've listened at Al-Anon, I know better than that! Then there's "inventory-taking," whereby I measure her progress or lack of it, give her a few helpful hints and hold her hand. The only time I'll contribute my opinion is when she asks me, point blank!

**"Q" — is for Quality of Human Relationship:** The "Q" factor, says Al-Anon, depends on how we communicate with one another. Not by what we say alone, but how we say it. Not by what we do but our motives for doing it. Tone of voice and even our smallest actions are elements in communication. (See "B.") If this marriage of ours is held together by love, respect and a desire to please and comfort, our communication just naturally will fall into patterns that express these feelings and give us confidence in one another. Grade A communication takes time and practice.

**"R" — is for Reality:** She's finally faced up to the fact that her drinking was an escape from reality and her sobriety is a return to reality. She's through playing games with me. Now if I'm tired of games and role-playing, I can drop my mask, shed my tin armor and let her and others see me as I am. Fantasies are fun if I recognize them for what they are. Reality can be fun, too. I won't pussyfoot now that she's sober. I won't blow my stack if she returns to drinking. I won't react or "show her." My honest actions can tell her that I respect her right to live the way she wants to, but that I also have that same right. My own actions must reflect honesty, with no element of blame or criticism attached. That's reality, chum!

**"S" — is for Sex and Self-Worth:** Part of good mental health is to love and be loved and to have a feeling of self-worth — to like yourself. Sex is an expression of love and a very natural one. To punish someone by physical withdrawal negates the self-worth of both individuals. Loss of self-worth results in guilt and fear. Guilt and fear can bring about impotency.

"Patience" is the key word. She won't expect perfection, and it will be easier for me as I honestly try to regain my self-esteem.

**"T" — is for Trust:** If she lied and cheated and conned me in the past, how can I trust her today? Doubts and fears that she'll stay sober and make the AA program require a change in my attitude — not a change to skeptical hope, but to plain old unadulterated trust. If that's too big an order in the beginning, use the "act as if" technique. As the technique works, genuine trust follows. Even if she has a relapse, it's *her* problem and my contribution is to stand by with patience, compassion and trust.

"U"—is for **Unbalanced Dependence:** Of course we need to depend on one another—marriage or any family relationship demands that. It's a two-way street, though. If she feels that she is "stuck" with the marriage and there are no alternatives, then the dependence is unbalanced. I can anticipate hostility and anger. It's equally unbalanced if I make excessive demands and am suspicious of her actions and motives. Balance is achieved by simply accepting one another, just for twenty-four hours at a time. Now we have a choice and can make a decision about tomorrow when tomorrow becomes today.

"V"—is for **Voice:** If I'm going to relearn the art of communication, I should push the pianissimo pedal on my vocal chords, try to come on low-key and pleasant. The surest way for her *not* to hear me is for me to roll it out in the loud, strong, authoritative I'm-so-right-and-you're-so-wrong tones which had brought her to tears and anger when I talked about her "damn drinking." I'll also avoid the over-solicitous ("you poor thing—you've been sick") and the super-supercilious ("I told you so, now see what you've done?").

"W"—is for **Watch and Worry:** The miracle of her sobriety is hers—not mine. It's not my responsibility to watch over her and worry about her drinking, to see that she hits the right number of AA meetings weekly and, in effect, to continue the old routine of management and supervision that made life hell for both of us when she was drinking. My responsibility is to let her manage her own sobriety, to be gentle and cooperative and to show my gratitude by keeping off her back.

"X"—is for **X-ray:** Not the kind we find in hospitals and clinics, old buddy, but the kind we can develop in Al-Anon. I need to learn how to look inside my own head and find an answer to the question, "Who am I?" What kind of a person am

I, what are my defects of character and what am I willing to do about them? What is my personal philosophy and does it make any sense? Once I can study my own X-ray, then I can start "getting my shit together" and I should become easier to live with, both for me and for her.

**"Y"—is for You Try Courtesy:** This one is so simple that it's easy to overlook, says Al-Anon. As a matter of course, I'm courteous to strangers and friends, but with my wife it's been the no-holds-barred fight, the scornful remark, the "Heaven help me" look of martyred patience. I've forgotten what it's like to treat her with real courtesy, to remember that she is a unique person with a soul and set of emotions that are all her own. We may have intimacy and togetherness running out our ears, but what I'm to look for is a particular un-smothering attitude of courtesy.

**"Z"—is for Zest:** If I've been running in the rut of routine, seeing nothing, feeling nothing, it's time that I make a determined effort to put a little zest for living in my life. This may be the end product of my change in attitude as I learn the art of empathy, to love people as they are and accept them, to find pleasure in the way the stars twinkle, the flight of a humming bird, the changes in the seasons. Zest is seeing, hearing, accepting. Zest is the joy of living, one day at a time, with a sober wife.

When Maggie's homecoming was a certainty, I was prepared. I had my notes covering the ABC's — Alcoholic Basic Convalescence — in good order. I had taken good care to remove temptation from the premises, cleaning out our liquor supply either by drinking it myself (neat, tidy and economical) or giving it away. That hurt. I had even donated my entire supply of homemade Cold Duck to one of my wine-drinking friends, a connoisseur of great vintages. That Cold Duck was pretty good stuff, aged for three weeks, and cheap, too — it cost only about a quarter per bottle. You buy concentrated grape juice, see, add sugar and water and bubble it in a five-gallon glass jug ... oh hell, ask your neighbor for the recipe.

Anyway, the house was bone dry, and I felt righteous and a little smug.

A few minutes in the kitchen and Maggie eyed the vacant shelf which had been the temporary resting place for the household vodka, blended whiskey and sherry. "Hey, where's the booze?" she asked.

"I got rid of it—the Cold Duck, too."

"Honey, listen. Whether I drink or not is *my* problem. Whether you drink or don't drink is *yours*. If you want a drink, you don't have to go to a bar—drink at home! And when we have friends in for dinner or bridge, if they drink, I want to offer them one. Just because I'm an alcoholic and can't drink is no reason why you and our friends shouldn't. If I want a drink and decide to take a drink, I will have gone to the liquor store and bought it. So please stock up, only this time buy some good stuff, not that junk that we used to buy."

Maggie had given me a taste of "C" with a shot of "R" thrown in.

I continued to drink moderately for a few weeks, but somehow it didn't taste so great or do much for me. Without any particular conscious effort, I quit drinking. Maggie asked why.

"Maybe because of 'M' and 'X' plus a lack of 'C.' I didn't have confidence that you wouldn't open a bottle if there was one around the house. Too, I thought I would be a big hero and quit drinking, so you wouldn't sit there with your tongue hanging out. Later, I thought that I had stopped because I had somehow just lost my taste for the stuff and it wasn't doing anything for me. Now that I'm getting to know myself a little better, I believe that the honest reason for quitting is that I'm scared. I have many, if not all, of the alcoholic's personality traits. I think my toes are pretty close to that invisible line that marks the difference between a social drinker and a compulsive drinker. You and I ran a race and you lost. It could have been me."

She leaned over and kissed me. We left for the bedroom to practice a little "S," with plenty of "Z" thrown in.

That's convalescence—mutual lessons in the ABC's!

# 13

## Whatever Became of the Baby?

"Bye-the-bye, whatever became of the baby?" said Cat.
"I'd nearly forgotten to ask."
"It turned into a pig," Alice answered quietly.
"I thought it would," said the Cat, and vanished again.

There's the story about a policeman in a suburban community who had the unpleasant duty of calling the parents of a youngster who had just totaled the family car at a downtown intersection. Fortunately, no one was badly injured, the policeman told the mother who had answered the phone, but her son and his companion were more than a little drunk, and there were three full bottles of wine on the front seat.

"Nothing else—just wine?" the mother inquired anxiously.

"Just three full bottles of wine and one empty, lady," the cop told her.

"Thank God," the mother exclaimed and lowering her voice, whispered, "I was afraid they were smoking pot or taking those awful pills!"

This parent and those like her would be comforted and pleased, no doubt, to learn that the younger generation seems to be getting the message and is turning away from the drug scene in favor of legal booze. Maggie told me that one of the lecturers at Hazelden had reported that treatment centers are seeing a startling growth in the number of young people appearing for treatment whose "chemical of choice" is alcohol. One reason, the lecturer explained, is that kids today grow up with the conviction that colas are cool because the bottlers din the message into their heads through the media of TV, radio and magazines.

Some deep thinker in the wine industry rightly concluded that if it's "pop" they want, then it's "pop" wine they'll get, and a whole new world opened. The industry brought out a wide range of low-proof, sweet-tasting, fruit-flavored wines that are cheap, heavily advertised and readily available.

So why fight it? The kids rightly reason that a possession rap for a couple of joints or a few stray seeds is hardly worth it when you can pick up this great stuff at almost any corner grocery store, where it's damn seldom that some officious clerk is going to ask for an ID. Man, it's easy, it's cool.

It's also addictive, the lecturer pointed out. Now maybe little Reggie will become a rummy instead of a drug freak like his older brother. Isn't that grand?

Yes, Virginia, young people become alcoholics, too. Elsie was the youngest member of AA that I've met, drinking compulsively from her eighth year until she came into AA at the ripe old age of eleven. When I first saw the kid, white knee socks, hair braided into two pigtails and braces on her teeth, I assumed that she was attending the meeting with her dad. That wasn't too unusual; once in a while a parent would bring a youngster along if a baby sitter wasn't handy. Some AA groups that cater to the family trade even operate a nursery or sitter service, often staffed with Al-Anon wives who look after the kids while mother or dad attends the meeting.

Elsie told me that it started with her taking a sip or two of daddy's drink, liking it, and helping herself when no one was looking. Besides, daddy didn't mind too much if she got a little tipsy—he enjoyed having someone to drink with. It wasn't so enjoyable when she became addicted. The shock was enough to help daddy hit bottom and they both came to AA together for help.

The kid had her favorite put-down and would wait with ironic anticipation for the newcomer who, on learning that Elsie was a member of AA, would approach her with the inevitable remark, "Honey, aren't you a little *young* to be an alcoholic?"

Elsie would bare her braces and smile as she shot back, "Oh, I don't know—aren't you a little *old*?"

Then there's the tale told in the circles of AA about the young man in his early twenties, suffering from a crashing hangover, who walked into the bar at ten in the morning for a little "hair of the dog," which someone had assured him would ease his pain. He settled on a bar stool next to an elderly gentleman who had very obviously been bitten by the same dog. The old gent was having some difficulty in guiding his drink to his lips. To steady his shaking hand, he had removed his tie, knotted the ends together and contrived a sling. With the sling to steady his arm, he was able to convey the drink more or less safely to its destination.

They sat in companionable silence for a few minutes, the young man following the oldster's effort with interest. "You know," he said, "this is the first time I've ever been in a bar before noon. I'm a little worried about myself. They say that if you drink in the morning, it's a good sign that you may be an alcoholic. What do you think?"

His companion eyed him with disgust and retorted scornfully, "Hell, kid—you *can't* be an alcoholic. I've *spilled* more than you've drunk in your entire life, and *I'm* not an alcoholic!"

We've heard references to the "twenty-year disease," inferring that it takes twenty years for the budding alcoholic to reach the status of a full-blown chronic drinker. Statistically, this may be true, but as with all averages, there are those who become addicted after a shorter period of drinking and those who take a bit longer. Maggie's experiences at Hazelden convinced her that age was no barrier to alcoholism and the length of time drinking no measurement in "qualifying" as an active alcoholic. She had met those nice little old ladies who had never taken more than an occasional glass of wine until they were in their sixties, then became chronic drunks within a year or two. She had lived with youngsters still in their teens who were addicted to alcohol within a year—or even less—from the time of their first drink. Maggie felt that she had been an alcoholic right from the time that she began to drink regularly at age fourteen. This was when she fell in love with the experience of intoxication, began to depend on it and became obsessed with the desire for a drink. It just took her a long time to admit it, she said.

It hadn't taken Judy nearly so long to admit her alcoholism. Now twenty-two, she had been sober in AA for almost a year. She had a trim, compact figure, the shape you associate with high-school cheerleaders or with majorettes strutting in front of a college band. Her face was devoid of make-up—with gray eyes that peered over the top of granny glasses, and even, white teeth. Her hair was a cap of glossy black curls. She was the kind of a girl that you would have been proud to introduce as your daughter.

But she never had been introduced that way, since her mother was dead, her father too occupied to take over the chore of raising a child, and she had grown up in a foster home. Her foster parents were kind people who brought up Judy as their own, dressing her nicely, protecting her, seeing to it that she had solid religious training. They had even paid for her violin lessons, and when she was big enough to wrap her arms around it, she had graduated to the viola. She had dreamed of becoming a cheerleader or a majorette or playing in the school band, but unfortunately, Judy sighed, there were no openings for viola players; she switched her dreams to performing, some day in the indefinite future, at Carnegie Hall.

Judy had related this background in her first turn at leading an AA group. Maggie and I were listening. Carnegie Hall seemed much closer, Judy said, after her boyfriend introduced her to pills when she was a junior in high school.

She liked the downers, which made the world turn a little slower, let her drift effortlessly to the stage, listen to the echos of applause when she made her debut, bow gracefully across the footlights to a receptive audience. Pills made it seem so real, so cool!

With the financial help and encouragement of her foster parents, she made it to college, where it was pizzas, pot and pop wine. Wine was fine, and she paid for her share by regularly tapping the till at the restaurant where she worked as a waitress. She just took enough for a couple of bottles, she said, and all the help took a few bucks when they needed it. The restaurant owner drank a bit too much himself and never missed the dollar bills from his cash register. But one day Judy was too greedy. She was caught and fired. The irate owner reported her to the Dean of Women, who put her on probation.

That was bad—no more bottles of sweet red wine to be poured over ice cubes, wine to quench the thirst that came with sharing a few joints rolled with Acapulco Gold, the finest Mexican marijuana. Her boyfriend suggested that maybe she could pick up a few bucks if she hung around a bar at a nearby motel, which had a steady clientele of out-of-town guests who were looking for a little excitement.

Judy didn't like being a part-time prostitute—her skin crawled and she felt dirty after the quickie sessions at the motel—but the ten and twenty dollar "gifts" bought plenty of bottles. Sometimes she felt so depressed and guilty that she would retreat to her room at the dorm, lock the door and get bombed out of her skull. One night she accidentally burned her fingers when she tried to pick up a lighted cigarette from the floor where it had fallen.

"It hurt, but it felt sorta good," said Judy, "so I deliberately touched the tip to my wrist and held it there. It gave me a feeling of satisfaction to punish myself for being a whore. God was going to burn me in hell, I thought, and I might as well get used to it."

But burning wasn't enough punishment, she decided. She would get loaded on wine and, behind locked doors, experiment with cutting herself with a razor blade, little slicing cuts on her arms and the inside of her thighs, feeling the pain and watching the blood trickle from the cut. But when she sobered up, she was disgusted with herself. What kind of a dirty, demented masochist was she? Why did she do these things? She began to think of death. "The ultimate experience," someone called it. She borrowed a handgun from her boyfriend, telling him that someone in the dorm was taking things, that she needed to protect herself.

One evening Judy was out with her boyfriend and two other students, riding around aimlessly, sharing a joint and a few bottles of wine. For some reason, she said, she couldn't drink as much as she could formerly and was inclined to get very noisy and abusive. She had trouble remembering where she had been and what had happened. She did remember something of this particular evening. She had argued with her boyfriend, he had stopped the car and unceremoniously pushed her out on the street.

She didn't remember how she had gotten back to her room and didn't remember shooting herself. The 22-caliber bullet entered her head just above her right ear, but the angle was bad. She had lots of time to think after the operation, in which they had shaved her head, opened her skull and removed the bullet lodged at the edge of her brain. When they let her out, would she go back to more of the same routine of pills, pot, pop wine, and the pain—not only the self-induced physical pain, but the agony of the mind, the guilt, fear and self-loathing?

Judy was more than ready to talk about it when an assistant to the Dean of Women stopped in her room at the hospital and told her about her experience with chemical dependency. "Can you imagine—she had been a double dipper just like me. She knew how I felt. She was only a few years older than I was and had learned to stay clean and sober in AA. Now she was working for the Dean of Women, for God's sake!"

When Judy was released from the hospital, she spent the next six months in a different set of classrooms, attending AA meetings and discussion groups, talking with other young men and women who were chemically dependent.

"At first I thought I was too young to be an alcoholic, and I thought that to be one, you had to drink the high-proof stuff. Maybe if I was an alcoholic and was ill, I just had a light case of the disease. I just couldn't imagine living the rest of my life without drinking and having a little fun.

"The people in the groups I visited finally convinced me that I could be free—truly free—only by accepting and surrendering to the fact that I was powerless over alcohol, powerless over drugs and I needed help from my Higher Power. So I started out by buying this wig," Judy patted her black curls, "and making all the meetings I could. I was a little turned off by some of the older men and women in AA, but after listening to their stories, I would think, 'If they can do it, I can too,' and I'm staying sober one day at a time."

Judy had been re-admitted to college, on probation, sawing away on her viola. "I'd like to start an AA group at school," she told us. "I know at least a dozen people that need it, and I think the Dean is willing to go along with me."

Most of the youngsters (anyone under thirty is a "youngster" to me) coming into AA follow a pattern. Initially, they're suspicious and defensive, a little hostile. They suspect that AA is "establishment," with a long list of "do's" and "don't do's," run by and for the "squares" of the world. Then they learn that they have joined something which requires no pledge of sobriety, that has no rules, just suggestions. In AA no one disapproves of their past conduct or really gives a damn about it. The name of the game is "now."

Maggie got along famously with these young ones, accepting them freely and naturally as peers, but it was harder for me. I was still inclined to slip on a mask to suit the occasion, and I would find myself playing the role of a kindly old uncle, wise, benevolent and maybe just a little condescending. After all, they were just kids and I was an adult!

I was going to have an opportunity to change all that. Maggie and I were going to learn very shortly that our younger son, our baby boy, seemed to have a problem!

Stan wasn't exactly a baby. At twenty-five, he was a big, rangy man with an engaging grin and a neat head of hair, not too long (he paid six dollars to have it styled!). He kept his shoes spit-shined and was polite to his elders. Sometimes he would sulk and sit for hours, strumming his guitar, sullen, morose and uncommunicative. "All sugar or all shit," was Maggie's description of Stan.

His first marriage had been a disaster, a marriage contracted during his military service with a teenager who was three months pregnant. The baby wasn't his, Stan declared. He had married her because, "I felt sorry for her and the baby could have been mine if I had met her earlier." Everyone breathed a sigh of relief when her father arrived one day to whisk bride and baby back to her mother.

Granted an uncontested divorce, Stan shortly thereafter had married Nancy, a demure, outwardly submissive girl, whose shyness belied a tough, bookkeeper's mind with a real flair for budgeting. With her help, Stan had pulled himself out from under a mountain of debt. He bought a VW, made a down payment on a condominium and filled it with furniture— including two TV's, stereo and Stan's guitar. The walls were thin, but the neighbors didn't complain—they liked loud music, too. Stan and Nancy lived near us, but not too near, and would stop by two or three times a week, usually close to dinner time.

Stan worked shifts as a lab technician in a process plant nearby, and Nancy came for a visit one evening, when he was working the graveyard shift, and announced a little nervously that she wanted to talk about "your son." This sounded like trouble. She huddled in the corner of the couch, legs drawn up under her, and peering at us shyly, she told us in a halting voice that Stan had a problem.

"He wets the bed," Nancy explained, "just like a baby. He goes out to a bar and spends the evening drinking beer. When he does get home and falls asleep, he can't seem to wake up and he just lies there and wets the bed. Sometimes when he does get up, he's all confused and goes over and pees in the corner of the room on our new carpeting. The whole place smells, and he says that he can't remember doing it."

Both of our sons drank rather moderately, I thought. Along with the obligatory lectures on sex and sin, I had given them my philosophy on drinking. "It's fun, if you know how to handle it," I had explained. "You don't have to sneak around when you think you're ready to start drinking. Just tell me, and I'll have a drink with you. I want you guys to be gentlemen, and a gentleman knows how to hold his liquor. Learn at home. If you think you want to get drunk, get drunk at home and we'll take care of you. A few drinks and a hangover won't hurt you."

Pete, our older son, was more perceptive than his father. He observed that drinking might be fun, but that his mother and dad were thick-tongued, loud and argumentative when *they* drank. He drew his own conclusions and grew up to be a social drinker. He enjoyed a beer or two, a glass of wine maybe, sometimes a mixed drink, but the whole shmear of drinking didn't turn him on, wasn't important to him.

Stan was different. He began his love affair with alcohol while still a toddler, sitting on his great-grandmother's knee, sharing sips of beer with her and grabbing eagerly at her glass for more. When he hit his mid-teens, he bypassed my standing invitation for a drink at home and went out with a group that always included an older boy who knew an accommodating bar where you could buy a few cold six-packs with no questions asked. However, his early experimentations always seemed to end up with Stan clutching the rim of the john, upchucking his evening's intake. Maggie and I, discussing this unfortunate tendency over our regular pitcher of martinis, agreed that Stan would never have a problem with booze because he couldn't drink worth a damn!

Stan never outgrew his love for clowns. Clarabelle-the-Clown, a rag doll, was his constant companion when he was a toddler. Later, Maggie made him a clown suit, and he would stand patiently while his mother made up his face with white grease paint, sad eyes dripping tears and a wide, red, smiling mouth. His shyness disappeared like magic when he could tell jokes, make funny faces or do tricks.

I was usually too busy to spend time playing with my boys, but did discharge my parental responsibilities punctiliously with a steady input of lectures, rules, rewards and punishments. There was my talk, "Dangers of Premarital Sex," that included vivid accounts of venereal disease, how to avoid "getting caught" and the consequent moral responsibility of "making her an honest woman" if you did. My repertoire included a lecture on "Getting Ahead," which set forth the need for hard work and for setting goals, also how to make money and how to save it. Stan was particularly impressed when I once brought home a bonus check in five figures. That was the reward of my steady grinding away at my job and the reason for my long trips away from home, I told him, and it would provide a sizeable chunk of college-education money for him and his older brother. Naturally, I expected both of them to attend college and prepare themselves for careers, preferably in business, where the opportunities for money-making were greatest.

Pete, it was decided, was to become a pharmacist, later own his own store and parlay it into a chain like Walgreens. He obediently entered college, flunked a few of his pre-pharmaceutical courses and then did what he wanted to do—took a degree in Liberal Arts. He disappointed me with his talk of teaching (everyone knows that teachers are overworked and underpaid) or studying theology (a preacher in the family? Jee-zus!).

Stan seemed more malleable, but even under my reward-and-punishment system (you won't leave the house until you've done your homework and I've checked it!), he managed to flunk the tenth grade. Alarmed, we submitted him to a battery of tests administered by an industrial psychologist, who declared Stan to be an "underachiever" but with great potential in some type of job "working with people," once he was properly motivated. Proper motivation in my book called for harsher discipline of the kind found, I thought, in military schools. Unfortunately, or perhaps fortunately, his poor scholastic record wasn't good enough to qualify him for the respectable schools where we made application.

The lad always fell just short of success. He learned to swim and dive well in the Junior Red Cross program, but failed to show up at the pool on the day he was to be tested for his lifesaving certificate. An excellent, careful driver, he smashed up Maggie's car twice within two months after being licensed. He was a strong wrestler, but didn't get his high school letter because of a hernia. He seemed to have a personal little black cloud that followed him patiently from one failure to another.

Stan stumbled along in high school, a mediocre student, passing some courses, failing a few. But when he flunked his required course in physical education, it was time for sterner measures. He admitted to failing because he didn't attend the classes. He didn't attend classes because he couldn't get his gym locker open. He had forgotten the combination on the lock and was too embarrassed to ask for help.

Somehow, some way, I had to "make a man" out of Stan. I persuaded him that his future might lie in military service, possibly in the Navy where he would travel the world and get paid for it, could finish his high school work and even continue with college courses, or learn a high-paying vocation. I knew because I had read the recruiting posters and the literature carefully. I won, and delivered him into the hands of the Navy recruiter and breathed a sigh of relief. Okay, Navy, you do it —the ball is in your court!

He liked the Navy and made a handsome sailor, with his wide shoulders and slim hips tightly encased in Navy blues, his cocky white hat perched perilously over one eye. He had found himself a new clown suit, but his black cloud pursued him doggedly: His training as an underwater specialist was terminated when his ear drum ruptured in the training tank. Lacking his high school diploma, he wasn't qualified for other specialty schools and ended up as a deck hand and later as a bosun's mate aboard a repair ship stationed on the East Coast.

Here he met and married his first wife, but the Navy promptly whisked him away on a training cruise in the Mediterranean. Our boy didn't like it. He was lonely, maybe a little scared, and life aboard ship was dull and monotonous. Our next word of Stan came from his new wife. "Stan's back here in the Navy hospital in the psycho ward," she told us, sobbing into the phone. "He says he just sort of went crazy on the ship, and they flew him back here for treatment."

Following tests and interviews with a psychiatrist, the Navy granted Stan a medical discharge. He "did not respond adequately under stress situations and is relieved from further active duty for the good of the service." Meaning, "We give up—here's your ball back—your odd-ball."

He had taken several jobs but had quit them, always for good and substantial reasons, according to Stan. Now that he was married to Nancy, he had settled down and talked blithely about his opportunities for advancement and company-paid training programs available to him.

But now he was wetting the bed.

Nancy was worried and uncertain; she knew of Stan's stay in the psycho ward. Did we think that possibly this was a recurrence of whatever it was that had driven him over the edge before? She burst into tears.

Maggie has a keen, perceptive mind and a great detective sense. She detected something that Nancy had mentioned in her recital—she detected alcohol. She questioned Nancy gently.

"How much does Stan drink?"

Nancy wasn't sure. "Well, at home, maybe a case or two of beer a week. He likes mixed drinks too. Sometimes he drinks a shot and a beer, but it's mostly beer." She had no idea of how much he drank in bars, but he was there three or four nights a week. Sometimes he stopped, she thought, at his favorite hangout for a beer or two on his way to work.

"How does he drink? Does he take a drink before you go out together? Does he like to get high?" Maggie continued her questioning.

Nancy said that he usually put away two or three cans of beer fast when he came home from work, just to relieve his thirst built up from a hard day of slaving over the test tubes. Then he slowed down, kept a beer open and handy while he played his guitar or turned on TV. Yes, they always had a drink before they went out to a party, and Stan usually had a couple. Sure, he liked to go out with friends that drank heavily, and the "boys" would end up getting pretty high. But that was the way men were—they drank because they were *men*.

The pattern of Maggie's questions was more than just motherly concern. She was checking the recognition points of an alcoholic, the identifying marks described by Dick Heilman in one of his Hazelden lectures. She was interested not only in how much or how often Stan drank, but more importantly, *how* did he use his drinking? Was he preoccupied with the use of alcohol—had he fallen in love with the effect, did he look forward with anticipation to the time of the next use?

"Does he ever drink alone?"

Nancy wasn't sure about what Stan did away from home, but when he arrived at the house, he had the door of the refrigerator open in a minute and could care less whether she joined him or not. Nancy would take a drink, but just to be sociable, just because everyone else was drinking.

"Does he ever get drunk when he hadn't planned to, maybe didn't even want to?"

"Sometimes," Nancy admitted, "but he always apologizes the next day—after he has a beer or two for his hangover. He thinks he's a little run-down and that the drinks hit him harder because of his condition."

"Does he ever seem concerned that he might run out of beer?"

"Oh, sure. He always keeps a full case in the basement and a half-dozen cold ones in the fridge. If anyone is coming over for the evening, he'll drive out to pick up a few extra six-packs. Then he makes sure that we always have some hard stuff around—rum, gin and whiskey—just in case someone wants a straight shot or a mixed drink."

"Does he keep anything hidden in the house?"

"I don't think so, but I've never looked," Nancy confessed.

"Does he drink much when he doesn't feel good, when he has a cold, for example?"

"I guess so. He'll drink a shot and a beer or a hot lemonade with whiskey in it. He says it helps him sweat it out. He says he learned that from you!" Nancy glanced at me, accusingly.

She was right—it *was* my standard treatment.

Maggie went on, "Does Stan seem to hold it better now than he used to? Does he drink more without showing it, maybe brag about his capacity?"

"Yeah, he says that he can drink more than anyone in the block, and he can really put it away when he wants to. I've seen him go through a case on his day off, then drink a lot more when we go out. He doesn't do that all the time, though," Nancy said.

"Does he ever forget what happened during his drinking—can't remember where he was, what he said, what he did?"

"Yes, he does, and then he says I'm lying when I tell him what he did. And he *never* remembers wetting the bed!" Her eyes filled with tears. "Why would he do a thing like that?"

"Honey," Maggie answered gently, "It looks like Stan might have the same illness that I have. I think maybe he has a problem with alcohol. He's sick."

Now the tears ran down Nancy's cheeks. "He can't be an alcoholic, Maggie! He doesn't drink that much hard stuff—just mostly beer. And he's too young—he's only twenty-five! He may drink a little too much but he's not that bad, not nearly as bad as you were!" Nancy bit her lip, conscience-stricken. "I'm sorry. I didn't mean it that way, but you know—he's not that bad!"

"That's all right, Nancy," Maggie said soothingly, "I know I was a mess. And I don't know for certain that Stan's an alcoholic. He has to decide that for himself."

"Anyway, this is one thing that Stan seems to be succeeding in," I thought, "He's becoming an alcoholic. He didn't plan to be one, didn't drink to become one, but it sure as hell sounds like he is one!" I didn't voice this judgment.

"If he is an alcoholic, what can you do about it?" demanded Nancy. "Can you send him to Hazelden or someplace or put him in AA? Can he be cured like you are, Maggie?"

We talked for another hour or so, and Nancy went home with some facts and suggestions spinning in her head. We couldn't force AA down Stan's throat or order him to a treatment center. Even if he quit drinking, he wouldn't be cured. The disease could be arrested but not cured. Meanwhile, we had a few practical suggestions. Don't nag him about his drinking. Walk away from any family fights he might try to start. Put rubber sheets on the bed. Don't cover for him if he's too hung over to make it to work. Most important—join Al-Anon. I would take her to meetings, introduce her to some girls in her age bracket, and she could hear what they might have to tell her. She would feel better.

I reckoned without considering her cash-register mind and her pride. Al-Anon definitely did *not* make her feel better, she announced after her second meeting. She felt worse! Those women just sat there, she said, talking about God and mouthing off about "Easy Does It," "One Day at a Time," that she had to learn to detach-with-love, and worst of all, they were telling her that she was sick, too! Was she just supposed to sit around and watch Stan drink up all the money they had saved, get fired, lose their car and maybe even lose their beautiful condominium with all their nice things?

"I just don't think it's fair!" she burst out, "We're saving money now, I'm going to start college in the fall, and then I want a baby! Stan won't even *talk* about having a baby—he just clams up. It just isn't fair that I have to sit around watching him swilling beer and I have to keep working until he does whatever it is he's supposed to do before he'll ask for help!"

"Come on, Nancy," I encouraged her, "Give Al-Anon a fair shake. Do like they ask you to: attend at least a half-dozen meetings before you make a decision. Look—if I can get help from Al-Anon after eight or so years of living with a compulsive drinker, you could do wonders for yourself and help Stan, too."

"Yes, but it was different with you—Maggie was already sober when you first went to Al-Anon," Nancy wailed, "and it's not so damn easy when somebody's still drinking! He's your son, and if you and Maggie are so damned smart, why don't you do something? Are you just gonna let him get worse and worse and worse and ..." her voice shook, and she began to cry.

Stan had upset her applecart, and she could see nothing but an uncertain future of work to support a drunken husband— no college, no baby, maybe even no house. It's hard enough to explain to an angry man that it's his own self-will that has him so frustrated and that he's projecting a future filled with problems—a future that he can't change. Trying to get through to an immature, frightened young woman who hadn't seen her twenty-first birthday was something else again. I could identify with Nancy—I knew how she felt inside—but Nancy couldn't identify with me. I was still the father figure, a man who was supposed to know how to deal with problems, a father whose kid was hurt and I was somehow supposed to make him well.

No more Al-Anon for her, Nancy declared firmly. She would stay with Stan, change the sheets daily, if necessary, but she was too tired after riding a bus to and from work, fixing dinner, cleaning house, just too tired to go to meetings. Besides, she was going to start her college courses, come hell or high water.

They continued to stop by the house, Nancy silent and sullen, Stan talking gaily and incessantly about every subject under the sun except how he felt inside. He would sit on the edge of his chair, outwardly calm with his legs crossed, and that leg on top would give him away—it shook like a feather dancing in the breeze. His hand trembled when he lit a cigarette. After a few minutes, he would pull Nancy to her feet. "Come on, Nancy, we gotta get home."

Maggie asked God for help and carried out His will as she understood it. From her wide circle of friends in AA, she selected Jerry as someone Stan might identify with and possibly trust. He was a tall, skinny guy with a gimpy leg, long black hair, intense eyes under heavy black eyebrows, a little hesitant in his speech but full of gratitude for his two years of sobriety. He was a few years older than Stan, married, with no children. He, too, was a high-school dropout, had spent time in the service and couldn't seem to find himself after his release. Jerry worked in the daytime and attended school at night with the help of the GI Bill. When and if Stan asked for help, Jerry might prove to be the sponsor in AA who could give him a helping hand. Jerry and his wife came to our house one evening, and we discussed Stan's problem as we saw it. It's not easy to detach and to view the illness of alcoholism objectively, particularly when it's your own kid that's hung up so badly. We agreed that Stan probably wasn't ready yet, but when he was, would Jerry make a Twelfth Step call? He would be delighted to.

Twelfth Stepping—carrying the message to others—is the key to continuing sobriety, the AA's declare. I once asked Scotty, Maggie's unofficial sponsor, about his percentage of success in Twelfth Step work.

"I never had a failure," Scotty grinned. Noting my look of disbelief, he explained, "Not every man I talk to agrees to try AA, and of those that do, some won't make the program. But I come away from every call remembering what it was like when I was drinking and how it is now. I need to be reminded. Those guys that attend a few meetings and don't come back— hell, I remember what that's like, too. I don't ever want to forget. The ones that stick and find sobriety—I take no personal credit for them. I've just been carrying out God's will as best I can, and that makes me feel good inside. You gotta give it away if you want to keep it, Jack. I'm supposed to carry the message, not stuff it down someone's throat, and as long as I do that, I'll never have a failure."

We had a Twelfth Step call set up by a potential AA sponsor for Stan, so what comes next? Where do we go from here? Asking God for guidance seemed like a logical approach. It's a little tricky for beginners like me to tap into God's line, but there's a test for the solutions that come to mind, seemingly inspired. The test is this: God's will or mine? My answers didn't seem to pass the test, but Maggie came up with an idea that she should do a little seed-planting. As a gardener, Maggie is cursed with a "black thumb." Plants just droop, blacken and die when she does the planting. The seed-planting she had in mind this time was to be different. She was going to talk to Stan about her experiences as a practicing alcoholic, how she felt and how AA had helped her maintain her sobriety —no more than that. All she hoped to do was to plant a seed of hope which might germinate in his mind.

Stan was working the graveyard shift again, and one evening Maggie called him at work. She was at loose ends, she said, and wondered if tonight would be a good time for a tour of his lab and the plant—he had offered to show her around, but for one reason or another she had never taken him up on the offer.

He was alone, bored and glad to see her. He led her through the dark, echoing reaches of the plant, pointing out the valves that he opened and closed, the gauges to be read, the samples to be taken. He then efficiently ran a battery of tests for her edification. It was a responsible job, he told her, but without much future in it, no real challenge, and the pay raises came too slowly. His boss didn't like him, he confided, and he was thinking about changing jobs, finding something where he would be appreciated and the money was better.

They settled down for a cup of coffee and a cigarette. "You know, Stan," Maggie began, "I've never told you what it was like with me when I was drinking," and she gave him a tour of her personal hell, pointing out the valves she had closed on the stream of reality, the gauges of happiness that she had misread and the tests she had run, faking the results, to measure her self-worth. She talked about her Hazelden experiences, the importance of AA to her and of her new friends.

"I don't know much about your drinking," she said, "and I don't want to know about it. What, when, why and where you drink is your personal business. But maybe some evening when you have the time, you might like to run a few tests for yourself. This copy of 'Who, Me?' can give you an insight as to whether or not alcohol is a problem for you. This booklet, 'Young People in AA,' has some stories about men and women in your age bracket who were hung up on alcohol or drugs and what they did about it. And last, here's a card with a name and a couple of phone numbers. Jerry is a little older than you are, is married. If you ever want to talk to someone about alcoholism, he'll meet you any time and tell you how it was with him. I think you might like him."

Stan casually tossed the pamphlets and card into an open drawer, thanked Maggie coolly and, very much the dutiful son, escorted her to her car. Nothing else.

Nothing happened during the first week following Maggie's visit. Nothing happened the second week or the third. But early one evening in the fourth week, Stan phoned. "Hey, Mom, you know that card with the name of the guy you thought I might like? I've lost it. Could you find his name and phone number for me?"

Stan was ready. He told us later that had Maggie been anyone but his mother, he would have thrown her out of the lab. He had been white-hot with anger and resentment that anyone—particularly his own mother—thought that *he* had a drinking problem! He had seethed and fumed, hidden the pamphlets in a file of old lab reports and stuck the card in his pocket. Then later, he had dug the pamphlets out of the file and took the "Who, Me?" test. He had qualified as an alcoholic all right, he told us, even though he had cheated on a few questions. He had read the ten little stories in "Young People and AA" and had felt a kinship with several of the authors. Then he tore up the pamphlets into tiny pieces. Goddammit— there wasn't anything wrong with him—he could quit any time he wanted to! But could he? Maggie's seed had germinated and was growing. What was happening? Well, he hadn't lost his job, but the boss was making noises like a fire-cracker fizzing—he was going to get canned, sure as hell. Nancy was pissed off at him and talking about a separation, maybe a divorce. He really couldn't blame her—changing pee-stained sheets was a bit much. He was drinking too much, he knew it, and even brought beer to the lab sometimes when he felt rotten. He was letting everyone down again, just the way he had in the past. He was a failure, and there didn't seem to be any way out, unless maybe this guy—the guy whose name was on that card—could tell him what to do.

Maggie had Jerry's phone number handy, and he was at the lab within fifteen minutes after getting Stan's call. Maggie was right: Stan did like Jerry. Here was a guy—maybe the first one he had ever met—who seemed to know just what he was thinking! "He crawled right inside my head," Stan marveled.

Since Jerry worked days, Stan walked into his first AA meeting the next morning by himself. He was scared when he opened the door down at the union hall, but his fear didn't last. "I felt that for the first time in my life I had found a home. There was no horseshit, no one gave me hell, preached a sermon or patted me on the head. The guy that spoke could have been me—he told my story. I cried and was ashamed of crying, but no one laughed at me. They were just glad that I had come and asked me to come back."

Our son took to AA as naturally as a duck takes to water. He listened and learned, attended six or seven meetings each week. He selected a second sponsor, a tough ex-con who told him in no uncertain terms, "Shut up—just keep your mouth shut and your ears open and listen, dummy!"

Stan, who had been a cocky boy, was now learning how to be a humble man. He traveled with a small group that made the meetings in the institutions—the workhouse, the reformatories and one of the state prisons. He sailed around on a pink cloud of sobriety, joined two AA groups and was put to work making the coffee, emptying ash trays and arranging folding chairs. He was happy, he was sober and he was making new friends who accepted and liked him no matter what he had done in the past. Life was great, just great!

Nancy thought that life was great, too, until the newness of a sober husband began to wear a little thin. She was still lonely and seemingly rather unimportant to Stan. He wasn't spending his evenings in the bars, there was room for milk in the refrigerator now that the beer was gone, the rubber sheet could be stored and the bed linen changed just once a week. But now he was out to all hours with "those AA guys." Stan couldn't very well take her with him to the AA meetings in the institutions, and the time of the evening meetings conflicted with her college classes. He had brought several of his AA buddies and their wives over to the house, but she wasn't particularly fond of them. All they ever wanted to do, she thought, was just talk about AA! Stan seemed more open and honest with her when they did get a chance to talk, but he still didn't want to discuss her ideas about having a family.

They were together again, but they were drifting apart. She wanted more from life than she had found in the past. She wanted a college degree, an executive-type job, plenty of money in the bank and a baby. Stan, she felt, didn't seem to need or want her or care about her needs. He just was content with his newfound sobriety and anxious to get away from her, to run around the country to a bunch of those damn AA meetings. She broached the subject of divorce, and Stan, surprisingly agreeable, told her that she was free to get one. He hoped she would stay with him and give them both a chance to get their feelings sorted out, but if she felt that their marriage had been a mistake, call a lawyer.

The edges of Stan's pretty pink cloud of sobriety were beginning to fray a bit, and we could see that he was noticeably edgy and morose, and the flutter had returned to his crossed leg. He was full of AA stories about the meetings he was attending and the problems others were having in making the program. Although he talked AA glibly, he wasn't leveling, at least not with us. He talked about the divorce, but it was surface conversation. It was apparent that he was deeply disturbed and was maintaining a brave front to cover his distress.

Maggie and I had a little chat one Sunday morning after Nancy and Stan had shared brunch with us and left. Stan had been withdrawn and impatient to get away. "I've talked to Jerry and several of Stan's friends," Maggie began, "and we agree that he's on a dry drunk. He's sober but not happily sober. He's still conning, still wearing his clown face. Now he's playing the role of an alcoholic who is successfully recovering."

"Are you taking his inventory?" I asked.

"Maybe," Maggie responded. "But one of these days he's going to take that first drink if he doesn't stop his stinkin' thinkin'. Physically he's doing all the right things: He makes a lot of meetings, spends most of his free time in AA bull sessions, keeps active. In spite of all this, he hasn't learned to be honest. He hasn't found a sense of self-worth. Underneath all his big talk, he still views himself as a born loser. The fact that Nancy has asked for a divorce just confirms it in his mind. He's changed on the surface, but not inside."

I knew more was coming. "So?" I asked.

"He's still expecting perfection in himself and others," Maggie continued. "Have you noticed that he's becoming a little critical of Jerry and Big Joe?" Big Joe was Stan's second sponsor, the hard-nosed ex-con who was active in the institutional meetings.

"But if he keeps active and makes a lot of meetings, don't you think he'll shape up?" I asked. "You know—'Keep Coming Back.'"

"It's possible," Maggie admitted, "but I'm wondering how Stan would feel about a visit to Hazelden. They keep pounding away at honesty and responsibility. It's sort of like a cram course in AA, where you work at it for almost twenty-four hours a day with no distractions and no excuses or alibis accepted." Maggie's eyes clouded as she remembered. "I'll never forget Hal the Cobra and his damn radar!"

Stan agreed that he was on a dry drunk, once the symptoms were laid out for him to examine, and yes, he would like very much to spend some time at Hazelden. He told us ruefully, "This divorce thing—I want it and I don't want it. It hurts me inside. I guess I still want things to go my way, but I'm not sure what direction that is."

He returned after a four-week stay at Hazelden considerably subdued but with an air of confidence. He could talk more easily about himself, acknowledged and accepted his limitations and the limitations of those around him. He didn't have that aura of serenity that I had seen about Maggie when she had returned, but certainly he had his head screwed on in the right direction. His knee shake had disappeared, the bravado was gone, and he was not only sober but happily sober. He had the tools in hand to face and deal with reality: Now it was up to him, he said, to do just that, one day at a time.

There are thousands of Stans in AA, finding their way to freedom by surrendering. Maybe our Stan still has some of the con man left to deal with, but Maggie and I think he'll work it out. We do our damndest to give him all the room and the time he needs to find his own way, with the help of his Higher Power.

# 14

## Keep Your Balance Properly

"The great art of riding, as I was saying, is — to keep your balance properly. Like this you know —" He let go the bridle and stretched out both of his arms to show Alice what he meant, and this time, he fell flat on his back, right under the horse's feet.

The doctors say that as we recover from an illness, there's the ever-present possibility of a relapse. There's a definition of alcoholism furnished by the American Medical Association which includes a statement that this disease is "characterized by a tendency to relapse." Check. She knows — and you and I had better learn — that she can "fall off the wagon," "backslide" or "tumble from Grace." The shorthand language of AA calls it a "slip." The ugly fact is that she's back to the bottle, popping pills, or both, and nine times out of ten, there is a knurd reaction, which ranges from discouragement and confusion to depression, anger or bitterness. Double check.

Charles W. Crewe, former chief therapist of continuation programs at Hazelden, in "A Look at Relapse," looks at the mechanics of recovery as a way to assess the *reasons* for relapse. A reasonable theory of alcoholism, he says, is that it's a learned, inadequate response to living, and it's been so well learned that the attitudes and responses are never unlearned. The disease is arrested by learning an entire new set of attitudes based on the AA Twelve Steps. Continued sobriety seems to depend on keeping the new attitudes strongly reinforced by a number of disciplines to prevent the re-emergence of the old attitudes. There are those who argue that a relapse is simply a highfalutin' copout, that the alcoholic drinks again because he wants the drink more than he wants to stay sober. Not true, says Crewe, because this implies that will power is the controlling factor, and his experience indicates that the person who has been sober must be temporarily insane to return to the hell of drinking. He feels that a person relapses "because he was not willing to do *everything* necessary for him to stay sober." Or, the alcoholic became too cocky, too sure of himself or too complacent. Things seemed to be going great, so he lowered his guard. Then came the dry drunk, a reversion to the AA "stinkin' thinkin'."

The key word is "happy," R. J. Solberg declares in *The Dry Drunk Syndrome*. Solberg, formerly supervisor of the treatment program at Hazelden, defines a dry drunk as an alcoholic who is sober, but not happy. He's "dry" because he isn't drinking, but "drunk" in that he hasn't changed his abnormal attitudes and behavior that he had learned in his boozing days.

Tim drove a truck, and Florence kept house, but these were sidelines to their main vocation of keeping an almost perpetual open house for AA's that congregated for coffee and conversation. Both were arrested alcoholics, and AA talk was the breath of life for them. Their five children, stair-stepping from sixteen down to four, accepted these conversations as calmly as they accepted brushing their teeth, but missed very little, including references to dry drunks.

According to Florence, early one morning before the AA invasion she was busy in the kitchen and heard four-year-old

Petey singing softly to himself in his room. She stopped her work for a moment to listen.

"Stinkin' thinkin' leads to drinkin'," Petey caroled, "Stinkin' thinkin' leads to drinkin'."

"Petey knows," Florence laughed, "and we listen to him!"

Solberg equates "stinkin' thinkin'" to intoxication without alcohol. Behavior traits include tense impatience, rigid judgments (it's either all good or all bad), overconfidence and just plain childish irrationality. These are the symptoms for the recovering alcoholic to learn and recognize in her own behavior.

Maggie's battered green stenographer's notebook was filled with hints on maintaining a happy sobriety, a condition she called "sobrenity"—the combination of sobriety and serenity. One such hint was Dr. Heilman's comment on the learned urge, the "tickle behind the eyeballs" that would come and go, and the need to vocalize the urge when it came. It shook me when Maggie once responded to my inquiry as to her preference in drinks with, "I'd like a double martini, but I'll settle for a Coke."

There were notes on the three bugaboos to "sobrenity," the "no-no's" of tension, hunger and exhaustion, which must be avoided whenever possible. Maggie kept emergency rations on hand for those times when a regular meal had to be postponed, carrying candy bars in her purse and seeing that the refrigerator was stocked with ice cream and more candy. In the past, alcohol had been her source of calories; now it was sweets.

When she felt that she was becoming overtired, she had learned to say "stop" and to pamper herself by getting all the rest she felt she needed. When an emergency arose, she consciously leaned on God's strength, following the AA maxim, "Let Go and Let God." She made a determined effort to avoid situations that engendered tension but, when this wasn't possible, she employed another AA maxim, "Easy Does It," as an aid to relaxation.

Maggie had never been big on cake, pie, ice cream and candy—they didn't mix well with drinks—but sober she became an ice cream and chocolate freak. Our freezer groaned under the load of French vanilla, chocolate ripple and the "Week's Special" from our friendly Baskin and Robbins store, where girls with forearms of steel cheerfully hand-packed half-gallons for Maggie and enticed her with those extras of thick chocolate syrup, butterscotch topping and synthetic whipped cream. If ice cream had been addictive, Maggie would have acquired a brand new set of problems.

She had also developed a near-passion for chocolate bars, and as she had once bought vodka in half-gallon bottles, she now bought big half-pound chocolate bars, with and without nuts, and six-packs of small bars to be tucked in her purse for use as necessary.

Since she was still underweight, the calorie-packed candy and ice cream did little more than add a few pounds where they were most needed, but this stage of her recovery was almost my undoing. I "helped" her as I had in the past, but rather than sharing a drink, we now shared sundaes and candy bars. My waist line bulged. I had two extra chins to shave in the morning and a fresh set of adolescent pimples to contend with. Maggie kept her hunger pangs under control and as for me, I went on the grapefruit diet.

Before Maggie returned from Hazelden, the staff made certain that she had a sponsor in AA. If she hadn't had one, an experienced woman in AA would have been found for her. Hazelden had learned from experience that between eighty and ninety percent of the repeaters treated for relapses reported one of the following: no attendance at AA meetings; brief attendance only; or dropping AA activities entirely. They felt that they could get along without AA.

My wife sure as hell didn't want to be a repeater, and she jumped into AA activities with enthusiasm. She attended regular meetings and joined a women's discussion group. She made the coffee and emptied the ash trays, served as group chairman when asked, made her Twelfth Step calls and callused her ear with phone calls to and from other AA's. As a volunteer worker in the women's alcoholic ward of a nearby hospital, Maggie had the opportunity to talk at length with the patients, some of them relapsed after long or short periods of sobriety. Aside from those who had never fully accepted their alcoholism, she found that those who had found sobriety and had been in the AA program, seemingly had failed in one or more of the three areas of the Twelve Steps. They had:

a. Lost faith, turned from God as they knew Him, taken back their will;

b. Failed to "clean house" daily;

c. Either attended AA meetings sporadically or dropped out of the progam altogether.

In *Barriers Against Recovery*, John O. Grimmett, Ph.D., director of the alcoholic rehabilitation program at the Salt Lake City VA Hospital, discusses five sets of circumstances that may lead to relapse:

There's the "Paralysis of Loneliness," manifest in such symptoms as depression, hopelessness, boredom and apathy. The relationships of the alcoholic are superficial—she (or he) hasn't learned how to express genuine feeling or affection toward others, and the "give and take" is virtually all "take." Lacking such honest relationships, the alcoholic never learns to like herself. "Poor me" leads to a "pity party," and unless the alcoholic can grow emotionally, the next step is to take a drink.

The "Perfectionist-Failure Bind" comes when the recovering alcoholic sets unrealistic goals because of her perfectionism, with built-in failure as the almost inevitable result. She can't make a mistake or be human, and neither can those around her. The family suffers as the alcoholic projects her perfectionism onto husband, children or parents. Those worthy parties are expected to perform at her level, and when they don't, she becomes bitter, angry, disillusioned and resentful. Now she has the excuse to take a drink.

"Tunnel Vision Dilemma" forces the alcoholic to view people and problems through a dark tunnel with just a peephole at the end. Brushing aside most aspects of a problem, she makes her decisions with incomplete information in an impulsive, short-sighted manner. She sees only what she wants to see, and her poor judgments simply add to her continuing frustration or failure. The answer, she concludes, is to take a drink.

A related aspect is the "Either/Or Myth," which describes the rigid thinking based on an either/or, black/white, go/no go approach to problem solving. Since our world is realistically complicated, the alcoholic is confused and helpless. There aren't any easy answers to be found in a simple either/or decision. Because of her failures in problem solving, she loses what little self-confidence she has gained and becomes sensitive to criticism. She rejects the rules of society, alienates friends and family and reacts with resentment, hostility, distrust and withdrawal. So she takes a drink.

Grimmett cites Paul Watzlawick's tape-book, *An Anthology of Human Communication,* in explaining the "Double Bind" in relation to marital and family relationships. A double bind is simply two opposing forces working on the alcoholic. She wants help and advice from others, but only under her own set of terms and conditions, and rejects the advice when it's given. She wants to live within a structured marriage, but fights strongly against it. She wants others to accept alcoholism as an illness, but refuses to accept her own alcoholism. She wants to cry for help, but disguises the cry in an irrational, often insane act. The tensions and anxieties built up by double binds can be relieved either through changing attitudes or a relapse.

Sometimes the relapse comes suddenly, inexplicably, seemingly from a very insignificant event. Maggie told of one such happening on her return from a tour of duty in the Women's Alcoholic Ward at the hospital. "We had a new admission today, a woman who had relapsed after almost eight years of sobriety. When she was settled in, I stopped by her bed to talk with her. 'What happened?' I asked. She looked at me helplessly with the tears rolling down her cheeks, 'It was my big toe. I had this awful ingrown toenail, you see ... and I took a drink.'"

Not every relapse comes as the seeming result of ingrown toenails, as Vera-the-Skinny-Dipper's experience pointed up. She had found only so-so sobriety in her first encounters with Alcoholics Anonymous and was still toting a load of guilt and fear when Maggie talked to her about what she had discovered in her stay at Hazelden. Vera's experiences paralleled Maggie's in many ways; she had tried the various avenues to sobriety through the medical and psychiatric routes, "will power," controlled drinking, the geographic cure, her church and AA—but she sobered up only to slip. Perhaps Vera might respond to the multidisciplinary approach used at Hazelden, Maggie suggested—respond honestly in an atmosphere free of day-to-day problems, in association with other women who were learning to admit their powerlessness over alcohol.

Vera thought that just might be the ticket, and her letters from Hazelden reflected her enthusiasm and growing self-confidence. She came home gung ho, with determination to live life just one day at a time, to work her Twelve Steps and to get into AA with both feet, just as she had been taught. She also came home to a major test of her sobriety.

One of her teen-age sons had experimented with drugs, including LSD, and was experiencing flashbacks from a "bad trip." He was a thoroughly confused, mixed-up kid in severe need of help. Vera and Mac (now in Al-Anon) were better able than many parents to cope with a problem of chemical dependency, and after a short stay in a hospital, their son had his turn at Hazelden. Although further treatment was recommended, he came home only to slide gradually away from AA and to return to the drug scene, with the help of a friendly pusher that serviced the high-school set.

The tensions were too much for Vera to handle, and her thinkin' turned stinkin' with a resultant slip. Back came the guilt, the fear, the uncertainty, the resentments and the pity parties. Gamely, she sobered up, insisted that she wanted nothing but "tough love" from Maggie and her friends in AA, and stayed sober—for a while. Some weeks later she attended a church conference, locked herself in her hotel room and got royally smashed. It was bad, Mac reported, but could have been worse. "At least she stayed the hell out of the hotel pool," he said.

As Vera continued to yo-yo between sobriety and compulsive drinking, Maggie tried to convince her that a return trip to Hazelden was in order, so that she might find what she had missed during her first stay, but the bane of the alcoholic, false pride, stood in her way. She just couldn't go back and face "them," she insisted. As her thinking changed under the influence of alcohol, she looked for and found a new sponsor. She was tired of Maggie's brand of "tough love."

However, near the end of another binge, she called Maggie and asked to be taken to a newly-opened ward for alcoholics in a nearby hospital. They could help her pull herself together, she felt, because she had been out there a few times as a volunteer and liked their approach. She phoned Maggie after a few days of detoxification and told her about the treatment. It was a short one, she explained, with daily meetings with the counselor, AA meetings in the ward, a carefully controlled diet and a regular exercise period. The program was still new and she was "helping out," she said. Would Maggie and Dottie please come to see her?

They found her bright-eyed and bushy-tailed, sitting at a desk, busily engaged with a pad of paper and a pencil. "I'm helping them work out new schedules," she announced. "Maggie, I want you to get me a set of the Hazelden lecture tapes—the patients aren't getting enough background information on alcoholism and drug dependency. I'm trying to get them to have regular therapy sessions, too. And can you believe—the hospital has been furnishing these women with a mouthwash that has *alcohol* in it? One of the gals here stashed several bottles away and then hung one on. They really need help here!"

Her stay was certainly worthwhile to the fledgling hospital program, but they couldn't produce the key to continuing sobriety for Vera. She continued her ding-dong periods of sobriety terminated with a few days or weeks of drinking for almost two years. Recently she wrote us, "I'm sober and I'm happy. I'm finally doing what I've been told to do—I'm living just twenty-four hours at a time, honestly accepting the fact that I'm an alcoholic."

I haven't heard from Mac, but I'm sure he's recovering from his obsession about hotel swimming pools—at least, for this particular twenty-four hours!

The subject of relapse wasn't uncommon at our stag meetings, and it wasn't unusual to hear a report of a slip, often only one or two drinks, then a call for help to a friend or sponsor in AA, and a return to continuing sobriety. In other instances, the relapse brought forth in the recovering alcoholic a gushing flood of guilt, defeat, and a hopelessness unmatched by any other tide of human emotion. Her self-esteem withered like a freshly planted flower in the hot sun and shame scalded her soul. Too often, the knurds in the family reflected her emotions with mirror accuracy.

Sully-the-Psychologist was delighted and grateful when wife Clara finally bottomed out and sought help from Alcoholics Anonymous. She responded wholeheartedly to the program and, after several months, seemed contented and happy in her newfound sobriety. Sully continued to attend our stag group meetings for a month or two, but then quit coming.

One evening he reappeared, white-lipped and holding himself under control with visible effort. Clara had slipped—not only slipped, but literally slid, smashing the family station wagon through one of the plate glass display windows of a neighborhood supermarket, he told us. The accident occurred only two doors away from the local police station, and the gendarmes had arrived moments later to pick his wife from the debris of a toppled mountain of Heinz pickle jars. She was scratched a bit, but not even the pungent aroma of pickle brine could cover the odor of booze. After due process of law, the police deposited Clara in the drunk tank and called Sully.

"They wanted me to post bond and take her home," Sully said, "but she wouldn't budge. She just sat there stony-faced, shaking her head back and forth. 'I could have killed some-body,' she kept repeating, and she wanted to be put away where she couldn't hurt anyone. She spent the night in jail and was sentenced the next day to thirty days in the workhouse. The judge was willing to suspend the sentence, but she insisted that she deserved to be punished and had to serve her time.

"She had been hitting the bottle hard for a week or so, and without detoxification she convulsed in the workhouse. The matron had her transferred to a hospital, where she was properly detoxified, then taken over to the women's alcoholic ward. But during the night she sneaked out of bed, stole a set of keys and unlocked a supply room, apparently looking for something to drink. There was a brown bottle that had the right shape, and Clara opened it and took a drink. It was some kind of acid, and she burned her mouth, throat and stomach. She's going to make it, I guess ..."

Sully's voice trailed off to a whisper. "She had been doing so well. We had settled down to normal around the house, and I really thought she had herself under control. I keep wondering if it was something that I said or did that set her off. I don't know what to do—she's crazy, I think. Maybe you guys have an idea."

"Has she talked to her sponsor or anyone from AA?" Nick inquired.

"She won't talk to me, she won't talk to her sponsor. She just says that the only way she can stay sober is behind bars. She *wants* to be punished," Sully replied dejectedly.

"Maybe she would talk to Mary," Nick suggested. "She's put damn near everything in her stomach at one time or another. Maybe they're on the same wave length. I think Mary would be glad to visit her, but let me phone her—I've quit making her decisions."

Sully was agreeable, and Nick left to find a phone. Mean-while, Health-Policy Harry pulled up a chair beside Sully. "Let's talk about you for a minute or two. I sort of think maybe you're having a relapse, too. You said that you must have done something to set her off. Sully, I think you're packing a load of guilt on your back again. I think you're depressed, confused and disappointed because Clara's slipped and not living up to your standard of sobriety for her. Dammit, it's *her* problem! But you did one thing right—you came to this meeting, where you can talk it out. You can't solve Clara's problem, but you can do something about yours, if you'll get off your ass and quit feeling so sorry for yourself. Okay, Sully?"

Nick returned with the expected word that Mary would be happy to talk with Clara and would try to see her in the morning. Clara was receptive, and it didn't take Mary too long to convince her that she had an alternative—that treatment in a rehabilitation center in the next state would be preferable to a stay in the workhouse or the state funny farm.

Sully now made our meetings with regularity and phoned several of us when he felt low. Clara seemed to have a good attitude, he said, and was feeling better about herself. Sully's attitude improved, too. He looked visibly better each week. But after four weeks, he came into our meeting, glum and dejected. Clara had relapsed in the treatment center!

"She likes nice things," he told us, "and I like to buy them for her. Before she left, I picked up a new nightgown and negligee for her, a couple of sweaters and a big bottle of *My Sin*—her favorite perfume. When I phoned her after her first week, she asked for another bottle of perfume—she said that some of the other women liked the scent and she'd given most of the bottle away. So, what-the-hell—I sent her another— she likes to smell nice, and if she wanted everyone in the place to smell good, too, that was okay with me. Then yesterday, I got this call from her counselor ..."

"Let me tell you what she did," Nick interrupted, "she *drank* the damn stuff!"

"Yeah, she drank the perfume—all three bottles." Sully confirmed. "The counselor said it was their first experience with a real perfume freak. She's back in the detox center, and the counselor said the room smells like the *My Sin* factory.

Clara reeks of the stuff. She should! Those three bottles cost me over a hundred bucks!"

Clara completed her treatment without smelling quite so nice, and when she was ready for her homecoming, Sully was aglow with excitement. "Know what I've bought her for a present? Three new perfumes in stick form, and they don't have alcohol as a base!"

Sam's wife didn't mess around with perfume, but spent ten years in a determined effort to outpace the distillers. Sam almost buried his wife alive as a consequence of this unequal contest. He was a stockbroker, he told us, and showed up at our stag group on the advice of his minister. Sam was a ruddy-faced, well-groomed man, portly, paunchy and perplexed. His wife had made repeated trips to a fashionable, out-of-the-way dry-out center in Connecticut that specialized in gentle detoxification of their "guests" and stern lectures on the evils of non-social drinking. Her last binge had been a three-week unescorted tour, which was terminated when she was discovered unconscious in a motel room fifty miles from their home. She was now hospitalized under heavy sedation in a private clinic.

Sam had just talked with her doctor. "He says I'm going to have to put her away somewhere. He tells me that her brain is badly damaged, her liver is shot and an institution is the only answer. I can have her committed to a state institution, or I can pay the clinic fifteen hundred a month to look after her. I just can't swing the clinic—you know how the market is now —and tomorrow I'm meeting with my attorney to arrange for commitment. I hate like hell to do it, but I don't see any other alternative. My minister suggested that I check with Al-Anon before I go ahead—that's why I'm here." His voice shook, and he brushed tears from his eyes. Sam was really a sad sack—he couldn't have been more dejected or confused if the Dow-Jones average had fallen under five hundred. He was whipped.

Beagle-ears Louie spoke up. "Sam, I have a suggestion. Before the meeting started, you said that you used to bowl with a league team. Why don't you go bowling before you make a decision?"

Sam eyed him with the same look of disgust and incredulity he would have reserved for a client who asked him to buy ten shares of a two-dollar stock on margin. "Look—I'm in trouble. What does bowling have to do with where I put my wife?"

"Sam, I can't tell you what to do about your wife, but I can see that you're in no condition to make a decision. You're confused, and you're beat to your knees. Have you read any of Hemingway's books?"

Sam allowed that he had and even remembered Hemingway's black-ass moods.

"Then you've read his description of a bullfight," Louie continued. "The matador works the bull around the ring, the banderillas are stuck in his neck, and the picador works him over with a lance. Finally the bull is so tired and confused and beat that he just stands there, head down and front feet together, almost hypnotized, and the matador can slip the sword over the horns and into the spot that drops him in his tracks. That bull made a bad decision. He should have kept his head moving and kept charging. You're like that bull, Sam—you're in no condition to make a decision. You can't think straight. You need to clear your mind, and a few frames of bowling will help.

"I know how you feel—I've felt the same way. Cool it for a week. Give me a call—or any of these guys a call—if you want to talk about it. There are other alternatives."

Sam agreed to postpone his decision for at least a week and returned to our next stag session. He had bowled several times and hadn't lost his touch—he had one game over two hundred.

"Have you ever considered calling in another doctor for consultation?" Louie asked. "I heard a doctor that really seems to know his stuff about alcoholism, an ex-drunk himself, talk at an AA meeting a while ago. He said that much of the physical damage that booze causes is reversible, and he described his own case as bad or worse than your wife's condition. He told about his hospitalization and his time in a good treatment center. It certainly wouldn't hurt to call him in professionally, would it?"

"It would cost too much," Sam answered flatly. "I told you that the market is lousy now and I just can't afford another hospital and a treatment center. If you guys knew how much I've spent on her over the past ten years, you wouldn't believe it." Sam shook his head heavily. "I just don't have the money."

Louie bored ahead. "What kind of a car do you drive, Sam?"

"I've got an Eldorado."

"Own your own home?"

"Of course."

"Could you sell some of your own stock?"

"Well—sure, but at today's prices I'd take a shellacking."

"Own any insurance you could borrow against?"

"Sure, I could do that, I guess."

"Sam, if your wife had cancer, would you stick her in an institution to die? Listen man, she's sick, and her sickness is just as real as cancer. Maybe there's still a chance for her. I can't tell you what to do, but there are alternatives. Don't sell her short—give her all of the chances she can have."

Louie made a strong case, but Sam was not convinced. I walked out to the parking lot with him, and we stood there talking. He eyed his year-old Eldorado speculatively. "I guess maybe I could trade it down on a good used VW," Sam said, half to himself, "or maybe ride a bus to work."

We didn't see Sam for a couple of weeks, but when he walked into the meeting, we could see that there was a fire lit and the little flicker of hope had blazed into confidence. "I called that doctor," he told Louie, "and he thinks there's a good chance for my wife. She's been moved to another hospital, and they're bringing her down from drugs. She's addicted to the pills they fed her at that clinic. The doc hopes she'll be able to go to a treatment center in a month or so. I must have been out of my mind to think about shoving her into a state institution!"

Sam continued reflectively, "You know, coping with an alcoholic is something like investing in the stock market. I keep telling my clients not to panic, not to dump good sound stocks just because the market dips a few points. I tell them to have confidence, to sit it out, take it easy and wait for the correction. I should have taken my own advice. I've been reading some of the Al-Anon literature, and I think I'm going to start passing it out to some of my clients.

"Louie," Sam went on, "your story about the bullfighter really hit home. I know just how that bull felt, standing there, paralyzed, waiting for the sword. I couldn't make a rational decision then. Thanks for your help."

"Not at all," Louie replied modestly, "we run a nice little bull market here. So keep coming back!"

# 15

## Is That All?

> "Come back!" the Caterpillar called after her, "I've something important to say!"
>
> This sounded promising, certainly; Alice turned and came back again.
>
> "Keep your temper," said the Caterpillar.
>
> "Is that all?" said Alice swallowing down her anger as well as she could.
>
> "No," said the Caterpillar.

Early on in Al-Anon I was disabused of the idea that "now that she's sober, everything is going to be just beautiful." This was tantamount to telling a kid that there is no Santa Claus, that Easter Bunnies are found only in Playboy Clubs and that turkeys will no longer be served on Thanksgiving since they are an endangered species. That wasn't the way I heard it. Back in the days when a good movie was ten cents and popcorn a nickel, the picture always ended with the cowboy riding down the trail into the sunset with the heroine riding alongside, their hands touching shyly. My mother said that if I worked hard, kept my nose clean and went to church on

Sunday, I would be rewarded. Now the guys in the stag group were telling me that life wasn't like that and some of the problems that bugged Maggie and me before and during her period of compulsive drinking wouldn't disappear with her sobriety. No happy ending!

A speaker didn't show up for one of our stag group meetings and, as chairman for the month, I was his substitute. The advantage of the chairmanship was the freedom to call the shots. "I'd like a discussion of what it's like after sobriety," I announced. I know that I should change, hopefully grow, as Maggie is changing and growing, and this improves the betting odds that our marriage will survive. Survive for what? I'm grateful that Maggie's sober and that I feel better. What I'd like to know is, when do I get my payoff? Where's the happy ending?

"You're getting your payoff right now, dad," Harry grinned, "and there ain't no happy ending—just today, right now, and whether it's happy or not is strictly up to you." He walked over to the table where the Al-Anon literature was displayed and pulled a pamphlet from the stack. "Here's the game plan —Al-Anon's Just for Today. May I take a couple of minutes and read it to you?"

Harry began reading: "Just for today, I will live one day only, forgetting yesterday and tomorrow and try not to solve the whole problem of life at once.

"Just for today I will be unafraid of life and death; unafraid to enjoy the beautiful and be happy. Lincoln said that people are as happy as they make up their minds to be.

"Just for today, I will adjust myself to what it is and not try to make everything over to suit me. If I cannot have what I like, I will try to like what I have.

"Just for today, I will be agreeable, cheerful, charitable, do my best, praise people for what they do, not criticize them for what they cannot do; and if I find fault, I will forgive and forget it. I will not try to improve or regulate anybody but myself.

"Just for today, I will have a plan. I may not follow it exactly, but I will have one. It will save me from worry, hurry and indecision.

"Just for today, I will get people off my nerves and not get on theirs. I will appreciate them for what they do and what they are.

"Just for today, I will not show it if my feelings are hurt.

"Just for today, I will find a little time for quiet, to relax and to realize what life is and can be; time to think about God and to get a better perspective of myself.

"Just for today, I will look at life with fresh eyes and discover the wonder of it; I will know that as I give to the world so the world will give to me."

Sully broke the silence that followed Harry's words. "That's great gut psychology. It's a funny thing, but now that Clara's sober, I'm discovering that I can put a better handle on my work and quit impressing the kids at school with professional double-talk. I've found some psychology reference books that talk the same language as AA and Al-Anon. I just picked up a new one—*I Ain't Much, Baby—But I'm All I've Got* by a Ph.D. at the University of Montana, a guy by the name of Jess Lair.

"He says that once you can accept yourself as something less than perfect, you can start changing, and credits Alcoholics Anonymous and Emotions Anonymous for showing people how to surrender, how to ask a Higher Power for help and how to change. He thinks that this process of changing is something like peeling an onion—you skin off one layer and then there's another one to peel back—you constantly discover new things about yourself. He's come up with what he calls "Lair's First Law: Bug ye not or ye will be bugged." Sounds like shorthand for part of 'Just for Today,' doesn't it?"

"I like what David Stewart has to say about changing and personal goals in *Thirst for Freedom*—you remember, Jack, you put me onto this book," Mac commented. "He went back to Plato for a description of an ideal experience called 'sophrosyne' and I memorized the definition: 'By this is meant an easy and graceful harmony among the three basic urges of man's inner nature and a delightful rapport with the world around him.' I'd like to think that when I peel Lair's onion I'll find Plato's sophrosyne."

Mac went on: "Stewart says that man's three basic urges are money, power and sex. Beyond those urges is a 'personal thing' that we all have, a desire to be free, to create and to love. He says that if we work at it, we can combine our basic urges with that personal thirst and then go beyond ourselves to live life freely, as an adventure, and take a taste of 'sophrosyne.' It beats the hell out of alcohol or pills as a thirst-quencher."

I dawdled my way home through the light late-evening traffic, bouncing these ideas through my mind like the marbles in a pinball game. No happy endings, just a daily game plan that could assure me of a steady succession of two cherries and a bar, sometimes three oranges or three plums lining up, even if there wasn't a big jackpot like in never-never land. Concentrate on my onion every day, and expect a few tears in the process—after all, I was peeling the damn thing, wasn't I? As I took it down, layer by layer, I'd get a little closer to that Greek thirst-quencher, Plato's "sophrosyne." Okay, I'd get with it, starting tomorrow.

Procrastination heads the list of my personal faults that could do with a change. Tomorrow was slow coming. Back in those days when drinking was fun for Maggie and me, one of our friends would keep us up until all hours, having "just one more for the road."

"We gotta have just one more lil' drink, ol' buddy," he would explain, pouring a round of shots a bit unsteadily, "because tomorrow never comes. You see, when we do go to bed and wake up, it's not tomorrow at all—it's today!"

And that was the way it went for me. My tomorrows became todays, then yesterdays, and I just didn't seem to get around to my plans for change. I was restless and a bit irritable and began a retreat into my own little world of dreams—my old pattern of putting off something that bugged me, something I should take care of but found easier to postpone.

Maggie read the symptoms correctly. "How are you doing with the Twelve Steps?" she asked.

"Oh, I'm doing fine. I'm pretty well satisfied that I've accepted the first three," I responded defensively.

"When are you going to tackle your Fourth—the moral inventory?"

"Look," I flashed, "I've learned to keep my hands off *your* program—don't tell me how to run mine! I'll get at it when I have some free time. I still have a living to make, you know. I'm busy, so stay off my back!"

"Okay, Okaaay!" Maggie soothed, "It's your program and your life, but when you go into your withdrawal act and bury your nose in a book or stare at the boob tube all evening, I get a little resentful. I'm going to pull my resentment out in the open and take a look at it. Something is bugging you, and maybe you should drag it out for examination. You're pretty uptight. But you work it out your own way."

Sometimes a little push helps, and the next evening I made the Big Announcement. "There's a three-day holiday coming up, and I'm going to do my Fourth. I'm going to check into a motel, take my typewriter, and when I've finished I'll come home. Not until!" I concluded firmly and a bit self-righteously.

I've always prided myself that I approached a new job, a new challenge, in a methodical, orderly fashion, and I intended to handle my Fourth Step Inventory in the same manner. I checked into a nearby motel, armed with Maggie's electric typewriter, two hundred sheets of white paper stolen from the office, a spare typewriter ribbon, shaving kit, clean socks, a copy of Hazelden's "Guide to Fourth Step Inventory for the Spouse" and an air of grim determination. I was going to knock this damn thing out in my usual workmanlike style—I'd show her.

Resisting the urge to turn on the ball game, I settled down to read the Guide. The inventory was to list assets and liabilities. I was to prepare a sort of moral balance sheet.

Balance sheets were my bag, and I could visualize the format —assets on the left, liabilities on the right, and the difference between the two would be net worth—in this case net self-worth. I shuddered, since my balance sheet was going to be heavy with liabilities and short on assets, which left self-worth far in the red. I thought of the remark I had heard that all alcoholics were bankrupt—physically, spiritually and morally. It looked like this comment referred to my case, too, except maybe the physical bit, and I wasn't too sure about that.

I read further. I was to examine myself in certain specific areas:

Virtues, attitudes and responsibilities,

Personality defects,

The Seven Cardinal Sins,

The Ten Commandments.

Write it all down, the directions said. Omit nothing because of shame, fear or embarrassment, starting with what bothered me most. I could destroy the inventory when I was finished if I liked. There was a check list with some very sticky questions. For example, under "Attitudes" there was this one: "Have I honestly faced myself or have I side-stepped by day-dreaming, wishful thinking, resentments or self-pity?" That ought to be good for at least a couple or three single-spaced pages. Or this one under "To My Duties:" "Have I maintained my ethical standards, or have I excused certain of my transgressions because of my spouse's behavior?" Under "Duties to God" there was: "Have I based my concept (or refusal) of God principally through training, hearsay, disappointments or emotional approaches? Would I prepare for a career or even a hobby in the same manner? In other words, have I ever sought God?"

This was mighty personal stuff, getting right down to the nitty-gritty. I recalled when one AA husband and Al-Anon wife co-led an AA meeting that the wife mentioned burying her pain and resentment in some deep corner of her mind. The husband chuckled and broke in with, "Yeah—sorta like dropping them in a cesspool." He had a point there. If I was going to do my inventory Hazelden's way, I was going to have to lift the lid off my personal septic tank, dredge out everything I could find there and list the contents—no matter how bad they smelled. I had vivid memories of septic systems, since several of our dwellings were equipped with these cranky necessities, which had the unfortunate facility of backing up at inopportune times. Like when we had house guests or a big party going. I knew from experience that septic tanks should be cleaned regularly, and if forgotten or disregarded, they *demanded* one's attention! I had been filling my mental septic tank for over fifty years and believe me, it was filled to overflowing.

I settled at the typewriter and gingerly lifted the lid to my mental tank. At first, I couldn't see much (it was dark down there), but gradually I could make out those dim shapes bobbing and turning, my old guilts, frustrations, lies, dirty tricks, sneaky cheating actions—all there waiting for me, and they stunk to high heaven.

"At least I haven't ever killed anybody," I consoled myself. "I haven't been that bad." Then I spotted floating over in one corner the note that I had written to Maggie after her first shot at suicide, the note that read in part, "If you ever decide to do it again, tell me and we'll go together."

Had I meant it or had I been grandstanding? I wasn't sure, but I remembered the details of my plan—I was going to take Maggie in the older of our two cars (a cheapie to the last), barrel down the Interstate as fast as the car would travel and smash into an unprotected bridge support. That would wipe us both out and then they (whoever "they" might be) would be sorry.

Then there were others, my "enemies" and Maggie's "enemies" who, I felt, deserved death if I could just figure out how to do it without getting caught.

My inventory or balance sheet was turning out to be a pretty lopsided affair. I had plenty of liabilities to dredge out of my cerebral cesspool, but the assets came hard. The Guide said that I should come up with some kind of a balance, and thirty-six hours later I completed my work. The self-worth section had edged over into the black, but I wasn't sure that the "Auditor" would approve of some of my entries. Was "I seldom kick cats and dogs" an asset?

Reading it over, I concluded that, if nothing else, it had the makings of a great dirty book. I had prepared a first-class list of liabilities, and it seemed a shame not to put them to some use.

I had listed among my assets that "I build a good patio." I had often complained that my day-to-day work was non-creative, that there wasn't much satisfaction in a job that dealt with pieces of paper—orders, financial statements, collection letters, sales letters, budgets and sales projections. I wanted something that could stand as a monument to my ingenuity, ability and power. So as we moved around the country, I built patios. I mixed concrete and cast paving blocks, laying them patiently in masterpieces that included spices growing between the blocks. I dug out a hillside, moving tons of dirt, paved the flattened terrace with sparkling pebbles, swung a hammock on the branches of an apple tree and opened a view to a little creek at the foot of the hill.

Then there was the beauty I built on the bank of a river, paved with slabs of river rock, edged with flowers and a fortune in ground cover. It was shaded, secluded and a real back-breaker. When we lived in a big old house situated on a narrow lot, I filled the backyard with a swimming pool and an artful Japanese garden. It was complete with waterfall— water was routed through a bamboo pipe to trickle into a reflective pool. The patios took a lot of sweat and muscle. Maybe I would never build a skyscraper or even a factory with my name on top, but I had left my monuments across the countryside.

Oddly enough, I hadn't built a patio at the house where we lived during Maggie's (and my own) worst years. Instead, we had added a screened porch at the rear, with drop blinds and further encased ourselves in a privacy fence around the yard. It was a good place to hide.

I was pooped when I came home, exhausted from my two days of septic-tank cleaning, but content. Maggie eyed me curiously, wondering, I suppose, what one says to a man who has been dredging up over fifty years of accumulated memories. "How did it go?" she asked cautiously.

"I feel better, I think. I started another patio."

"Oh? Where?"

"Inside me. I'm going to start the paving with the few good qualities that I've got and keep adding new ones as I can acquire them. It's kinda small now but I hope it will grow, with God's help." I walked over to her chair, bent over and kissed her. "I love you. That's the first paving stone in my new patio."

My inventory told me that I was not a compulsive—or even a big-time—liar and cheat but simply misrepresented the facts or bent them into more attractive shapes to avoid trouble, to improve my image in the eye of others or to make an extra dollar or two. I was to replace these actions with honesty. Taking honesty to the office would be difficult. Doing business with people outside the country is often based on a premise of mutual distrust. My First Law: "Screw others before they screw thee." A little misrepresentation, a few extra charges here and there, a little document falsification—these were standard practices for me, along with a little double dealing on the side with the profits hidden in another country.

Changing those practices came hard. I refunded several hundreds of dollars to a customer in one of the Arabian countries, money advanced for ocean transportation. The refund was not required; ordinarily it was just "gravy" for the company.

The customer wrote, "I don't understand why you sent us this refund. No other supplier that I do business with has ever returned any of our advances. What are you trying to do?"

My partners were wondering the same thing, but two months later we received another order, a very big order, from this buyer. Maybe he thought we were a little crazy, but it looked like this kind of craziness was going to pay off.

As I consciously tried to change myself, I felt very naked, very alone, very unsure of myself. It was like learning to walk again after a long illness, and I needed some help. Someone told me that I should pick out people that I respected and admired, then imitate their good qualities until I had developed similar qualities of my own, that I should, in AA parlance, "Get in bed with the winners." Maggie and I talked about it. "I think it's a great idea," Maggie said, "only remember that the advice is figurative—when you literally feel like getting in bed, be sure it's with me!"

And *that* was another good idea.

I looked both to AA and Al-Anon, as well as to other friends, for men and women with strong senses of personal identity. One such man was Fred, a big guy with an engaging grin, whom in the past I had viewed with dark suspicion. He was scrupulously honest. For example, he didn't even cheat on his federal income tax return! He drove a company car and once, when filling it with gasoline, won a five-dollar prize in the oil company's weekly jackpot drawing. Damned if he didn't deduct the five bucks when he turned in his next expense account! You know—nobody is *that* honest.

He had a strong sense of fair play and didn't even nudge his ball to a better lie on the fairway of the golf course. He had developed, he related, a personal philosophy, which he called "Practical Idealism," a concept whereby he accepted others at their own valuation, expected them to be honest and responsible, was willing to overlook their mistakes and, in return, asked for the same treatment. Idealistic? Certainly. Practically, when he bumped up against the fakes, cheats and liars in the world, he accepted these qualities, too, but kept his guard up.

Fred was the kind of guy who didn't mind serving as Aquila for the Cub Scout troop, working his tail off as Sunday School Superintendent or acting as the peacemaker in a neighborhood squabble. Despite all this, he was a guy with a great, earthy sense of humor, who loved a good dirty story and even more, a lurid limerick.

"One of the times when I wasn't honest," Fred related, "was when I was courting Diane. She was such a lady, so poised and correct, that I tried to play the role of a perfect gentleman. I had this absolutely enormous collection of limericks, 'The Old Man from Kent' and all the rest—they were considered very risque then. I thought that Diane would be shocked if she knew about this side of my character and, like an idiot, I burned them. I was going to be as pure as the driven snow. Then, after we were married, it turned out that she could recite some limericks that even I hadn't heard before." He turned to Diane, "Isn't that right, lady?"

"Shut up, Fred," Diane replied, knitting furiously and blushing a little.

Fred enjoyed equally a day in the woods, a night on the town, or sweating himself silly in his half-acre garden, but he really surprised me when he announced that he was going to quit his job with the company for which he had worked for over twenty years. He had advanced to an executive position in the company, drove a company car, was well paid, and there was a good retirement program if he held on for a few more years. But Fred quit.

"I may be crazy to do this, but I'm not happy there now. I hate to go to the office. Top management has changed, and they're more concerned about looking good than they are about doing good. I'm losing my self-respect. I know it's going to be tough to try something new now that I'm past fifty, but I'm going to do it anyway."

It wasn't going to be too long before I would be considering the same decision. During the past two years, three of my friends, guys I had known for twenty years or longer, died unexpectedly. These were men in my age bracket, late fifties, one in his early sixties, men who had kept their noses clean, went to work every day, raised their kids and saved their money for retirement, victims of the "happily ever after" myth. They had it made—almost.

I didn't have it made, not by a damn sight, but there was a happily-ever-after plan that someday was to take us to a little hill down in Costa Rica, a hill with a spectacular 180-degree view of the Pacific and miles of deserted beach, green mountains rising behind us, an ecologist's dream. We had purchased our hill impulsively, dreaming of the time when we could build a snug white house under the shady old trees and could measure time with the rise and fall of the tides, a place where the major event of the day would be watching the after-glow of the sunset. Since our nest egg was too small to hatch fat dividend or interest checks, this dream was out there somewhere in the future ... maybe when we hit the winning number in the lottery.

Maggie hesitantly unfolded her idea during one of our ice-cream sundae sessions: "Why don't we sell our house, you quit your job, and let's go to Costa Rica?"

Just like that. We would sell most of our furniture, store the things we couldn't or wouldn't part with, dispose of our two cars, buy a four-wheel drive truck and a trailer, and take off. Our beach was in a remote corner of Costa Rica, accessible by plane, and during the dry season, trucks and some cars could make it over the gravel and dirt roads, fording a few rivers and creek beds. We could try it on for size, Maggie argued, spending a year, living in our trailer during both the wet and dry seasons. Our kids were grown, she reasoned; there was nothing to stop us. The cold, gloomy weather in our area did little for Maggie's arthritis, and I had chronic sinusitis, more than a touch of arthritis in my knees and a growing aversion to snow, slush and sleet.

Nothing to stop us! Almost automatically I reverted to the old reactions that were so standard for Jack-the-Knurd. Any ideas other than my own were subject to chicken-pickin'. I would pick up the idea, examine it and pick away the feathers and fuzz. "See, this part is no good," I'd say, and "this smells funny," sniffing suspiciously at the meat of the idea and discarding it. Finally I'm down to the bones and could exclaim with some logic, "See, there's nothing to your idea—it's just a pile of old bones and, hell, they're no good to anyone!"

Mentally, I picked Maggie's chicken. What would we live on? What would happen if either of us become seriously ill? What if someone in our family needed us? How could we possibly sell the house in these times of high interest rates? What did I know about pulling a trailer—suppose I piled it in a ditch, wrecked the car, hit a cow and marched off to jail? Could we get along with the little Spanish that I knew? And, after a year, if it didn't work out and we had to come back to the States, what would we do? Could we live on food stamps and public relief, or would I maybe end up racking balls in a pool hall for the tips? Wouldn't we miss our kids, particularly our grandchildren? Could we *really* pull a trailer across those rivers and ditches, navigate the dirt roads, power our way up and over mountains?

Maggie sat quietly while I worked my way down to the bones, but as I did so, a thought intruded and shoved its way into my mind. "Hey, jerk, aren't you back at the old management racket again? Is the idea no good because you didn't think of it first? Why not get honest and admit that the idea scares the hell out of you, that you want to say 'no' because then you won't have to face up to your fear and your uncertainty? Why don't you admit that you're still projecting, still worrying about tomorrow, that you don't have the faith and trust in a Higher Power, and that all your Al-Anon talk is just another mask you're wearing? Come on—tell her honestly how you feel!"

I said slowly, "I'm afraid, Maggie. I don't know whether I can handle it. Let me think about it for a few days."

"Okay," Maggie answered, "and while you're thinking about it, why don't you open your mind and see if God wants to tell you something?"

The trouble with listening to God when you haven't had much practice is the uncertainty: He didn't suddenly appear at my side and shake His finger in my face and say, "No way, Jack," or clap me on the back, sending me on the way to Costa

Rica with His best wishes and a made-in-heaven road map. Instead, he just let me sit there, sweating it out and thinking about my problem.

But that newly emerging man, naked and without masks, stumbled around in my head, coughed apologetically and seemed to mutter, "If you're so all fired up with the Al-Anon philosophy, why don't you measure this idea in its framework? You have already admitted that you're scared, and that's a start. Now then, why are you scared? Because you are afraid that you can't handle tomorrow by yourself—right? Man, can you handle today by yourself? If you look at your track record, you doubt it. Okay, you're being honest up to here, anyway. Now, how about those Second and Third Steps—the belief that a Power greater than yourself can square away your thinking, that you're ready to put your will and your life in His hands? If you're able to believe that, Jack, you can handle today, and that's all that counts—just today. All those worries about tomorrow that bug you will be taken care of one day at a time."

There wasn't any question that I welcomed the thought of dumping the dullsville routine of money-grubbing and going on a trip with Maggie, just because we wanted to have ourselves a "great adventure," like those brawny men and beautiful babes in the beer ads who insist that we "only go around once" in life. Maybe we could even experience it without the reward of a can of beer—who knows?

Still, there are considerations, very real ones, that we must face.

How well are we going to get along in our daily lives without the support of AA and Al-Anon? They're mighty important to us.

There are groups listed in the International Directories for every state in the Union and in each of the countries we will traverse—Mexico, Guatemala, El Salvador, Honduras, Nicaragua and Costa Rica. We could find one or more groups meeting in almost any town where we might stop. In Costa

Rica there were 360 AA groups and ninety Al-Anon groups for us to choose from.

How would we make out financially?

Not too bad. Traveling by car and trailer would cost us less than flying. We had a place to park our trailer once we arrived, could have electricity and water brought to our property, and food, particularly fresh fruits, vegetables and meat would be less expensive than Stateside. Allowing for unforeseen expenses and the return trip, we wouldn't be broke—dented, but not broke.

What happens if one or the other of us get sick?

We go to the doctor or to a hospital. Our beach colony was served by plane; good doctors and good hospitals were thirty-five minutes away by air. A semi-private room in a hospital cost about sixteen dollars per day, we were told, and the doctors' fees were correspondingly low.

Would we miss our families and friends?

Of course we would, but perhaps some of them might visit us. Furthermore, it was not our intention to stay away forever! Sure, we would miss them, particularly our grand-children, but Costa Rica did have direct-dial phone service to the United States, and the mail service was good.

We concluded that our plan was feasible and the trip a part of a "great adventure," a step in the direction of freedom, happiness and fulfillment. Or—was it an impulsive cop-out, a running away from reality? We could use a little guidance, and my answer to Maggie was, "Let's try it, open-door, closed-door style."

We were both wary of impulsive decisions. Somebody has described alcoholic behavior as "self-will run riot," and in my case at least, the description applied equally as well to a knurd. We needed some help with this decision, and we were going to ask the question, "Hey God—about this particular problem we're trying to solve—my will or Yours?"

If God would only appear as a big traffic signal, flashing green for "go," red for "stop" and yellow for "caution," we could move with more assurance. Lacking this, we were going to practice the technique described in both AA and Al-Anon as "open-door, closed-door" for our insight to God's will. Imagine a long hallway with a series of identical closed doors lining both sides—something like a Holiday Inn hallway, but without the room numbers on the doors. We're going to walk down the hallway, trying the doors. There's no house detective in sight, so it's all right. If the first door is locked or doesn't open easily, we try another door. We keep trying until we find one that opens easily, swings wide on oiled hinges—nothing to block our way—and we enter.

In decision-making, if obstacles keep popping up or if we have to push, jam our way forward, beat down all the opposition, it's time to back off and try another door. But if things go smoothly and each door swings open at our touch, we keep moving through the doors. The decision, then, is not irrevocable. We can always try a new course of action. Simple? Well not exactly, but you begin to get the hang of it with practice!

We list our home with a realtor. Money is tight, he tells us, interest rates are high, and there are plenty of homes on the market, but there are still buyers. While we were waiting for this door to edge open, we went trailer-shopping. One of our neighbors, a seasoned veteran of trailering, with a big motor home parked in his driveway, told us, "If I were going to take your trip, I'd go for an Airstream trailer. They're big enough to live in, but are beautifully balanced and will go anywhere your tow vehicle will travel. They cost a bundle, but they're really put together to stay, the equipment is all first-class, and they have good resale value. They have caravaned them around the world, so anything you might encounter on your trip is old stuff to an Airstream."

We phoned a dealer who was located just a few miles from our home (open door) and, yes, they had several models available at year-end prices (open door) and why didn't we drive out and take a look? The doors (the real ones), were open from ten in the morning until ten at night. Our experience with the recreational vehicle industry had been limited to a one-week rental of a seventeen-foot motor home and four days in a state park, alternately folding down the table so we could sit on the bed, or shoving all the cushions in place somewhere else so we could open up the table to play cards.

Now, at the dealer's lot, we had a choice of little tent-type trailers that popped open like a telescope, monster motor homes with picture windows—complete with shower and tub and carpet so thick that one expected a lawnmower as an accessory—and a raft of sturdy, functional two-wheelers that would be great for a weekend of fishing. These were jammed side by side on the outdoor lot, but the Airstreams were displayed in the huge, air-conditioned showroom. This was a warning in itself. We entered, eyeing the big silver beetles that we had seen before only on the highway, often hurtling along behind big Cadillacs, Lincolns and Buicks. Airstreams were apparently allergic to plain old Fords, Chevvies and compact Oldsmobiles, and would refuse even to squat beside a small foreign car.

"Just look around," the soft-sell sales manager said, all teeth and smiles, "if you have any questions, just call me over."

We started with the bottom of the line, the nineteen-foot model. Nice. Functional, but there was a couch that converted into a double bed, a gas stove, refrigerator, john, shower, air conditioner, radio and even a TV antenna. Very nice indeed. I approached the neatly-typed price ticket displayed on a window and sneaked an apprehensive peek. "$7,000 plus taxes," a nice round number. SEVEN THOUSAND DOL-LARS? Hell, that was almost twice as much as we had paid for our first house, which had five rooms, a wooded lot and a view of the lake. True, that had been over thirty years ago, and prices had gone up, but SEVEN THOUSAND DOLLARS for a nineteen-foot travel trailer?

The sales manager was conferring busily with Maggie, who had been drawn irresistibly to the far end of the showroom, where the biggie, the thirty-one-foot model, gleamed splendid-ly. I joined them reluctantly. If we planned to live in a trailer for any length of time, the salesman was saying, we should consider a larger model such as this, the Land Yacht. He pronounced the name reverently, and visions of polished brass, captain's hats and ships' bells flickered through my mind. It slept four in comfort, he said, six if we wanted the optional double-decker bunks. This one had an electronic oven, color TV, retractable rotating antenna, plus a host of other goodies, including a telephone jack, which would make life bearable away from home.

Taking me by the arm (me, the practical guy who has trouble operating an electric can opener), the sales manager demonstrated the hydraulic jack, pointed out the magnesium wheels, jiggled the leveling-jack controls and led me back inside to the "Master Control Center." There I could scrutinize a bewildering array of dials and meters—adequate instrumentation, I assumed, to navigate it by radar in case of foggy weather. It was so well-balanced, he said, I could tow it as easily as a smaller one—in fact, I would even forget I had a trailer behind me.

How could I ever forget a five-thousand-pound monster of aluminum, glass and steel relentlessly pursuing me down a ribbon of concrete? Not only would a nice big tent be closer to my price bracket, but a tent would lie quietly in the back of the car until I needed it. I sidled up to the price tag. J.P. Morgan once said that if a man had to ask the price of a yacht, he shouldn't own one. Maybe he was right, since this baby cost $12,500 plus extras, plus federal, state and city taxes. Now then, I should reach my decision quickly, the sales manager observed, since it was the end of the model year, they had only two Land Yachts in stock and the new models were going to cost in the range of $15,000. "Inflation, you know," he said, spreading his hands helplessly.

"Maybe you have something used?" I asked weakly.

"Not a one," was the firm and decisive answer. "An Airstream will last almost forever. People who buy them, keep them, use them for second homes." The average Airstream buyer was sixty-three, he said. The units were designed for men and women who wanted luxury, comfort, style, ease of maintenance. I reflected glumly that they must also make damn fine coffins. Like an Indian whose worldly goods share his final resting place, the owner could be buried in luxury, comfort and style in his Airstream out in back of the trailer park, the antenna above ground, rotating slowly with a wreath of artificial flowers wired to it. R.I.P.

It seemed to me that this particular door was closing—the cost would take a big chunk of our capital—too big a chunk. Maybe we would be back later, I told the sales manager. (Much later, when I was old enough to make the purchase without disturbing the "average age of buyer" statistics.)

A few weeks later, I spotted the little ad under "RV Vehicles, Trailers" in the classified section of the Sunday paper, an offer of a "1969 Airstream, 31-ft., like new." A quick call gave us the information that this trailer was the property of an elderly gentleman, recovering from a bout of illness, who had bought it to make a last pilgrimage around the country before his impending death. To his surprise, he felt better and better, returned to work and bought a boat, and the trailer had sat gathering dust in the "carriage barn" for the past two years. We made the trip to carriage-barn country and, as advertised, the trailer was immaculate except for a few "dings" and some exterior corrosion that could be cleaned up. After the expected horse-trading session, the price was less than half of the cost of a new model.

That particular door had opened, but we needed our patience while we waited for that "right buyer" to come along, the one that would want our house and maybe even the draperies and furniture we planned to sell, the one who could offer a sufficiently large down payment with income enough to satisfy the increasingly picky mortgage banker. It happened. A young executive on his way up, with a wife who liked Maggie's taste in decorating and furniture, offered to buy our house at our asking price and accommodatingly arranged his move to coincide with our departure plans.

The doors continued to swing wide. My partners allowed as how they could manage without me, and my suggested quitting date was fine by them. "I just wish I had your guts, Jack," the senior partner told me wistfully, "I have this little farm, you know, and keep thinking that maybe next year ..."

Our tow vehicle, a Dodge Ramcharger, was purchased after a crash course with truck salesmen, who thoroughly confused me with their talk of gross vehicle weights, tongue weights, drawbar weights, heavy duty options, transmission coolers and oil coolers. All I wanted was something that would tow the trailer safely to Costa Rica and back again. "El Toro" was a two-door station wagon on a truck chassis, a stubby, powerful-looking vehicle with an intermediate eight-cylinder engine, four-wheel drive and most of the heavy-duty options that we concluded were necessary. With power steering and power brakes, plus special seats to cradle our "bad backs," it was comfortable and easy to handle and might give us eight or nine miles to the gallon of gasoline. There was a substantial discount to cheer my chintzy heart.

Maggie is a string-saver and a sentimentalist. We had an attic full of dusty books, my old love letters, all the Christmas cards we had received since 1945, my WWII mementos and outgrown uniforms, football shoes, baseball mitts, ice skates, 78 rpm records, broken chairs and tables that I was going to fix some day and the assorted junk of over thirty years of marriage. There were also boxes on boxes of books and other personal possessions belonging to our sons, who found it convenient to leave them with us and not clutter up their own places.

One reason for buying our house had been the closets, big roomy closets that could easily accommodate the belongings of a family of six. Maggie simply couldn't bear the thought of discarding anything wearable. Our granddaughters loved to drag out the boxes of old shoes and parade precariously through the house, tottering on high heels of ancient vintage. "Styles run in cycles, and in a few years I can wear them again," was Maggie's defense over my demand that she sort them out so there would be more space for my stuff. Then there was the silverware. There were wedding gifts that were kept carefully wrapped and stored away except for the annual unwrapping and polishing. There were also a few heirloom plates and several pieces of Swedish glass. Maggie had supplemented these when she was on her cut-glass kick, buying bowls and tumblers, pitchers and vases at farm auctions. "Someday they will be worth a lot of money," Maggie declared.

Books, bed linen, kitchenware, a four-drawer file filled with priceless wastepaper — all must be sorted and a decision made to (A) store them, (B) sell them, (C) give them away or (D) cram them in the trailer as absolute essentials. Our friends Honest Fred and Blushing Diane took a look at the mounting piles of (C) and the growing mountain of (D). "Everybody ought to do a little personal root-pruning," Fred observed, "but you two are conducting radical surgery!"

Our trailer had been towed to the dealer's service department for reconditioning, and we were to be trained in the care and feeding of this silver beast, now named "La Tortuga" (the turtle), which was, hopefully, to follow us faithfully down the highway for five thousand miles. "It's very simple," our instructor explained, smoothly jacking up the front end, backing El Toro (the bull) into place under the ball hitch, plugging in the power cable, snapping sway bars in place, connecting the safety chains and a break-away cable, then lowering the trailer — all in about two minutes. "I went slow, so you could get it the first time," he told us.

My mind boggled. I was going to do all *that*, every day? What if I failed to connect the whatchamacallit and the trailer should suddenly pass me on the highway, or maybe obstinately squat dead-still on the road while I cruised along blithely, like the man said, forgetting that I had a trailer behind me?

It went a little better inside. "You turn this valve, see," our instructor was checking me out on the gas-electric refrigerator, "and push this here little toggle switch up and you give this spark lighter a twirl or two and you're all switched over from electric to gas. Nothing to it. It's idiot-proof," he concluded, eyeing me kindly and, I'm sure, knowingly.

There was an hour spent in actual driver training: how to tow on the interstate highways (watch for the big trucks — when they pass, she's going to sway a little — so just touch the brakes lightly and she'll straighten out); taking the turns (remember to swing wide, watch your mirrors — if you turn her too tight, she'll jackknife on you); going through underpasses or coming in to a service station with a canopy roof (you're ten-foot-six high, so watch it — we had one guy that damn near tore the top of his trailer off when he pulled into a service station); backing up (just turn your wheel the reverse of the way you turn when you back a car and gooooo sloooow, watch your mirrors).

Both Maggie and I had our turns on a short test run over highways and back roads (watch for low-hanging branches), peering anxiously into the big rear view mirrors that we had strapped on El Toro's sides. Miraculously, we avoided any contact with oncoming cars, trucks, curbs, tree branches, livestock or pedestrians. Backing up was not so successful, since La Tortuga had a mind of her own and obstinately refused to enter the lined area designated as the parking slot. "Don't worry," our instructor reassured us, "when you've done it a few times, it will come easy. Your biggest problem will be to remember that you've got a trailer behind you!"

Yeah.

Our last days before departure were a mad rush of last-minute details. There was the unbelievable experience of a garage sale, where housewives fought to buy junk jewelry at boutique prices, but turned up their noses at nearly-new electrical appliances marked at five to ten percent of our cost. Still — we were $500 richer when the last package of paperbacks was carted out the door. Then there was my frantic shopping for sturdy no-iron clothing — summerweight, please — to be searched out from shops featuring topcoats, tweed jackets and wool shirts. Worst of all were Maggie's brisk parades from the house toting still another load of absolute necessities, such as a full case of instant iced tea, a twelve-inch cast-iron skillet and our vintage 1961 tape recorder, net weight, sixty pounds. Too, there was my big tin trunk with three hundred pounds of service tools and assorted bolts and nuts, things that we really might need someday.

The new owner of our house was on hand with a thirty-foot moving van of his possessions, and he waved good-bye to us as we pulled away early one morning. "Have a great trip and don't drive too fast," he admonished us, sitting in what was once *my* chair and drinking coffee from *my* big cup.

Determinedly, I adjusted the rear view mirrors one more time, trying for the angle which would let me see the side of the trailer and the road behind. We were moving at a brisk fifteen miles per hour enroute to our first stop, the Airstream dealer's, to have the new curtains for the trailer installed, curtains ordered two months ago and hopefully arriving from the factory today. Four hours later, exhausted and sweaty from installing the curtains with the help of a mechanic, we rolled down the ramp into the roar of interstate traffic. My thin cloak of serenity rippled and waved dangerously, threatening to rip into rags and scatter on the berm along with the empty beer cans, candy wrappers and paper cartons that complemented the "Keep Our Highways Clean" signs.

A truck and trailer rig, big as a boxcar, roared up behind us, and I tensed, hunched over the wheel, waiting for that "little sway." The rig was around us in seconds, taking with him most of the air that properly belonged around us, and irresistibly, uncomfortably, we edged maybe six inches closer to the center line.

"That wasn't so bad, was it?" Maggie asked solicitously.

"Can I open my eyes now?" I responded gamely.

I learned as we drove and parked, learned all of those little things that other trailer owners seemed to do so easily and so well. I mastered the driving techniques, the routine of hitching and unhitching the trailer, everything except backing the damn thing. I could park only after ten minutes of anxious forward and backward maneuvers, always accompanied by frantic waves from Maggie and much shouted advice from the five or six veteran trailer owners who sprang up like toad-stools wherever I struggled to park.

"Dammit, if you think it's so easy, *you* do it!" I told Maggie after five frustrating minutes of low and reverse, the trailer never quite settling on the concrete pad of our selected site.

Maggie climbed behind the wheel. Up—back, up a little and there it was, level, square on the pad and ready for unhitching.

"You cheated—you *conned* the thing into place," I accused. Maggie wisely said nothing. From that point on, I drove the rig forward and when it was time to park, Maggie took over. We *had* to go to Costa Rica—I couldn't turn us around to go back where we came from!

Still, by the time we arrived at the Texas-Mexican border, I was confident and even comfortable, and we rolled steadily southward down the good and sometimes not-so-good highways leading to Mexico City. "Everybody gets lost in Mexico City," experienced trailerites assured us, "but you just stop and ask any policeman or soldier in uniform for directions. Some of them speak a little English."

I was determined that I would definitely not get lost in Mexico City. After all, I'd been there plenty of times, arriving by plane, but I had covered much of the city by cab, and certainly I knew the *zona roja*, the tourist zone in the center of town. I studied the maps, traced our course with a purple-tipped pen and instructed Maggie, who was navigator, coffee-pourer, cigarette-lighter and front-seat homemaker. "Just watch for the signs," I told her (directional signs in Mexico are best read from a distance of five feet since they are placed, with a nice Latin touch, in unobtrusive places), "and when we get onto Avenida Reforma I'll show you some of the points of interest."

We were to follow, our AAA map and directions said, *Ruta* 95 through the city, pick up a new toll road, and then it was just a short distance to Cuernavaca, our next stop. We joined the approximate eight million Mexican drivers fighting their way in or out of the city at noon one Saturday. Maggie waved and shouted at them, and they waved and shouted back, sliding in front of, and around me like a school of dusty tropical fish with traffic-battered fins. Suddenly there was one of those little signs with an arrow indicating we should swing left onto another street, if we wished to believe the "A 95" direction. In the wrong lane of course, I nosed my way across, amid squealing brakes and sounds of Spanish curses, and onto a three-lane snake of a road that dipped and twisted its way through the city.

"Where's Avenida Reforma?" I demanded, "We're supposed to be on Avenida Reforma."

"How the hell would I know?" Maggie responded inelegantly but pleasantly, "You're the one that knows Mexico City like the palm of your hand."

Forty minutes later without any warning, there it was, the line of traffic pulling slowly forward to the entrance of the Cuernavaca-Acapulco toll road. Somebody had stolen one of the biggest avenues in Mexico City, I concluded, since we hadn't seen the slightest trace of the wide, tree-lined Avenida Reforma. Later, we learned that we had correctly taken a *periferico*, a bypass that led us around the crush of stop-and-go downtown traffic. The AAA mapmakers hadn't caught up to that change.

"From here on, it's a breeze," I assured Maggie confidently, "It's almost a straight shot to Cuernavaca, and with the little detour I've marked, we'll bypass the center of the city and should be at the trailer park in an hour."

The road was straight, but the map didn't show that the first sixteen miles of the highway was straight up a mountain to an elevation of over two miles. El Toro complained about the quality of Mexican gasoline and belched threateningly from time to time. This was our first test of mountain driving, but we gained the summit, overtaking less fortunate stalled and overheated cars and trucks, then slid gratefully through groves of pine and green fields, enjoying the pleasant vistas in the cool crisp air of the mountains.

We just overshot the turnoff to the secondary road by a few yards, and I managed a weaving back-up to the exit. We would be at the park in a few mintues—another ten miles or so, all straight road, the map indicated. But we awakened to the realities of Mexican roads with a jolt. The jolt came from a spring-testing traverse of an *etope*, a ridge of steel or six-inch cobblestones built into the road to slow traffic to a crawl through the villages that dotted our route. Even the weakest, most emaciated Mexican dog found time to stagger across the road in front of us when we inched across each successive *etope*.

We rolled through flat country along the narrow blacktop, which is not too bad if the lack of a shoulder on either side doesn't bug you. Then we came to a little squiggle on the map. A sign informed us that we were entering Wolf Canyon, and the highway narrowed even further. It careened drunkenly around the side of a mountain, clinging desperately to the edge, no more than a paved ox-cart path. Traffic, naturally, was heavy. Cars and buses raced along the road, forcing us to the edge—an edge unprotected by safety rails—and I caught glimpses of sharp white rocks, pointed like the fangs of a wolf, ready to tear at us if we had to go one more inch closer to the side. I pulled behind an asthmatic truck and let it run interference for me as it wheezed its way around the hairpin turns leading to the top.

The road leveled, and we drove on, searching for the trailer park shown by the perfidious map as just beyond the squiggle of Wolf Canyon. Nothing. I found a spot where I could pull over. I shook a pencil at the defenseless map. "See? It's supposed to be *right here!*"

Maggie and the map maintained a discreet silence.

"Right here!" I raged, jabbing the pencil into the map.

Maggie spoke quietly, "I didn't make the damn map, I didn't build the damn road, I didn't put the *etopes* and Wolf Canyon here, and I didn't move the trailer park! Would you kindly SHUT UP."

The park was about a half-mile up the road, and we drove in grim, smouldering silence through the entrance. I slumped over the wheel dramatically and announced that Maggie could park the trailer wherever she liked, in the middle of the pool if it suited her. I had had it!

It took two days for me to recover my cool and to make my apologies. "I'm sorry I blew my stack. When things didn't go my way, I fought it. Then I was scared. Then I tried to put the blame on your back. I forgot 'Easy Does It.'"

Maggie told me that she had violated all three of her "no-nos," allowing herself to get too hungry, too tired and too tense. "When we start south again, let's really 'Let Go and Let God,'" she suggested.

One of my friends from the stag group had told me that when he found himself uptight because of a business problem or a bad scene at home, he would repeat the Serenity Prayer silently perhaps three or four times and always seemed to feel a bit better. Then somehow he could handle his problems in a sane and sensible manner.

"Okay God, here's Your chance," I muttered as we pulled out a few days later. I visualized God sitting at my elbow as we took the curves of Wolf Canyon and I ran the phrases of the Serenity Prayer through my mind. The road was a little wider, the traffic was light and the curves less abrupt. I remembered the *etopes*, and it was a pleasant trip back to the main highway.

God did a very creditable job of piloting for the remainder of our trip. The border crossings were slow, but we relaxed and practiced our Spanish, laughing and waving our arms when the going was rough. Unmarked highways became the rule rather than the exception, which wasn't so bad, considering that if we stayed on the paved highway we were on the right route it was that simple. We disregarded the Auto Club route prepared by someone who simply traced green lines between cities on our route, but who had obviously never driven in Central America. We relied instead on reports and recommendations of north-bound tourists that we met at our overnight stops. Nobody robbed us, customs officials were polite, and we relaxed, holding our daily travel to 150 to 175 miles and stopping when we felt like it. God took good care of us, but the last leg of the trip was His crucial test.

There were three routes from the end of the paved highway back into the boonies to our hill overlooking the Pacific beach. One route led directly over the mountains, we were told, suitable only for mounted horsemen with a great sense of daring. The recommended route was a little longer and followed the coastline, and we decided to make a trial run in El Toro before braving the trip with our trailer in tow. From the end of the concrete, we rattled over washboard gravel, which was soon replaced by red dirt and dust. We counted thirty semi-dry creeks, each with a sharp dip, four rivers to ford and a couple of tight turns that might or might not accommodate our rig. We would need a crew to precede us to build temporary bridges over some of the creek beds and to haul us through the rivers if the gravel bottoms proved unstable under our five tons of weight.

One of the building contractors at the beach colony suggested the third route, which he described as comparatively level, recently graded, with only one river to cross. *"No problemas,"* he promised, and agreed to meet us at the turn-off where the gravel road ended and to escort us with his big German-made four-wheel-drive truck across the last section of unmarked dirt road and the final approach over three miles of beach.

There was only one river, but the contractor failed to mention that we were to cross it twelve times. We made it to the rendezvous point with only minor damage to La Tortuga's fat behind and waited patiently for our escort in a tiny bar and grocery at Las Vegas, population fourteen. We passed the time consuming oranges and twelve-ounce bottles of Coke, seated on feed bags on the tin-roofed porch, which we shared with a flock of chickens and an occasional pig that wandered up grunting a request for an orange peel. We talked with several people who stopped to admire our trailer, and as we interpreted their voluble Spanish there were indeed, *no problemas* on the dirt road. It had been recently graded—only six or perhaps eight miles to the next village. Rivers, *si*, but only six very small ones. It was all *muy facile* —very easy.

Our Texaco map of Costa Rica showed no road at all, so this was welcome news. Since our escort failed to show after a two-hour wait, we decided to go it alone. If we got stuck, somebody would help us. We crawled along cautiously, and in a few spots, Maggie crouched in front of El Toro, directing me, foot by foot, in our progress on dried mud ridges with deep ruts in between. The six rivers turned out to be only one, but—as I mentioned—we crossed it twelve times. The six miles were, instead, about sixteen, perhaps an error in translation, but we made it to the village and stopped for another Coke and more advice about the final stretch of beach. We had three miles of it to cross, once we had made it down an ox-cart trail from the village.

We were happy to find, seated at the bar in the cantina, a retired Air Force colonel now turned land developer, and he cheerfully volunteered to guide us on this last stretch when the tide went out.

So God, Maggie and I sailed majestically across the hard-packed sand. Following faithfully in the tire tracks of the colonel's Land Rover, we churned through the soft sand at the top of the beach and onto the welcome gravel roads of the colony. Then, relying on memory, we made all of the right turns on the unmarked roads, strained up the mountain in low-low and pulled up under the shade of a massive, old tree that graces our property.

"We made it!" I exclaimed jubilantly, "We did it, we did it!"

"That we did," Maggie agreed, "but we had a lot of help."

We pulled our two folding lounge chairs out of the back of the truck, and we watched the sun nuzzle the rim of the placid Pacific and dip quickly below the horizon, marveling at the afterglow—a full 360 degrees of vibrant pinks, oranges and lavenders that were reflected in the sea and bathed the mountains behind us in muted tones of the same colors. The breeze dropped to a whisper. We heard the roar of the surf on the beach below us, the sleepy call of the owls and the soft, dry rustle of the palms. The stars appeared and loomed large above us, millions of them shimmering and winking, and the moon rose, hanging so close overhead that we could almost count the craters.

I squeezed Maggie's hand and thought of the Hand of God — first extended by Dr. Tom, who had heard and correctly identified Maggie's third suicide attempt as the cry of an alcoholic pleading for help the only way she could. Then there was the warm reassurance of Connie on the phone and the patience of the Hazelden staff, particularly the Cobra, with his radar that kept pinging against Maggie's anger and my own egotism. I remembered the cheerful and understanding help of our many friends in Alcoholics Anonymous and Al-Anon who sustained and educated us in the art of living one day at a time. I felt a deep gratitude to these Hands.

Maggie stirred. "I've got to fix us something to eat — how about a steak, fried potatoes and fried onions?"

Onions, reality. We had reached our destination in Costa Rica, but along with that pile of (D) neatly stowed in the trailer, I had brought along with me all of those things that still needed to be changed, my masks that had to come off, my onion that had to be peeled away, layer by layer, if I was to discover the man underneath.

"Let's go," I said, pulling her to her feet, "You cook the steak and potatoes, and I'll start peeling an onion."

# 16

# Be What You Would Seem To Be

"I quite agree with you," said the Duchess, "and the moral of that is ... 'Be what you would seem to be,' ... or, if you'd like it put more simply ... 'Never imagine yourself not to be otherwise than what it might appear to others that what you were or might have been was not otherwise than what you had been would have appeared to them to be otherwise.'"

"What's it like," you ask, "living in the bush of Costa Rica? Has your 'Great Adventure' been the ideal experience of Plato's sophrosyne or a bust?"

Some of our friends, who have the idea of sobriety firmly planted in their heads, are a little hazy about their geography and write to us, wondering just how we managed to get ourselves, El Toro and La Tortuga across all those miles of ocean to a little country that they dimly associate with Robert Vesco and Chiquita Banana.

You know. It was simply a matter of plunging south from the Mexican border until we saw a sign "Bienvenidos a Costa Rica." Since I couldn't back up and there was no room to turn around, the choice was made for us. Costa Rica, population about two million, is in Central America, the next to last stop before you come to the sturdy wire fence that marks the edge of the Panama Canal Zone, a country known as the "little Switzerland of the Americas." The central valley around the capital, San Jose, looks much like central Indiana or Ohio, with its checkerboard of small farms that produce almost every vegetable you'll see in your nearest supermarket, plus a host of fruits and vegetables that you will see only in the bustling, big central market in downtown San Jose. Over on the Atlantic side of the country are the big banana and palm-nut plantations, while the northwest sector is a different world, big cattle spreads, cowboys and a population descended from the Choretega Indians. The cities are choked with traffic, and there are jungles where it's easy to get lost; there are flatlands, rolling hills, blue mountains and some of the loveliest, loneliest, unspoiled beaches in the world.

Every Eden has its snake, and here it's alcoholism. Liquor production and distribution of the imported stuff, except for the bootleg guara, a heady concoction that guarantees stomach ulcers and worse, is closely controlled by the government and is a substantial source of revenue. However, five percent of the profit is set aside for education, treatment and rehabilitation of alcoholics. Here the illness seems reserved principally for men—the women are too busy with household chores, raising families and sobering up their drunks.

Though Maggie still has trouble with the Spanish language in AA meetings, she observes that the guilt, anger, resentments and fears are completely understandable. The hangovers, our friends in AA report, are just as shattering, the blackouts are just as black, and alcoholics lie, cheat, brag and wreck their lives just as thoroughly as they do Stateside.

The National Commission on Alcoholism, headed by the charming and indefatigable Dr. Irma Morales, operates treatment centers and halfway houses, spearheads a continuing educational program and trains leaders for AA and Al-Anon groups in the remote villages. Some of the AA groups hold meetings seven nights per week. An English-speaking group caters to the emigrants and retirees who came here only to find that they brought the problem of alcoholism with them. Al-Anon groups, so far all Spanish-speaking and 99 percent female, are spread across the country in all of the big towns and in many of the small villages.

Drinking starts at an early age, about the time the young man gets his first machete and begins to whistle at the girls. The average age of the alcoholic here is twenty-five!

Maggie and I have learned patience. The mail is inexplicably delayed. Mechanical repairs are agonizingly slow. Directions are given in terms of distance from well-known landmarks (well-known to everybody but us) instead of by street address and house number. "Two hundred varas (a vara is 33 inches) north of the Kentucky Fried Chicken restaurant," they tell us. (The fast-food franchises are here, too.) Here in the colony, I work out my resentments with a machete session, swinging the razor-edged, two-foot-long knife for an hour or so, fighting back the jungle that threatens to reoccupy our hill. My swivel-chair flab has melted away in the ninety-degree heat. I've dropped thirty pounds, and my three chins have merged into one.

Kahlil Gibran suggests in *The Prophet* that married couples should leave a few spaces in their "togetherness," and this advice goes double for folks who live in trailers. We added a roomy screened porch to ours, and it helps, but not enough. We solved this problem by my spending the mornings at my "office," the vacant home of a friend, atop the mountain with a sweeping panoramic view of the beach. I give Maggie a kiss and trudge up the mountain with my thermos of hot coffee and greet our neighbors as I pass.

The Green Feather Gang, a flock of two hundred or so parrots, wings overhead and spreads the word that the Gringo is on his way. There's an exchange of greetings with a tribe of black howler monkeys—a word or two with Dominant Male, the patriarch; Ringtail, the scout; Cry-Baby, the most vocal of the family. When we moved onto the hill, Cry-Baby told the tribe, "There goes the neighborhood," but we have a good understanding—they keep out of my garden and I stay out of their trees. I keep an eye peeled for our cleaning crew, the army ants who periodically inspect our porch and trailer for scorpions and other small insects, destroying them mercilessly and hauling away their eggs and bodies for later consumption. They are hard-working, single-minded ants, and we sincerely appreciate their help. Maggie does find some fault with their sudden appearance. She would like them to send a note the day before their arrival, but this communication problem is still unsolved.

I watch for Deer who still distrusts me, bounding away with his white flag of a tail bobbing, and for Iguana, a scaley-eyed miniature dinosaur that suns sedately on his favorite rock near the road. I wave at Hawk who soars overhead and seems to invite me to join him for a leisurely aerial survey of the colony and the beaches.

Maggie spends much of her free time on the five miles of beach at the foot of the mountain, shopping for the latest specials from the shell supermarket brought in by the waves from the offshore reefs. She creates jewelry, weaves palm hats and baskets, polishes pre-Colombian jade acquired from her Tico suppliers, writes poetry, works at her easel, reads and bakes bread and chocolate cakes.

In addition to our animal and insect neighbors, we have been drawn close to the handful of pioneers who have built homes in the colony. Some live here just during the dry season, others are residents for the full year. We accept each other, depend on one another, play bridge, poker and dominoes, watch the sunsets together. We learn Spanish from the local schoolteachers and, in turn, teach them English. We go to the village to see a soccer game and visit our Tico friends; we listen to short-wave radio, Voice of America from the States, BBC from London, Radio Canada. We tune to Radio Moscow and Radio Havana to hear the news with a different slant.

Life is as simple as we can make it be, but life is also reality. Reality for us is that the humidity of the six-month rainy season here plays hell with arthritic aches and pains, so we'll be hitching up El Toro before the next rainy season and heading north for the United States—somewhere in the southwest where the weather is hot and dry. But we'll be hoping to return to our hill in Costa Rica during the dry season.

Perhaps the most remarkable thing that we've learned is that we really never had to leave home to experience a "Great Adventure." We've learned how to live each day to its fullest, to accept ourselves and others uncritically. We believe that we could have done this wherever we happened to be. "Great Adventures," then, are the opportunities to find out what's under the next layer of onion, to experience the intoxication of happy sobriety and the serenity that it brings—the "sobrenity" of Plato's sophrosyne. Happiness for us isn't confined to Costa Rica or someplace in Arizona. It doesn't come as the end product of living in a luxurious house or an aluminum trailer, but from love, respect and keeping it simple, one day at a time, with the help of God as we know Him.

# BIBLIOGRAPHY AND READING LIST

These are the books, pamphlets and taped lectures that helped me understand the illness of chemical dependency, evolve a workable plan for living with an arrested alcoholic and possibly most important to me, find some answers to the question, "Who am I?"

## Books

*Alcoholics Anonymous* (New York, Alcoholics Anonymous World Services, Inc., 2nd Ed., 1955)

*An American Woman and Alcohol* by Patricia Kent. (New York, Holt, Rinehart & Winston, 1967)

*The Booze Battle* by Ruth Maxwell. (New York, Praeger Publishers, 1976)

*The Cracker Factory* by Joyce Rebeta-Burditt (New York, Collier books, 1977)

*The Dilemma of the Alcoholic Marriage* (New York, Al-Anon Family Group Headquarters, Inc., 1971)

*The God Players* by Earl Jabay. (Grand Rapids, MI, Zondervan Publishing House, 1969)

*I Ain't Much, Baby — But I'm All I've Got* by Jess Lair, Ph.D. (Garden City, NY, Doubleday & Company, Inc., 1969)

*The Identity Society* by William Glasser, M.D. (New York, Harper & Row, Publishers, 1972)

*I'll Quit Tomorrow* by Vernon E. Johnson. (New York, Harper & Row, Publishers, 1973)

*I'm Black and I'm Sober* by Chaney Allen. (Minneapolis, CompCare Publications, 1977)

*Living with an Alcoholic* (New York, Al-Anon Family Group Headquarters, Inc., 1976)

*Love and Addiction* by Stanton Peele with Archie Brodsky. (New York, New American Library, 1976)

---

*Editors' note: these are books which have been published since the author's experiences. They have been selected by the editors because they also may be of help to the reader.

*One Day At a Time in Al-Anon* (New York, Al-Anon Family Group Headquarters, Inc., 1972)

*The Prophet* by Kahlil Gibran. (New York, Alfred A. Knopf, Inc., 1923)

*Reality Therapy* by William Glasser, M.D. (New York, Harper & Row, Publishers, Inc., 1965)

*Search for Serenity* by Lewis F. Presnall. (Salt Lake City, U.A.F., 1959)

*Thirst for Freedom* by David A. Stewart. (Toronto, The Munson Book Company Ltd., 1960)

*Twelve Steps for Everyone ... Who Really Wants Them* by Grateful Members. (Minneapolis, CompCare Publications, 1977)

## Pamphlets, Booklets and Articles

"Alcoholism and the Empty Nest" by Joan Curlee. (Center City, MN, The Hazelden Foundation)

"Alcoholism—the Family Disease" (New York, Al-Anon Family Group Headquarters, Inc.)

"Another Look at Step One" by James G. Jenson. (Center City, MN, The Hazelden Foundation)

"Arresting Alcoholism" (New York, The Christopher D. Smithers Foundation, Inc.)

"Barriers Against Recovery" by John O. Grimmett, Ph.D. (Center City, MN, The Hazelden Foundation)

*"Career Woman/Going Up Fast: Alcoholic/Going Down Fast" by Dodie Gust. (Minneapolis, CompCare Publications, 1976)

"The Dry Drunk Syndrome" by R. J. Solberg. (Center City, MN, The Hazelden Foundation)

*"For Silent Sippers ... A Way Out of Hiding" by Muriel Zink. (Minneapolis, CompCare Publications, 1977)

"Guidelines for Admission of Alcoholics to Hospitals" (New York, The Christopher D. Smithers Foundation, Inc.)

---

*Editors' note: these are books which have been published since the author's experiences. They have been selected by the editors because they also may be of help to the reader.

"Guide to Fourth Step Inventory for the Spouse" (Center City, MN, The Hazelden Foundation)

"How to Help an Alcoholic Who Insists He Doesn't *Need* Any Help" (Fairfield County, CT, Fairfield Publication No. I)

"A Look at Relapse" by Charles W. Crewe. (Center City, MN, The Hazelden Foundation)

*"So Your Alcoholic Is Sober" by Muriel Zink. (Minneapolis, CompCare Publications, 1976)

"Surrender Versus Compliance in Therapy with Special Reference to Alcoholism" by Harry M. Tiebout, Ph.D. (Quarterly Journal of Studies on Alcohol, Vol. 14, pp. 58-68, 1953—reprinted by the Hazelden Foundation)

"Triple A Family Group"( Tuscon, AZ, Triple A Family Group, 1951)

*"Up, Down and Sideways On Wet and Dry Booze" by Dodie Gust. (Minneapolis, CompCare Publications, 1977)

*"Ways to Live More Comfortably With Your Alcoholic" by Muriel Zink. (Minneapolis, CompCare Publications, 1976)

*"What's a Nice Girl Like You Doing With An Illness Like This?" by Anne Ludcke. (Minneapolis, CompCare Publications, 1976)

"Who ... Me?" (New York, Alcoholics Anonymous World Services, Inc.)

"Young People and AA" (New York, Alcoholics Anonymous World Services, Inc.)


**Taped Lectures**

These tapes, available from the Hazelden Literature Department, Center City, Minnesota, include lectures heard by the patients at Hazelden. Informative and witty, they cover background, diagnosis and treatment of chemical dependency as well as mental attitudes, an excellent description of Alcoholics Anonymous, plus a comprehensive discussion of the "mind-bender" drugs. No knurd should be without these tapes!

By Daniel J. Anderson, Ph.D., Director of Hazelden:

"Historical and Cultural Attitudes."

"Anxiety" and "Conflict."

"The Revolution in Psychotherapy."

By Richard O. Heilman, M.D., Consulting Staff Psychiatrist at Hazelden:

"A Consideration for Heredity in Drug Dependency."

"Use of Drugs in Our Society."

"Nature of Drug Dependency."

"Diagnosis of Drug Dependency."

By Dee Smith, R.N., Supervisor, Medical Services at Hazelden:

"Mood Altering Drugs."

A Division of the Comprehensive Care Corporation
Post Office Box 27777, Minneapolis, Minnesota 55427

for faster service on charge orders
call us toll free at:

# 800/328-3330
In Minnesota, call collect 612/559-4800

# ORDER FORM

Date _____

| | | | | | | ☐ ☐ ☐ ☐ ☐ | **For Office Use Only** |
|---|---|---|---|---|---|---|---|
| | | | | | 1 2 3 4 5 | |

Order Number     Customer Number     Customer P.O.

| UPS 1 ☐ | PP 2 ☐ | PPD 3 ☐ | PPD CHGS 4 ☐ | WILL CALL 5 ☐ | OUR TRUCK 6 ☐ | CARRIER _____ |

BILL ORDER TO:

Name _____

Address _____

City/State/Zip _____

Non-profit organization, please show tax exemption number [_____]

Signature _____ Sales and use tax number _____

SHIP ORDER TO: (If other than above)

Name _____

Address _____

City/State/Zip _____

Telephone _____ Purchase Order (if required) _____

☐ Please ship back-ordered items as soon as possible

☐ Please cancel order for items out of stock

☐ Please send _____ copies of *Drink Like A Lady, Cry Like A Man* at $6.95 each. (Catalog number 03004.)

☐ Please send me the CompCare Catalog of more books and materials for growth-centered living. (No charge.)

**PLEASE FILL IN BELOW FOR CHARGE ORDERS**
Or enclose check for total amount of order.

Prices subject to change without notice.

Account No. (12 or more digits) from your credit card.

| | | | | | | | | | | | | | | | |
|---|---|---|---|---|---|---|---|---|---|---|---|---|---|---|---|

Check one:

☐ VISA     ☐ MASTER CHARGE   Master Charge—also enter 4 digits below your account no

Your Card
Issuing Bank _____ Expiration Date of Card _____

Credit Card
Signature _____

TOTAL PRICE _____

4% Sales Tax _____
(Minnesota residents only)

Postage & Handling charge _____
Add 45 cents to orders totaling less than $15.00
Add 3% to orders totaling $15.00 or more

GRAND TOTAL _____

All orders shipped outside continental
U.S.A. will be billed actual shipping costs.

**VISA**     master charge